D. Stanlake.

MW01140105

Complete Canadian Curriculum

8

- Math
- Language
- History
- Geography
- Science

Printed in China

Content

Mathematics

English

History

Geography

Science

Answers

Exponents

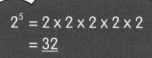

- write integers as powers
- evaluate expressions using the order of operation
- find volume and side length of cubes
- write numbers as a product of prime factors
- find common factors using prime factors

We double ourselves every minute. There'll be 32 of us after 5 minutes.

Write each as a product of powers.

1. $3 \times 3 \times 3 \times 4 \times 4 = \underline{3^{\square} \times 4^{\square}}$

2. $6 \times 6 \times 6 \times 6 \times 8 \times 8 = \underline{6^{\square} \times 8^{\square}}$

3. $2.5 \times 2.5 \times 8 \times 8 = \underline{\qquad}$

4. $1.7 \times 1.7 \times 1.7 \times 1.7 \times 5 \times 5 = \underline{\qquad}$

5. $9 \times 5 \times 5 \times 9 \times 9 = \underline{\qquad}$

6. $4.6 \times 7 \times 7 \times 4.6 \times 7 = \underline{\qquad}$

7. $10 \times 7.8 \times 7.8 \times 10 \times 2 \times 2 \times 10 \times 7.8 \times 7.8 = \underline{\qquad}$

8. $6.3 \times 5 \times 5 \times 5 \times 6.3 \times 6.3 \times 13 \times 14^2 = \underline{\qquad}$

9. $3 \times 3 \times 3^2 \times 4 \times 4 \times 5.5 \times 4^3 \times 5.5 = \underline{\qquad}$

Write the integers as powers.

10. $81 = 3 \times \underline{\qquad}$

$= 3 \times \underline{\qquad} \times \underline{\qquad}$

$= 3 \times \underline{\qquad} \times \underline{\qquad} \times \underline{\qquad}$

$= \underline{\qquad}$

Hint

Write 16 as a power of 2.

$16 = 2 \times 8$
$= 2 \times 2 \times 4$
$= 2 \times 2 \times 2 \times 2$
$= 2^4$

11. 125 as a power of 5 $\underline{\qquad}$

12. 1296 as a power of 6 $\underline{\qquad}$

13. 243 as a power of 3 $\underline{\qquad}$

14. 10 000 as a power of 10 $\underline{\qquad}$

15. 1024 as a power of 4 $\underline{\qquad}$

16. 128 as a power of 2 $\underline{\qquad}$

Follow the order of operations to evaluate, commonly called: **BEDMAS**

        B - Brackets
        E - Exponents
        D - Divide
        M- Multiply
        A - Add
        S - Subtract

e.g. $20 \div (8 - 6)^2 + 10$

$= 20 \div (\mathbf{2})^2 + 10$ ← Do the brackets first.

$= 20 \div \mathbf{4} + 10$ ← Evaluate the exponent.

$= \mathbf{5} + 10$ ← Divide.

$= \mathbf{15}$ ← Add.

Evaluate.

17. $2^4 = 2 \times 2 \times 2 \times$ _____ = _____

18. $7^3 =$ _____ = _____

19. $1.5^3 =$ _____ = _____

20. $(\frac{1}{3})^4 =$ _____ = _____

Follow the order of operation to evaluate.

21. $2^3 \times 3$

    $=$ _____ $\times 3$ ← Evaluate 2^3 first.

    $=$ _____

22. $6^3 - (2 + 1)^2$

    $=$ _____ $-$ _____

    $=$ _____

23. $10 + 1.2^2 \times 5$

    $=$

24. $(5 - 2)^4 \div 9^0 + 8$

    $=$

25. $(3 + 1)^2 \div 2^2 - 1$ $=$ _____

26. $45 \div (2 + 1)^2 - 3$ $=$ _____

27. $(10 - 3)^4 \div (3 + 4)$ $=$ _____

28. $(7^2 - 4^2) \times 2 + 10$ $=$ _____

29. $36 - (5^2 - 4^2) \times 4$ $=$ _____

30. $5^2 \times (31 - 3^3) + 99^0$ $=$ _____

31. $(6^2 - 5^2)^2 \div 11$ $=$ _____

32. $(4^3 - 5^2 \times 2)^2 \times 5$ $=$ _____

Find the volume of each cube.

33.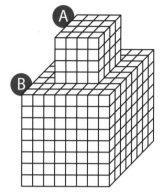

Volume of A

= ▢³ = _____ (unit cube)

Volume of B

= ▢³ = _____ (unit cube)

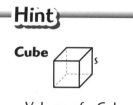

Hint

Cube

Volume of a Cube
= s^3 (unit cube)

34.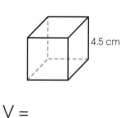
4.5 cm

V =

35.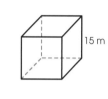
15 m

V =

36.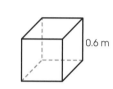
0.6 m

V =

Evaluate the cube of each number. Find the side length of each cube with the help of the evaluated answers. Then fill in the blank.

37. $1^3 =$ _____ $\quad 2^3 =$ _____ $\quad 3^3 =$ _____ $\quad 4^3 =$ _____ $\quad 5^3 =$ _____

$0.5^3 =$ _____ $\quad 1.2^3 =$ _____ $\quad 2.5^3 =$ _____ $\quad 3.4^3 =$ _____ $\quad 4.2^3 =$ _____

38. **8 cm³** Think: 8 = _____³

side length = _____ cm

39. 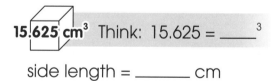 **15.625 cm³** Think: 15.625 = _____³

side length = _____ cm

40.  **64 cm³** Think: 64 = _____³

side length = _____ cm

41. 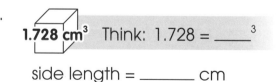 **1.728 cm³** Think: 1.728 = _____³

side length = _____ cm

42. The side length of a cube is the value of the _____ of the power.

<u>base / exponent</u>

Finding common factors of 2 or more numbers using prime factors:

1st Find the prime factors of each number.

2nd Multiply any 2 or more common factors to form another common factor.

e.g. Find the common factors of 24 and 36.
Write each number as a product of prime factors.

$24 = 2 \times 2 \times 2 \times 3$ ← 2, 2, and 3 are common factors.
$36 = 2 \times 2 \times 3 \times 3$

So, the common factors of 24 and 36 are 2, 3, 4 (2 x 2), 6 (2 x 3), and 12 (2 x 2 x 3).

Write each number as a product of prime factors.

43. 25 = _____

44. 40 = _____

45. 42 = _____

46. 18 = _____

47. 72 = _____

48. 56 = _____

49. 96 = _____

50. 100 = _____

51. 300 = _____

Hint

You can use a factor tree to find all the prime factors of a composite number.

e.g.
```
        63
       / \
      7   9
         / \
        3   3
```
$63 = \underline{3 \times 3 \times 7}$
$= \underline{3^2 \times 7}$

Write each number as a product of prime factors. Then find the common factors of each pair of numbers.

52. **30** = 2 x _____

   45 = _____

   common factors of 30 and 45: _____

53. **120** = _____

   420 = _____

   common factors of 120 and 420: _____

Don't you know that 120 and 420 have 10 common factors excluding 1?

Square Roots

- evaluate square roots
- estimate square roots
- find area and dimension of squares and triangles involving square roots
- solve problems involving square roots

This wall is in the shape of a square and its area is 7 m². How long is this wall border?

Guess (square – side length)	Square of Guess (area)
2.6	6.76 (< 7)
2.7	7.29 (> 7)
2.65	7.02 (> 7) ✔
2.64	6.97 (< 7)
7.02 is closer to 7.	

The border should be about 2.65 m long.

Use a calculator to evaluate.

1. $\sqrt{81}$ = _____

2. $\sqrt{121}$ = _____   3. $\sqrt{361}$ = _____   4. $\sqrt{625}$ = _____

5. $\sqrt{900}$ = _____   6. $\sqrt{1.69}$ = _____   7. $\sqrt{0.25}$ = _____

Write the answers and circle the correct answer for each sentence.

8. $(\sqrt{16})^2$ = ( )² = _____   9. $(\sqrt{100})^2$ =

10. $(\sqrt{2.25})^2$ =   11. $(\sqrt{a})^2$ =

12. *The square of the square root of a number is the number   itself / squared   .*

13. $\sqrt{3^2}$ = $\sqrt{}$ = _____   14. $\sqrt{11^2}$ =

15. $\sqrt{100^2}$ =   16. $\sqrt{b^2}$ =

17. *The square root of a number squared is the number times 2 / itself .*

Approximating square roots by a guess-and-check method:

1st Find the two perfect squares that are closest to the number.

2nd Find the square roots of the two perfect squares.

3rd Choose a number that lies between the square roots and find the answer by guessing and checking.

e.g. Evaluate $\sqrt{21}$,

1st the two square roots closest to 21 are 16 and 25

2nd $\sqrt{16} = 4$ and $\sqrt{25} = 5$

3rd root: between 4 and 5

Guess	Check
4.5	$4.5^2 = 20.25$
4.6	$4.6^2 = 21.16$ ← closest to 21
4.7	$4.7^2 = 22.09$

So, the value of $\sqrt{21}$ is about 4.6.

Complete the number line. Find the value that each square root lies between. Then find the square root and round it to 1 decimal place.

18.
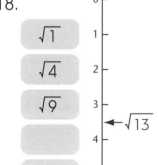
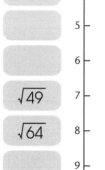

19. $\sqrt{13}$: between $\sqrt{9}$ and $\sqrt{16}$ — Guess — Check

$\sqrt{9}$ = _____ and $\sqrt{16}$ = _____

$\sqrt{13}$ ≈ _____

20. $\sqrt{28}$: between ____ and ____ — Guess — Check

21. $\sqrt{150}$: between ____ and ____ — Guess — Check

22. $\sqrt{85}$: between ____ and ____ — Guess — Check

Put "<", "=", or ">" in the circles to make the statements true.

23. $\sqrt{25}$ ◯ $\sqrt{40}$ 24. $\sqrt{44}$ ◯ 7

25. $\sqrt{510}$ ◯ $\sqrt{300}$ 26. $\sqrt{250}$ ◯ 18

27. $\sqrt{100}$ ◯ $\sqrt{10^2}$ 28. $(\sqrt{40})^2$ ◯ 14

> **Hint**
>
> If $a > b$, then $\sqrt{a} > \sqrt{b}$.
>
> e.g. $16 > 9$, so $\sqrt{16} > \sqrt{9}$.

Put the numbers in order from least to greatest.

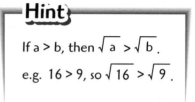

29. $\sqrt{100}$ 11 4^2 30. $\boxed{7^2}$ $\boxed{14}$ $\boxed{\sqrt{13^2}}$ $\boxed{\sqrt{225}}$

_____   _____

31. $\sqrt{33^2}$ 5^2 $(\sqrt{26})^2$ 32. $\sqrt{169}$ 12 $\sqrt{11^2}$ $(\sqrt{10})^2$

_____   _____

Look at the figure. Find the area and dimensions of each shape.

33. The figure is formed by a rectangle, 2 small squares, and 1 big square.

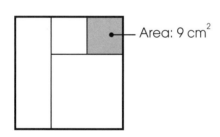

— Area: 9 cm²

	Area
small square	
big square	
rectangle	
whole figure	

34. The figure is formed by 1 square, 2 small triangles, and 1 big triangle.

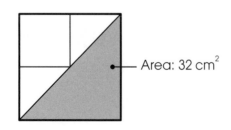

— Area: 32 cm²

	Area
big triangle	
small triangle	
square	
whole figure	

Help the children find the side lengths of the squares. Then solve the problems.

35.

> I have a spool of ribbon with a length of 1.5 m. Do I have enough ribbon to give each piece of cardboard a border? If so, how much ribbon will I have left?

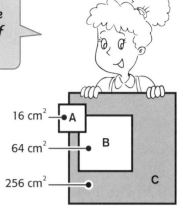

16 cm^2 — A

64 cm^2 — B

256 cm^2 — C

_____

36. Farmer Jack wants to fence his two fields.

   a.   About how much fencing is needed in total?

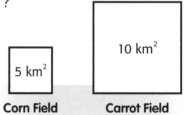

5 km^2

10 km^2

Corn Field   **Carrot Field**

_____

   b.   The total amount of fencing for both corn and carrot field is the same as that needed for the wheat field. If the wheat field is also in the shape of a square, what is its side length?

_____

   c.

> My field is in the shape of a square, too. The side length of my field is 2 times that of Farmer Jack's wheat field. Is the area of my field two times that of Farmer Jack's wheat field?

Tom

_____

Pythagorean Theorem

- identify legs and hypotenuse of a right triangle
- find the lengths of sides of a right triangle using Pythagorean Theorem
- determine whether or not a triangle is a right triangle using Pythagorean Theorem
- solve problems using Pythagorean Theorem

hypotenuse = ladder (ℓ)

$\ell^2 = 36^2 + 48^2$
$\ell^2 = 1296 + 2304$
$\ell^2 = 3600$
$\ell = 60$

48 cm

ladder

36 cm

If we have a 60-cm ladder, we will be able to get the slice of cake.

Fill in the blanks with the given words in the diagram. Then trace the hypotenuse of each triangle red and the legs blue.

1.

A Right Triangle

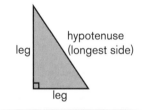

leg
hypotenuse (longest side)
leg

In a right triangle, the _____ form the right angle. The side opposite to the right angle is called the _____ , which is always the _____ side in a right triangle.

2.

Draw a line to cut the rectangle into two identical right triangles. Then measure and record the lengths of the legs and hypotenuse of one of the triangles.

3.

leg: _____

hypotenuse: _____

4.

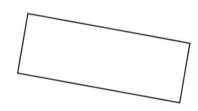

leg: _____

hypotenuse: _____

Pythagorean Theorem:

In any right triangle, the square of the hypotenuse equals to the sum of the square of each of its legs.

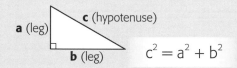

a (leg) **c** (hypotenuse)
b (leg)

$$c^2 = a^2 + b^2$$

e.g. Find the length of the hypotenuse.

$$h^2 = 3^2 + 4^2$$
$$h^2 = 9 + 16$$
$$h^2 = 25$$
$$h = 5$$

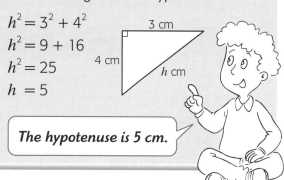

3 cm
4 cm
h cm

The hypotenuse is 5 cm.

Choose the correct equations.

5.

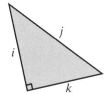

i j k

  A $i^2 = j^2 + k^2$

  B $j^2 = i^2 + k^2$

6.

q r s

  A $s = \sqrt{r^2 + q^2}$

  B $s = \sqrt{r^2} + \sqrt{q^2}$

7.

t v u

  A $u^2 = t^2 - v^2$

  B $u^2 = v^2 - t^2$

Find the lengths of the missing sides. Show your work.

8.

3 h 2

$$h^2 = \underline{\qquad} + \underline{\qquad}$$

9.

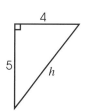

4 5 h

10.

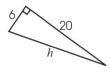

6 20 h

11.

h 5 8

12.

9 h

It is an isosceles triangle.

15

Find the lengths of the missing sides. Round the decimals to 2 decimal places.

13.

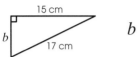

$b = $ _____

14.

$a = $ _____

15.

$k = $ _____

16.

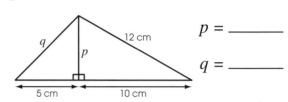

$p = $ _____

$q = $ _____

17.

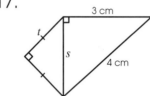

$s = $ _____

$t = $ _____

The lengths of the three sides of each triangle are given. Decide whether or not each is a right triangle. Explain.

18.

19.

20. 7 cm, 11 cm, 5 cm

21. 6 cm, 10 cm, 8 cm

Hint

You may use Pythagorean Theorem $a^2 + b^2 = c^2$ to tell whether or not a triangle is a right triangle.

e.g.

1.

$a^2 + b^2$	c^2
$5^2 + 3^2$	6^2
$25 + 9$	36
34	36 ✗

It is not a right triangle.

2. lengths of a triangle:

4 cm, **5 cm**, 3 cm
  └─ hypotenuse (the longest)

$a^2 + b^2$	c^2
$4^2 + 3^2$	5^2
$16 + 9$	25
25	25 ✔

"4 cm, 5 cm, 3 cm" forms a right triangle.

Find the area of each shaded part. Round the decimals to 2 decimal places.

22.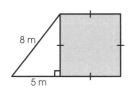

23.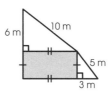

24.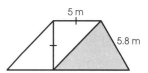

Solve the problems.

25. A ramp is attached to a truck for loading. What is the length of the ramp?

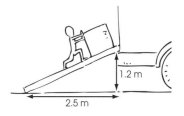

_____

26. If Janet walks across the court diagonally instead of walking along the border to reach the flag, how many fewer metres will she walk?

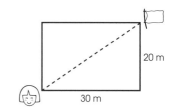

_____

27.

A slice of cake is 20 m due east and 10 m due south. Another slice is 15 m due west and 15 m due north. Which slice of cake am I closer to?

(You may draw a diagram to help you.)

_____

4

Integers

- add and subtract integers with the help of number lines
- multiply and divide positive and negative integers
- identify pattern rules and complete patterns
- solve problems involving negative integers

We are at B2, which is 2 floors below the ground level. How many floors do we go up to get to my apartment on the 5th floor?

5 – (-2)
= 5 + 2
= 7

We need to go 7 floors up.

Do the addition and subtraction with the help of the number line.

1. (-3) + 5 = _____

2. -5 – (-8) = _____

3. -2 – (-3) + 5 = _____

4. 1 – 6 + 7 = _____

Find the answers.

5. -9 + 5 – (-2) = -9 + 5 + _____ = _____

6. 13 – 19 + (-4) = 13 – 19 – _____ = _____

7. 21 – (-6) + (-3) = _____ = _____

8. -9 + (-7) – (-4) = _____ = _____

9. 4 – 15 + (-7) = _____ = _____

10. (-19) – 7 + 8 = _____ = _____

Hint

- Adding a negative integer means subtracting its opposite.

  e.g. 7 + (-2) = 7 – 2
           = <u>5</u>

- Subtracting a negative integer means adding its opposite.

  e.g. 7 – (-2) = 7 + 2
           = <u>9</u>

Multiplying Integers:

- **(+) x (+) ➡ (+)**
  e.g. (+2)(+3) = +6

- **(+) x (–) ➡ (–)**
  e.g. (+2)(-3) = -6

- **(–) x (+) ➡ (–)**
  e.g. (-2)(+3) = -6

- **(–) x (–) ➡ (+)**
  e.g. (-2)(-3) = +6

> *When 2 integers with the same sign are multiplied, the product is always positive.*

Fill in the blanks with "positive" or "negative".

11. a positive integer   x a positive integer   = a _____ integer

12. a positive integer   x a negative integer = a _____ integer

13. a negative integer x a positive integer   = a _____ integer

14. a negative integer x a negative integer = a _____ integer

15. a negative integer x a negative integer x a positive integer

    = a _____ integer

16. a positive integer x a negative integer x a positive integer

    = a _____ integer

Do the multiplication.

17. (-3) x 5 = _____

18. (-7) x (-8) = _____

19. 6 x (-12) = _____

20. 6 x (-4) = _____

21. (-9) x (-5) = _____

22. (-10) x 7 = _____

23. (-8) x 2 x (-3) = _____

24. (-4) x (-2) x (-8) = _____

25. 9 x (-3) x (-1) = _____

26. 3 x 4 x (-9) = _____

Fill in the missing integers.

27. 9 x _____ = -45

28. _____ x (-3) = 15

29. _____ x (-6) = -36

30. 8 x _____ = -16

31. (-5) x (-2) x _____ = -40

32. _____ x 7 x (-3) = 42

Fill in the blanks with "positive" or "negative". Then write the sign of each quotient.

33. **Dividing Integers**

    • The quotient of 2 integers with the same sign is _____ .

    e.g. (+12) ÷ (+2) = ▨ 6   and   (-12) ÷ (-2) = ▨ 6

    • The quotient of 2 integers with different signs is _____ .

    e.g. (+12) ÷ (-2) = ▨ 6   and   (-12) ÷ (+2) = ▨ 6

Do the division.

34. (+12) ÷ (-3) = _____

35. (-10) ÷ 2 = _____

36. (-78) ÷ (-6) = _____

37. 81 ÷ (-3) = _____

38. (-98) ÷ 7 = _____

39. (-76) ÷ (-2) = _____

40. 24 ÷ (-2) ÷ (-6) = _____

41. 10 ÷ (-2) ÷ (-1) = _____

42. (-32) ÷ 4 ÷ (-2) = _____

43. 48 ÷ (-6) ÷ 2 = _____

Circle the part that you do first. Then find the answer.

44. (-12) + (-4) x 8

    = (-12) + _____

    = _____

45. 13 x (-5) ÷ 2

    = _____

    = _____

46. (-20) ÷ (-4) + (-18)

    = _____

    = _____

47. (-11) x (-4 + 2)

    = _____

    = _____

48. $(3^2 - 21)$ ÷ (-2)

    = _____

    = _____

49. (-30) ÷ 6 + (-5)

    = _____

    = _____

Find the pattern rule for each pattern. Then write the next three terms.

50. 1, -2, 4, -8, 16, _____ , _____ , _____

    pattern rule: _____

51. 2, -5, 9, -19, 37, _____ , _____ , _____

    pattern rule: _____

52. 128, -64, 32, -16, 8, _____ , _____ , _____

    pattern rule: _____

53. -1276, 425, -142, 47, _____ , _____ , _____

    pattern rule: _____

54. -3, -12, -48, -192, _____ , _____ , _____

    pattern rule: _____

Solve the problems.

55. Each of the 7 members has a score of -6 in the first round.

    a. What is their total score?   _____

    b. They got a score of 35 in the second round. What is
        the total score of the two rounds?   _____

56. Jason recorded the temperatures of the last five days.

    -21°C   -18°C   -17°C   -11°C   -23°C

    a. What is the mean temperature?   _____

    b. Today's temperature is 3°C lower than the old mean.
        What is the new mean temperature?

    _____

Order of Operations

- apply order of operations to integers
- evaluate expressions involving decimals
- evaluate expressions involving negative numbers
- identify the correct expressions to solve problems

No. of Dark Chocolates

$(7^2 - 9) + 4^2 \times 6$

$= (49 - 9) + 16 \times 6$

$= 40 + 96$

$= 136$

$7^2 - 9$

$4^2 \times 6$

Tim, let me give you all my dark chocolate.

Thank you, Jane. So I'll have 136 dark chocolates.

Evaluate each expression.

1. $(12 - 4)^2 + 4^2 \div 2$

    = _____^{2} + $4^2 \div 2$ ← brackets

    = _____ + _____ $\div 2$ ← exponents

    = _____ + _____ ← divide

    = _____ ← add

> **Hint**
>
> When solving an expression that has multiple operations, there is an order to follow, often referred to as "BEDMAS".
>
> **Brackets**
> **Exponents**
> **Divide**
> **Multiply**
> **Add**
> **Subtract**

2. $5^2 \times 8 - (10 - 5)^2$

    =

3. $4^3 \div 16 + 2^4 \times 3$ = _____

4. $10 \div (7 - 2) + 3^2$ = _____

5. $51 \div (5^2 - 2^3) + 4$ = _____

6. $(11 - 2) \times 4 - 6^2$ = _____

7. $(4^2 + 2^2) - 2 \times 3$ = _____

8. $5^2 \times 6 + (7 - 5)^2$ = _____

9. $(17 - 2)^2 \div (4 + 1)^2$ = _____

10. $(28 + 12) \times 3 + 2^3$ = _____

Evaluate without using calculators. Show your work.

11. $(1.2 + 0.8)^2 - 9.9^0$

12. $22 - (1.7 + 2.3)^2$

13. $1.8^3 - (0.2^2 \times 5)$

14. $1.5^2 \times (0.1^3 + 9.999)^2$

15. $(10 - 8.5)^2 \times 2^2$

16. $1.1^3 + 3 \times 1.1$

17. $9^3 \div (5^2 - 4^2) + 11^2 =$ _____

18. $2^3 \times (8.25 - 3.75)^2 =$ _____

19. $(5 + 6.4 + 0.27)^0 \div 2 + 1.5 =$ _____

Evaluate each power. Then put "+" or "–" in the circles.

20.   **$(-4)^2$**   **-4^2**

    $= -4 \times$ _____ $= -(4 \times$ $)$

    $= +$ _____ $= -$ _____

21.   **$(-2)^3$**   **-2^3**

    $= -2 \times$ _____ $= -($ $)$

    $=$ _____ $=$ _____

22. $(-3)^4 =$ _____

    $-3^4 \;\;=$ _____

23. $(-5)^2 =$ _____

    $-5^2 \;\;=$ _____

24. $(-4)^5 =$ _____

    $-4^5 \;\;=$ _____

25.   a negative number with an even number exponent ➡ ◯ integer

26.   a negative number with an odd number exponent ➡ ◯ integer

Check the next step for each expression.

27. $(-8)^2 - (-3)^3 \times 2$

     Ⓐ $-64 + 27 \times 2$

     Ⓑ $64 - 27 \times 2$

     Ⓒ $64 - (-27) \times 2$

28. $(-5^3) \div (-2)^2 + 8$

     Ⓐ $(-125) \div 4 + 8$

     Ⓑ $125 \div 4 + 8$

     Ⓒ $(-125) \div (-4) + 8$

29. $(-14) - (-4)^3 \div 5^2$

     Ⓐ $(-14) - 64 \div 25$

     Ⓑ $(-14) - (-64) \div 25$

     Ⓒ $(-14) + (-64) \div 25$

30. $(-3)^2 \times (-5)^2 - (-7)^3$

     Ⓐ $9 \times (-25) - 343$

     Ⓑ $9 \times 25 - (-343)$

     Ⓒ $9 \times 25 - 343$

Evaluate the expressions.

31. $-5^3 - 7^2 \times (-6)^3$

     $=$

32. $(-2 - 3^2) \times (-3)^2$

     $=$

33. $(6^2 - (-2)^3) \div 2^2$

     $=$

34. $(-8^2 + 10^2) \div (5^2 - 4^2)$

     $=$

35. $2 \div (1 - 0.5)^2 = $ _____

36. $(0.96 + 0.2^2)^8 + (-3)^0 = $ _____

37. $(-4.5 - 1.5)^3 + (5 - 2^2)^{99} = $ _____

38. $(-7^2 + 5 \times 10)^9 \times (2^8 - 8^2) = $ _____

1 to the power of any number is always 1.

$$(1)^n = 1$$

Check the correct expression for each question. Then find the answer.

39. Annie folds a piece of paper that measures 50 cm by 50 cm into two halves 6 times. What is the area of each small rectangle?

　Ⓐ $50^2 \div 2^6$

　Ⓑ $50^2 \div (2 \times 6)$

　Ⓒ $50^2 \div 6^2$

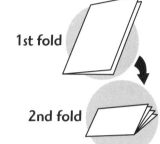

1st fold

2nd fold

Each small rectangle has an area of _____ .

40. A technician puts each of the two types of bacteria in a test tube. One type doubles itself every 10 minutes and another type triples itself every 15 minutes. After one hour, a drop of chemical is added and the number of bacteria is reduced by 40%. What is the total number of bacteria left in the jar?

　Ⓐ $(2 \times 6 + 3 \times 4) \times (1 - 0.4)$

　Ⓑ $0.4 \times (2^6 + 3^4)$

　Ⓒ $(2^6 + 3^4) \times (1 - 0.4)$

The number of bacteria left in the jar is _____ .

41.

I cut out 2 blocks from this modelling clay, each having a volume of 17.5 cm³. Then I cut out another 3 cubes from the remaining clay, each having a side length of 4 cm. How much has the volume of the original clay been reduced?

　Ⓐ $17.5 \times 2 - 3 \times 4^3$

　Ⓑ $17.5 \times 2 + 3 \times 4^3$

　Ⓒ $17.5 \times (2 + 3) \times 4^3$

The volume of the clay has been reduced _____ .

Expanded Form and Scientific Notation

- write numbers in expanded form
- identify numbers that are written in scientific notation
- write numbers in scientific notation
- order numbers that are written in scientific notation
- solve problems involving scientific notation

What? Only $5.31 was raised!

No, Sam. They raised $531 000 000.

$5.31 \times 10^8 = \underline{531\ 000\ 000}$ ← scientific notation

$\underset{\sim}{5.3\,1\,0\,0\,0\,0\,0\,0}$

Move the decimal point 8 places to the right.

Write each number in expanded form three different ways.

1. $724 = 700 + \underline{\hspace{1cm}} + \underline{\hspace{1cm}}$

    $= 7 \times 100 + \underline{\hspace{1cm}} + \underline{\hspace{1cm}}$

    $= 7 \times 10^2 + \underline{\hspace{1cm}} \times 10^1 + \underline{\hspace{1cm}} \times 10^0$

2. $253 =$

3. $896 =$

4. $1625 =$

5. $47\ 000 =$

Hint

Quick Reference:

$$1 = 10^0$$
$$10 = 10^1$$
$$100 = 10^2$$
$$1000 = 10^3$$
$$10\ 000 = 10^4$$

$$100\ 000\ 000 = \underline{10^8}$$

Think: $1\underset{\sim}{.0\,0\,0\,0\,0\,0\,0\,0}$

8 places to the left

Numbers in Scientific Notation*:

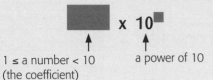 x $10^{\blacksquare}$

↑
1 ≤ a number < 10
(the coefficient)

↑
a power of 10

* Scientific notation is used to express very large numbers.

e.g. Write 625 000 in scientific notation.

Think: 6$\underbrace{25\ 000}$ Move the decimal point 5 places to the left to get the number 6.25 (which is greater than 1 and less than 10)

625 000 = $\underline{6.25 \times 10^5}$ ← the number 5 indicates how many places the decimal point moved

Circle the number written in scientific notation in each group.

6. 1.75×10^8
   17.5×10^7
   1.75×2^{10}

7. 106×10^3
   1.06×10^5
   10.6×10^4

8. 0.04×10^6
   4×10^4
   4×100^2

9. 0.097×10^8
   9.7×10^6
   9.7×100^3

10. 1.52×100^2
    15.2×10^3
    1.52×10^4

11. 7.06×10^4
    0.706×10^5
    7.06×4^{10}

Fill in the blanks.

12. $3\underbrace{4\,000}$ = 3.4 x _____
    = 3.4 x $10^{\blacksquare}$

13. 9210   = _____
    = _____

14. 70 800 = _____
    = _____

15. 31 450 = _____
    = _____

Hint

Draw an arrow to help you count the number of places that the decimal point has moved.

e.g. 2$\overset{}{6\,0\,0\,0}$
     4 3 2 1

The decimal point has moved 4 places to the left.

Fill in the blanks.

16. $250\,000\,000 = \underline{\hspace{1cm}} \times 10^8$

17. $3.27 \times 10^9 = \underline{\hspace{2cm}}$

18. $31\,450\,000 = \underline{\hspace{2cm}}$

19. $1.008 \times 10^6 = \underline{\hspace{2cm}}$

20. $8\,012\,000 = \underline{\hspace{2cm}}$

21. $6.324 \times 10^7 = \underline{\hspace{2cm}}$

22. $19.27 \times 10^8 = \underline{\hspace{1cm}} \times 10^9$

23. $372 \times 10^{11} = 3.72 \times \underline{\hspace{1cm}}$

24. $0.8507 \times 10^{10} = 8.507 \times \underline{\hspace{1cm}}$

25. $200.86 \times 10^5 = 2.0086 \times \underline{\hspace{1cm}}$

Write the numbers in standard form. Then complete the table.

26. $2 \times 10^2 + 4 \times 10^1$

$= 2 \times 100 + 4 \times \underline{\hspace{1cm}}$

$= \underline{\hspace{2cm}}$

27. $5 \times 10^3 + 2 \times 10^2 + 8 \times 10^1$

$= \underline{\hspace{3cm}}$

$= \underline{\hspace{2cm}}$

28. $8 \times 10^4 + 2 \times 10^2 + 3 \times 10^1 + 2 \times 10^0 = \underline{\hspace{2cm}}$

29. $3 \times 10^5 + 2 \times 10^3 + 2 \times 10^1 + 1 \times 10^0 = \underline{\hspace{2cm}}$

30. $2 \times 10^5 + 1 \times 10^4 + 2 \times 10^3 + 7 \times 10^1 = \underline{\hspace{2cm}}$

31. The number of marbles produced in a factory on Tuesday was 10 times the number it produced on Monday. The number of marbles produced on Monday was 10 times the number it produced on Wednesday.

	Monday	Tuesday	Wednesday
Number of Marbles Produced	3.7×10^5		

32. The total number of marbles produced in the past three days is $\underline{\hspace{2cm}}$.

Comparing Numbers in Scientific Notation:

1st Compare the powers of 10. The greater the power, the greater the number.

2nd If the exponents are the same, compare the coefficients.

e.g. 2.3×10^6 and 9.8×10^3

2.3×10^6
9.8×10^3 $\rightarrow$ 6 > 3, so 2.3×10^6 is greater.

$2.3 \times 10^6 > 9.8 \times 10^3$

e.g. 6.9×10^6 and 7.3×10^6

6.9×10^6
7.3×10^6 Compare the coefficients.
7.3 > 6.9, so 7.3×10^6 is greater.

$6.9 \times 10^6 < 7.3 \times 10^6$

Put each set of numbers in order from least to greatest.

33. 5.46×10^3
6.54×10^2 4.56×10^4

_____

34. 1.09×10^8
9.01×10^7 1.09×10^7

_____

35. 2.43×10^a
$2.34 \times 10^{a+2}$ 3.42×10^a

_____

36. 4.65×10^b
6.54×10^b 4.56×10^b

_____

Put the planets in order according to their masses.
Then answer the question.

37. Planets (from heaviest to lightest)

_____

38. The mass of Saturn is about 100 times the mass of Earth. How heavy is Saturn?

_____

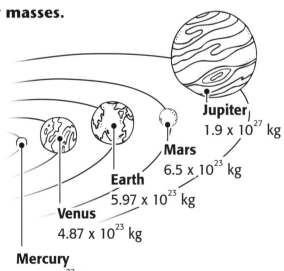

Jupiter
1.9×10^{27} kg

Mars
6.5×10^{23} kg

Earth
5.97×10^{23} kg

Venus
4.87×10^{23} kg

Mercury
3.3×10^{22} kg

Ratio and Proportion

- write ratios in different ways
- use proportions to find missing terms
- find measurements of shapes using proportion
- find distances on map with scale
- solve problems using proportion

Sam, the ratio of the number of hearts on my designed hat to yours is 2:3. There are 24 hearts on my hat.

$$\frac{2}{3} = \frac{24}{n}$$ (×12)

$$n = 36$$

Do you mean that you are going to put 36 hearts on this hat?

Write the ratios in simplest form and in two different ways.

1.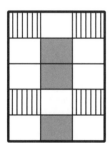

 to ☐ = 1:2 = _____

☐ to = _____ = _____

▨ to all = _____ = _____

2.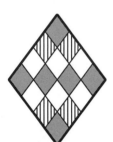

◇ to ◆ = _____ = _____

◈ to ◆ = _____ = _____

◇ to all = _____ = _____

Design a pattern with the given ratios.

3. to all = 2:15

 to = 5:2

 to = 7:10

all to = 5:1

Proportion:

an equation that has two equal ratios

> *There are 2 ways to find the missing term in a proportion.*

e.g. k:6 = 15:18

Way 1

using equivalent fraction

$$\frac{k}{6} = \frac{15}{18}$$

$\times 3$ (top), $\times 3$ (bottom)

k = <u>5</u>

Way 2

multiplying both sides by a number to isolate k

$$\frac{k}{6} \times 6 = \frac{15}{18} \times 6$$

k = <u>5</u>

Find the missing terms. Show your work.

4. 2:p = 12:6

5. 8:3 = s:9

6. 3:7 = q:14

7. n:10 = 8:20

8. *3 is to 4 as b is to 24*

Look at the ratio of different coloured balls in the bag. Then solve it with proportion.

9. There are 10 red balls. Find the number of

   a. blue balls

   b. green balls

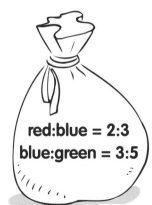

red:blue = 2:3
blue:green = 3:5

10. The ratio of the total number of balls to red balls is 11:2. How many balls are there in the bag?

Look at each pair of similar figures. Find the length of the missing side. Show your work.

11.

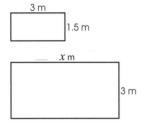

12.

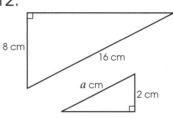

13.

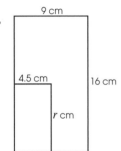

14.

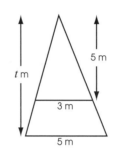

Find the distance between the cities with the given scale. Show your work.

15. The scale tells us that 1 cm on the map represents _____ cm of actual distance.

16. Find the distance between

a. the school and library

_____

b. Mary's house and the theatre

_____

c. the library and theatre

_____

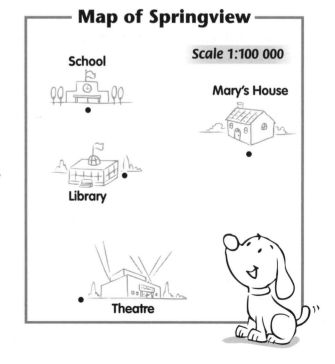

Find the scale of the map with the given information. Then find the distances.

17. a. The scale of the map is _____ .

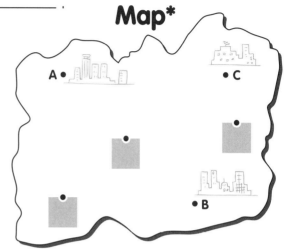

Map*

A

C

B

    b. The actual distance between

        • City A and City C is _____ .

        • City B and City C is _____ .

    c. The actual distance between City C and City D is 132 km. Mark "D" on the map.

* The actual distance between City A and City B is 120 km.

Solve the problems using proportion. Show your work.

18. The number of the star stickers to the heart stickers in a box is in the ratio of 4:5. There are 320 star stickers. How many more heart stickers than star stickers are there?

_____

19.

> The ratio of star stickers to heart stickers on this hat is 3:6 and the ratio of heart stickers to flower stickers is 2:7. There are 14 flower stickers on the hat. How many star stickers are there?

_____

Rate

- find simple rates
- compare rates
- find exchange rates
- solve problems involving rates

My eating rate is 12.5 g/day. How long will this block of cheese last?

No. of Days = 200 ÷ 12.5
= 16

It will last 16 days.

CHEESE 200 g

Find the unit rate for each situation.

1. typing 34 words in half a minute

   _____ words/min

2. earning $385 a week

   $_____ /day

3. a dozen eggs for $2.04

   _____ ¢/egg

4. running 5 tracks in 7 minutes

   _____ min/track

5. printing 20 copies in 45 seconds

   _____ s/copy

6. serving 4 customers in 1 hour

   _____ min/customer

Find the unit rates. Then check the best buy.

7.

A $6.90
B $3
1.5 L
Juice
3.75 L
300 mL
C 63¢

Unit Price

A) $_____ /L

B) $_____

C) $_____

8.

A $6.88
Flour
Flour 600 g
4.3 kg
Flour 2.25 kg
B $1.44
C $4.50

Unit Price

A) $_____ /kg

B) $_____

C) $_____

Find the food items that the children bought. Show your work.

9. Katie bought 3 L of juice that cost $3.90.

 $1.28/L

 0.13¢/mL

 $1.42/L

Cost of 3 L =

Katie bought _____ juice.

10. Joe bought 200 g of cold cut that cost $3.60.

 2¢/g

 $21/kg

 1.8¢/g

Joe bought _____ .

Complete the table and find the exchange rates. Then answer the question.

11.

Exchange Rate

USD ($)	CAD ($)	HKD ($)
1		7.75
3	3.69	
5		
7		
9		
10		
20		
30		

12. Write the exchange rates.

a. USD $1 = CAN $_____

b. CAD $1 = HKD $_____

c. HKD $1 = USD $_____

13.

> I have USD $4, HKD $70, and CAD $21. How much do I have in total in CAD?

_____

35

Look at the recipe and read what Karen says. Help her solve the problems.

14.

> I want to make a loaf of banana bread of 15 servings. How much of each ingredient do I need?

Karen needs:

- butter: _____

- sugar: _____

- banana: _____

- salt: _____

- baking powder: _____

Banana Bread
(10 servings)

- 3 teaspoons of baking powder
- 3 bananas
- 120 g of butter
- $\frac{1}{2}$ teaspoon of salt
- 2 cups of flour
- $\frac{1}{2}$ cup of sugar

15. A tub of 500 g of butter costs $5.48. How much does the butter cost for Karen's loaf? _____

16. How much salt does Karen need if she makes 20 servings? _____

17. How many servings can Karen make with 2 cups of sugar? _____

18. How many bananas are needed for

   a. 6 cups of flour?   b. 240 g of butter?

   _____   _____

Solve the problems.

19. Look at the price of pebbles.

$4.50/kg

a. How many kilograms of pebbles can be bought with $10?

_____

b. How much do $3\frac{1}{5}$ kg of pebbles cost?

_____

20. A customer gets one free pack of correction pens for every purchase of 5 packs. How much does each correction pen cost if a customer

$5.75/pack

a. buys 1 pack?

_____

b. buys 5 packs and gets 1 pack for free?

_____

21. Michelle makes 19 cookies in 30 minutes and Jane makes 30 in 45 minutes.

a. What is the total number of cookies made by both girls in 1.5 hours?

_____

b.

What is the ratio of the number of cookies that Michelle makes to what I make in 3 hours?

Jane

_____

Application of Percent

- find percent change
- find sale price of items in different ways
- find sale tax on items
- calculate simple interest using the formula

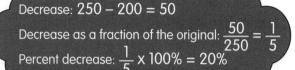

Decrease: 250 − 200 = 50

Decrease as a fraction of the original: $\frac{50}{250} = \frac{1}{5}$

Percent decrease: $\frac{1}{5} \times 100\% = 20\%$

How come the weight of the cookies deceased by 20%?

Fill in the blanks and find the percent change.

1. The average test score increases from 78 to 87.

    - Increase: _____

    - Increase as a fraction of the original: _____

    - Percent increase: _____ x 100% = _____

The test score increases by about _____ .

2. To drop from 51 kg to 46 kg

    - Decrease: _____

    - Decrease as a fraction of the original:

      _____

    - Percent decrease:

      _____ = _____

3. To grow from 160 cm to 178 cm

    - Increase: _____

    - Increase as a fraction of the original:

      _____

    - Percent increase:

      _____ = _____

Finding the Sale Price Using Two Different Ways:

e.g.   The regular price of a circus show ticket is $95. If the ticket is sold at a 25% discount, what is its sale price?

Way 1 Find the discount. Then subtract.

Discount: $95 x 25% = $23.75

Sale Price: $\underline{\$95}$ − $\underline{\$23.75}$ = $71.25
　　　　　　regular　　discount
　　　　　　price

Way 2 Find the percent. Then multiply.

Discount in Percent: 1 − 25% = 75%

Sale Price: $\underline{\$95}$ x $\underline{75\%}$ = $71.25
　　　　　　regular　discount
　　　　　　price　in percent

The sale price of the ticket is $71.25.

Find the sale price of each item. Then answer the question.

	Way 1	Way 2

Ideal Clothing

*Get **30%** off Regular Price*

4.

• $110.50

5.

• $59.24

6.

• $82.88

7.   Ms. Collins buys a 3-piece suit set. How much does it cost? (You may use either method to find the answer.)

Get an extra 10% off on a 3-piece set.

The suit set costs _____ .

9

Finding Sales Tax:

e.g. A printer costs $112. How much does it cost including the PST and GST?

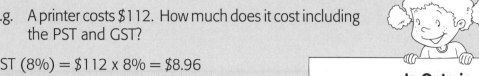

PST (8%) = $112 x 8% = $8.96
GST (5%) = $112 x 5% = $5.60
Total Cost: $112 + $8.96 + $5.60 = $126.56

The total cost of the printer is $126.56.

In Ontario

PST (Provincial Sales Tax) = 8%

GST (Goods and Services Tax) = 5%

Find the taxes and total cost of each item.

8.

 $59.50    $98.70    $110.54

PST _____ x 8% = _____

GST _____ x 5% = _____

**Total
Cost**

All the appliances and toys are 15% and 35% off the regular price respectively. Complete the information chart and answer the question.

9. **Stove Top: $1340**   **Oven: $1780**   **Bike: $218.50**

Sale Price: _____   Sale Price: _____   Sale Price: _____

PST: _____   PST: _____   PST: _____

GST: _____   GST: _____   GST: _____

Total: _____   Total: _____   Total: _____

10. The regular price of an oven in another store is $1690 and is selling at a discount of 10%. Is this oven a better buy than the one above? Explain.

_____

Simple interest – interest that is calculated only on the principal

Simple interest formula:

$$I = P \times r \times t$$

Interest ($)

Principal ($)

Interest Rate (%)

Time (year)

e.g. Galie deposited $500 into a bank account at the simple interest rate of 6%. How much interest does Galie earn in 3 years?

P = $500   I = P x r x t
r = 6%   = $500 x 6% x 3
t = 3   = $90

Galie earns $90 interest in 3 years.

Find the values of the missing terms.

11. **P = $2500   r = 9%   t = 5**

I = _____ x _____ x _____

= _____

12. **P = $39 000   r = 5%   t = 3**

I = _____

= _____

13. P = $180

r = 5.5%

t = 2

I = _____

14. P = $3600

r = 7.25%

t = _____

I = $1957.50

15. P = $8300

r = _____

$t = 1\frac{1}{4}$ ← 1 year 3 months

I = $207.50

Solve the problems.

16. I deposited $5800 into a simple interest savings account $2\frac{1}{2}$ years ago and earned $522. What was the interest rate?

_____

17.

I borrowed $19 385 at a simple interest rate of 5.5% for the car. If I wait 9 months to repay the loan in full, how much interest will I be paying back?

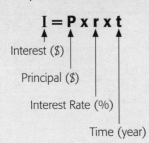

_____

Fractions

- add and subtract fractions that have different denominators
- multiply fractions and mixed numbers
- divide fractions and mixed numbers
- solve problems involving operations on fractions

James, I'm going to make a bowl of fruit punch for you with these two bottles of juice.

Total amount of juice:

$$2\frac{1}{3} + 1\frac{1}{6} = 2\frac{2}{6} + 1\frac{1}{6}$$
$$= 3\frac{3}{6}$$
$$= 3\frac{1}{2} > 3$$

3 L

$2\frac{1}{3}$ L

$1\frac{1}{6}$ L

Thank you, Sue. There will be $3\frac{1}{2}$ L of fruit punch. I think you need a bigger bowl.

Add or subtract the fractions. Write the answers in simplest form.

1. $\dfrac{3}{8} - \dfrac{2}{7}$ = _____ – _____ = _____

2. $\dfrac{7}{12} + \dfrac{1}{6}$ = _____ = _____

3. $2\dfrac{3}{7} + \dfrac{16}{21}$ = _____ = _____

4. $1\dfrac{1}{3} - \dfrac{1}{12}$ = _____ = _____

5. $3\dfrac{4}{15} + 1\dfrac{7}{30}$ = _____ = _____

6. $1\dfrac{3}{4} + 1\dfrac{1}{2}$ = _____ = _____

Hint

To add mixed numbers, add the fractions first; then add the whole numbers.

e.g. $1\dfrac{1}{2} + 2\dfrac{2}{5} = 1\dfrac{5}{10} + 2\dfrac{4}{10}$
$$= 3\dfrac{9}{10}$$

add whole numbers
(1 + 2 = 3)

add fractions
$(\dfrac{5}{10} + \dfrac{4}{10} = \dfrac{9}{10})$

Find the sum and difference of each pair.

		Sum	Difference
7. $2\frac{1}{2}$	$5\frac{4}{6}$	_____	_____
8. 10	$3\frac{7}{9}$	_____	_____
9. $3\frac{7}{10}$	$1\frac{2}{15}$	_____	_____
10. $1\frac{3}{8}$	$1\frac{1}{4}$	_____	_____

Multiplying Fractions:

1st Change all mixed numbers to improper fractions.

2nd Divide the numerators and the denominators by their common factors.

3rd Multiply the numerators and the denominators.

e.g. $\frac{9}{14} \times 1\frac{1}{6}$

$= \frac{9}{14} \times \frac{7}{6}$ ← Change the mixed number to improper fraction.

$= \frac{\overset{3}{\cancel{9}}}{\underset{2}{\cancel{14}}} \times \frac{\overset{1}{\cancel{7}}}{\underset{2}{\cancel{6}}}$ ← Divide the numerator and the denominators by their common factors, 3 and 7. Then multiply.

$= \frac{3}{4}$

Multiply the fractions

11. $\frac{3}{7} \times \frac{2}{9}$

12. $\frac{5}{22} \times 2\frac{3}{4}$

13. $1\frac{7}{12} \times \frac{2}{5}$

14. $\frac{7}{10} \times 3\frac{4}{7} = $ _____

15. $2\frac{5}{8} \times 1\frac{3}{14} = $ _____

16. $1\frac{9}{13} \times 1\frac{5}{11} = $ _____

17. $6\frac{4}{5} \times 2\frac{10}{17} = $ _____

Answer the questions.

18. Joe walked $\frac{1}{3}$ of the journey to the library from his house to meet his cousin, Lucy. How far has he travelled?

Library

$1\frac{3}{4}$ km

Joe's House

_____

19. A bag of flour weighs $3\frac{3}{4}$ kg. Aunt Katie used $\frac{1}{3}$ of the bag of flour to make a cake. How much flour is needed to make the cake?

_____

Dividing Fractions:

1st Change all mixed numbers to improper fractions.

2nd Find the reciprocal of the divisor.

3rd Multiply the dividend by the reciprocal of the divisor.

e.g. $\frac{3}{4} \div 1\frac{1}{8}$

$= \frac{3}{4} \times \frac{8}{9}$ ← $1\frac{1}{8} = \frac{9}{8}$, reciprocal of $\frac{9}{8}$ is $\frac{8}{9}$

$= \frac{3}{4} \times \frac{8}{9}$

$= \frac{2}{3}$

> To find the reciprocal of a fraction, swap the denominator and the numerator. If it is a mixed number, change it to an improper fraction first.

Find the reciprocal of each fraction.

20. $\frac{14}{19}$ _____

21. $\frac{6}{5}$ _____

22. $1\frac{2}{7}$ _____

23. $4\frac{6}{11}$ _____

24. $\frac{1}{3}$ _____

25. 5 _____

Do the division.

26. $14 \div \frac{7}{8} =$ _____

27. $\frac{9}{13} \div 1\frac{1}{8} =$ _____

28. $\frac{3}{11} \div 9 =$ _____

29. $\frac{6}{13} \div \frac{12}{26} =$ _____

30. $27 \div 4\frac{10}{11} =$ _____

31. $1\frac{3}{14} \div 6\frac{4}{5} =$ _____

Solve the problems.

32.
> I'll pack this box of apples into bags each holding $1\frac{1}{4}$ kg of apples. How many bags do I need?

_____

33. There are about 5 apples in a bag. How heavy is an apple on average?

_____

Evaluate each expression and write the answers in simplest form.

34. $(\frac{2}{7} + \frac{5}{14}) \times \frac{8}{15}$

35. $3\frac{1}{3} \div 2\frac{2}{3} - \frac{6}{7}$

36. $1\frac{3}{8} - \frac{1}{2} \times \frac{4}{5}$

37. $\frac{7}{16} \div \frac{1}{4} \times \frac{10}{21} = $ _____

38. $4\frac{7}{8} \times \frac{4}{13} - \frac{9}{10} \div 3 = $ _____

39. $1\frac{5}{13} \times (3\frac{7}{9} - \frac{7}{2}) = $ _____

40. $\frac{6}{7} + \frac{1}{3} \times \frac{9}{10} - \frac{13}{35} = $ _____

Solve the problems.

41. Kary has bought 3 pizzas. She saves $\frac{1}{2}$ of a pizza for her family and serves each guest $\frac{1}{6}$ of a pizza. How many guests are there?

_____

42. How much juice does Kary have?

_____

43. How many cups can all of the jars fill?

_____

Each jar holds $3\frac{2}{3}$ L of juice.

$\frac{3}{8}$ L

4 full jars and 1 half-filled jar of juice

Decimals, Fractions, and Percents

- identify the repeated digits in repeating decimals
- identify terminating and repeating decimals
- put numbers in order
- divide numbers by decimal numbers
- solve word problems

Sue, I'm tired out having to keep writing "3".

decimal of $\frac{1}{3}$

0.333333333...

$0.\overline{3}$

You can just put a bar over the repeated digit "3" to show that $\frac{1}{3}$ is a repeating decimal.

Circle the digit that repeat in each repeating decimal. Then rewrite it with a bar over the repeated digits.

1. $0.99999... = 0.\overline{9}$

2. $1.1313131... = \underline{\hspace{2cm}}$

3. $1.02402402... = \underline{\hspace{2cm}}$

4. $5.08181818... = \underline{\hspace{2cm}}$

5. $3.12342342... = \underline{\hspace{2cm}}$

6. $2.781321321... = \underline{\hspace{2cm}}$

7. $1.1718418418... = \underline{\hspace{2cm}}$

8. $4.053053053... = \underline{\hspace{2cm}}$

Convert the fractions to decimals. Then write "T" for terminating decimals and "R" for repeating decimals in the circles.

9. $\frac{3}{5} = \underline{\hspace{2cm}} \bigcirc$

10. $\frac{2}{9} = \underline{\hspace{2cm}} \bigcirc$

11. $\frac{5}{74} = \underline{\hspace{2cm}} \bigcirc$

12. $2\frac{7}{8} = \underline{\hspace{2cm}} \bigcirc$

13. $\frac{7}{12} = \underline{\hspace{2cm}} \bigcirc$

14. $1\frac{12}{25} = \underline{\hspace{2cm}} \bigcirc$

15. $3\frac{8}{11} = \underline{\hspace{2cm}} \bigcirc$

16. $4\frac{5}{6} = \underline{\hspace{2cm}} \bigcirc$

> **Hint**
>
> **Terminating decimal**: a decimal having a finite number of digits
>
> e.g. 0.85, 2.459
>
> **Repeating decimal**: a decimal having an infinite number of digits
>
> e.g. $0.8888... = 0.\overline{8}$
> $3.181818... = 3.\overline{18}$

Write the fraction, decimal, and percent for the shaded part of each figure.

17.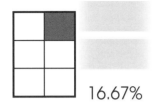

16.67%

18.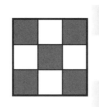

$0.\overline{5}$

19.

$\dfrac{2}{3}$

20.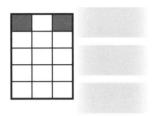

21.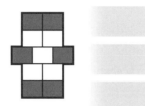

22.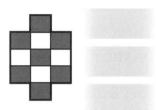

Put ">", "<", or "=" to make each statement true.

23. $\dfrac{2}{9}$ ◯ $0.\overline{2}$

24. 0.4 ◯ $0.4\overline{1}$

25. $\dfrac{1}{8}$ ◯ $0.12\overline{5}$

26. $0.1\overline{9}$ ◯ $1.\overline{19}$

27. $0.\overline{3}$ ◯ $\dfrac{4}{11}$

28. $2\dfrac{1}{3}$ ◯ $2.0\overline{3}$

29. $\dfrac{2}{11}$ ◯ $0.00\overline{8}$

30. $0.5\overline{3}$ ◯ $\dfrac{8}{15}$

31. $0.\overline{07}$ ◯ $\dfrac{7}{90}$

Order each set of numbers from least to greatest. Then do what the girl says.

32. 206% $2.0\overline{6}$ $2.0\overline{06}$ $2.00\overline{6}$ _____

33. 1.16 $1\dfrac{1}{6}$ $1.0\overline{6}$ $1\dfrac{6}{9}$ _____

34. $\dfrac{7}{11}$ $0.6\overline{3}$ 63.3% $\dfrac{33}{90}$ _____

35.

Change 1.207 into different repeating decimals by putting a bar over the digit(s). Then put them in order.

_____

Dividing Decimals by 0.1, 0.01, 0.001:

$$a\ decimal \div \begin{matrix}\div 0.1\\ \div 0.01\\ \div 0.001\end{matrix} = the\ decimal \begin{matrix}\times 10\\ \times 100\\ \times 1000\end{matrix}$$

e.g. $8.9 \div 0.1 = 8.9 \times 10$
$$= 89$$

$$0.21 \div 0.03 = 0.21 \div \frac{3}{100}$$
$$= 0.21 \times \frac{100}{3}$$
$$= 7$$

Do the division.

36. $0.281 \div 0.1 =$ _____

37. $8.07 \div 0.001 =$ _____

38. $0.506 \div 0.01 =$ _____

39. $1.13 \div 0.001 =$ _____

40. $14 \div 0.1 =$ _____

41. $2.8 \div 0.7 =$ _____

42. $0.8 \div 0.02 =$ _____

43. $1.6 \div 0.4 =$ _____

44. $0.09 \div 0.3 =$ _____

45. $0.81 \div 0.009 =$ _____

Find the missing numbers.

46. $0.078 \div$ _____ $= 7.8$

47. _____ $\div 0.001 = 2023$

48. _____ $\div 0.1 = 10.8$

49. $0.73 \div$ _____ $= 14.6$

50. $3.6 \div$ _____ $= 9$

51. _____ $\div 0.09 = 80$

52. $\frac{2.5}{\rule{1cm}{0.4pt}} = 5$

53. $\frac{4}{\rule{1cm}{0.4pt}} = 8$

54. $\frac{\rule{1cm}{0.4pt}}{0.03} = 40$

55. $\frac{\rule{1cm}{0.4pt}}{0.005} = 30$

Hint

A fraction can be rewritten as a division.

e.g. $\frac{0.8}{\rule{0.7cm}{0.4pt}} = 4$ ← equivalent

$0.8 \div$ ___ $= 4$

Complete the charts.

56.

÷ 10	
0.25	
	4.5
3.4	

57.

÷ 0.01	
1.4	
	27.9
0.26	

58.

÷ 0.1	
0.7	
	18.6
	0.29

59.

÷ 0.2	
0.18	
	4
1.56	

60.

÷ 0.05	
0.15	
	10
1.2	

61.

÷ 0.003	
0.9	
	60
1.8	

Help Mr. Welly solve the problems.

62. Mr. Welly had 1.78 kg of ground beef and he used 35% of it to make a shepherd's pie. How many kilograms of ground beef are left?

63.

> 0.65 L of water and $\frac{7}{12}$ of a box of beef stock are needed to make a tasty soup base.

a. How many litres of soup base will Mr. Welly get?

b. Mr. Welly used 45% of the remaining stock to make the shepherd's pie. How much beef stock is left?

Nets

- identify the top, front, and side views of different solids
- match the views with the solids
- sketch solids with given views
- draw nets of prisms
- understand the Euler's formula

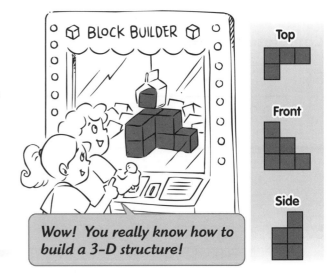

Wow! You really know how to build a 3-D structure!

Label the views of the solids. Write "top", "side", or "front" on the lines.

1.

2.

3.

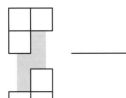

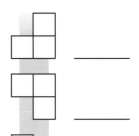

Match the solids with the given views. Write the letters.

4.

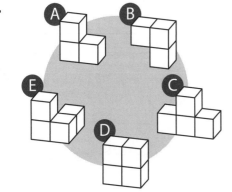

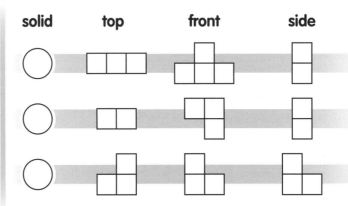

Put a cross on the wrong view of each solid. Then draw the correct one in the circle.

5.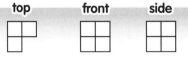

6.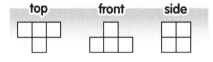

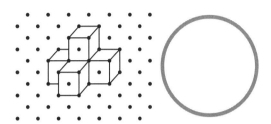

7.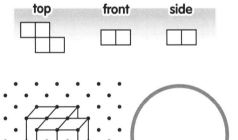

8.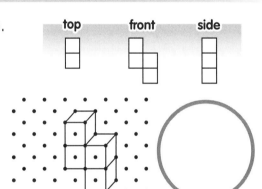

Sketch the objects on the isometric dot paper.

9.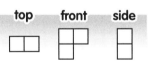

10.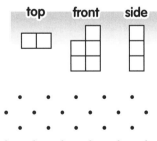

11.

Draw the missing faces to complete the net of each prism. Label the measurements of the sides in bold. Then draw another net that can be folded to give the same prism.

12.

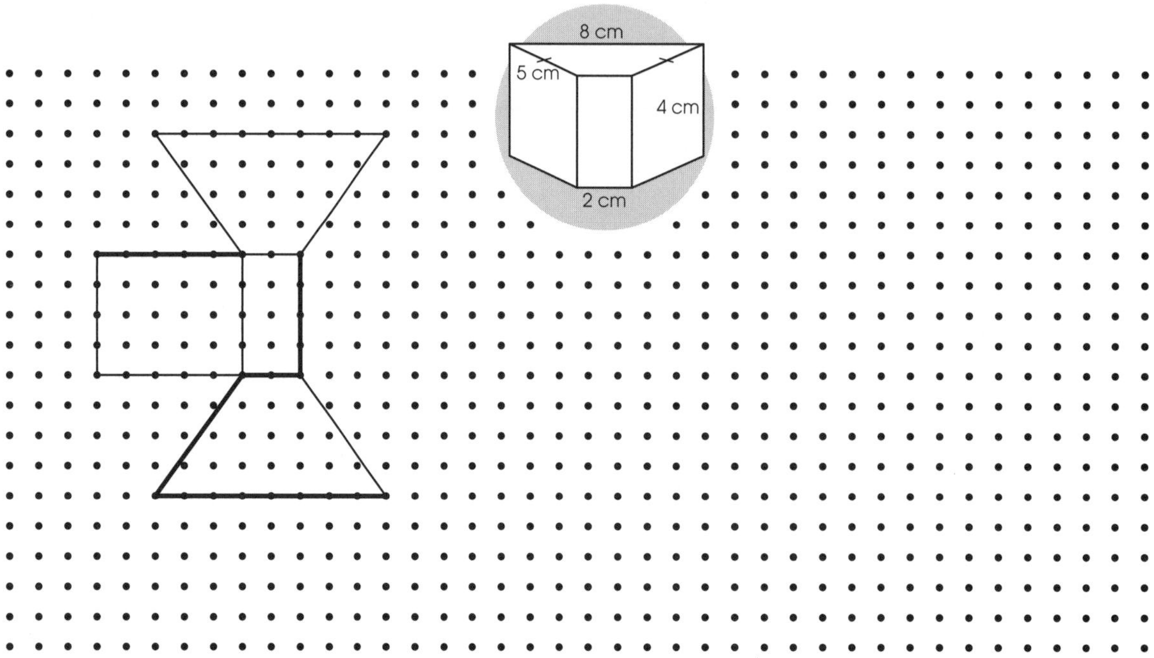

8 cm
5 cm
4 cm
2 cm

Description: _____

_____

13.

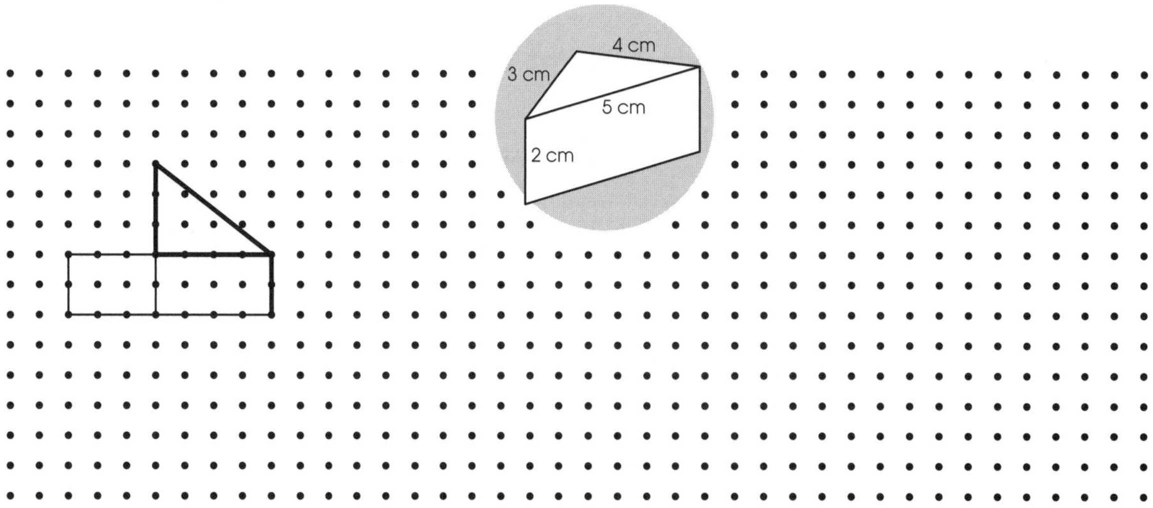

4 cm
3 cm
5 cm
2 cm

Description: _____

_____

MATHEMATICS

Match the views of the correct object. Then sketch a possible net and name the object.

14.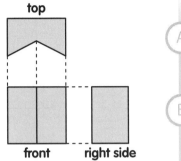

15.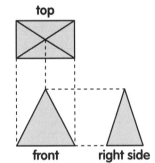

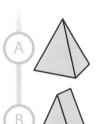

Complete the chart and the Euler's formula to show the relationships among vertices, faces, and edges of a solid. Then answer the question.

16. a.

Solid	Rectangular Prism	Triangular Pyramid	Pentagonal Pyramid
No. of Vertices (V)			
No. of Faces (F)			
No. of Edges (E)			
V + F – E			

b.   Euler's fomula: V + F – E = _____

17.

There are 7 vertices and 7 faces in a solid. How many edges does it have? Name the solid.

_____

53

13

Circumference and Area

- identify the radius and diameter of a circle
- find the circumference and area of a circle
- solve problems involving circumference and area
- draw circles with given information

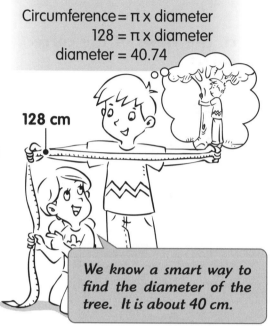

Circumference = π x diameter
128 = π x diameter
diameter = 40.74

128 cm

We know a smart way to find the diameter of the tree. It is about 40 cm.

Fill in the blanks with the help of the words given in the diagram.

1. _____ (r):
   the length of any line segment from the centre of a circle to its edge

2. _____ (d):
   the length of any line segment that passes through the centre where its endpoints are on the edge

3. _____ (C):
   the perimeter of a circle

4. *pi* (π):
   a number, 3.141592... , which is the ratio of

   circumference to _____

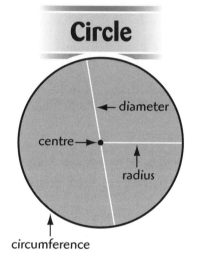

Circle

diameter
centre
radius
circumference

Draw a radius with a red pen and a diameter with a blue pen on each circle. Measure and record the lengths. Then answer the questions.

5. **A** r = _____   d = _____
   B r = _____   d = _____

6. What is the relationship between radius and diameter?

   _____

   _____

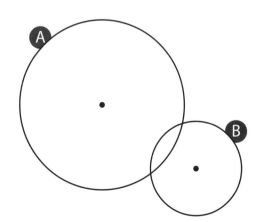

Finding the Circumference of a Circle:

$$C = \pi d$$

or

$$C = 2\pi r$$

e.g. What is the circumference of the circle with a diameter of 4 cm?

$C = \pi d$
$= \pi \times 4$
≈ 12.57 (cm)

π = 3.14

You may find the answer using the "π" button on your calculator or by substituting π with 3.14.

Find the circumference of each circle.

7. d = 3 cm

    C = _____ x _____

    = _____

8. r = 10 m

    C = _____

    = _____

9. r = 0.5 cm

    C = _____

    = _____

10. d = 0.68 m

    C = _____

    = _____

11. 7 cm   C = _____

    = _____

12. 1 m   C = _____

    = _____

Solve the problems.

13. The circumference of a circle is 46 cm. What is its radius?   _____

14. 50.27 cm of string was needed to wrap around a circular object twice. What is the radius of the object?   _____

15. Molly makes 3 identical circles with a string of 152 cm long. What is the diameter of each circle?   _____

16. The circumference of a big circle is 62.83 cm and it is twice as long as that of a small circle. What is the radius of the small circle?   _____

Finding the Area of a Circle:

A = πr²

or

A = π(d/2)²

e.g.   Find the areas.

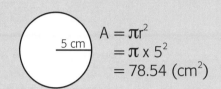

$A = \pi r^2$
$= \pi \times 5^2$
$= 78.54 \ (cm^2)$

$A = \pi(\frac{d}{2})^2$
$= \pi(\frac{12}{2})^2$
$= \pi \times 6^2$
$= 113.1 \ (cm^2)$

Find the area of each circle.

17. r = 1 cm

A =

18. r = 3.9 cm

A =

19. r = 20 cm

A =

Sally has made 3 circles out of modelling clay. Find the areas of the circles. Then answer the questions.

20.

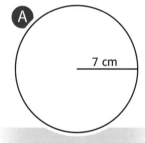

A — 7 cm

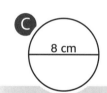

B — 4.5 cm

C — 8 cm

21.

I make one big circle that has the same area as the sum of the 3 circles. What is the radius of the big circle?

_____

22.

I'm making 3 identical circles. Their total area is the same as the big circle's. What is the radius of each circle?

_____

Drawing Circles:

e.g. Draw a circle with a radius of 5 cm.

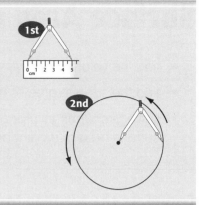

1st Use a ruler to set the point of the compass and the point of the pencil to be 5 cm apart.

2nd Place the point of the compass at the centre of the circle and turn the compass 360°.

Draw circles with the given dots as their centres. Then answer the questions.

23. **A**: centre at A with r = 2.5 cm

    B: centre at B with r = 2 cm

    C: centre at C with d = 3 cm

24. Points A, B, and C are the vertices of △ABC. Explain how to find the side lengths of △ABC without using a ruler.

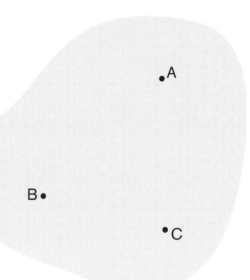

Solve the problems.

25. Tom wants to cut out the largest circle possible from the cardboard to make a spinner. What is the area of the spinner?

_____

26. Timmy the Dog will put a ribbon around the spinner. How much ribbon will be needed?

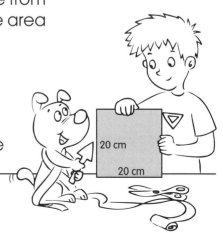

_____

Surface Area and Volume

- find the volume of a cylinder
- find the surface area of a cylinder
- solve problems involving volume and surface area of a cylinder

Volume = $\pi r^2 h$
= $\pi \times 8^2 \times 25$
= 5027 (cm³)
≈ 5 (L)

His water bottle can hold about 5 L of water.

Complete the formula for finding the volume of a cylinder. Then find the volume of each cylinder.

1.

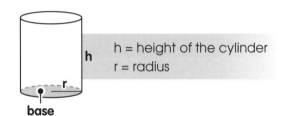

h = height of the cylinder
r = radius

base

Volume of a Cylinder

= base area x height

= _____ x _____

2. **r = 5, h = 4**

V =

3. **r = 3.5, h = 6**

V =

4. **r = 9.2, h = 5.5**

V =

5.

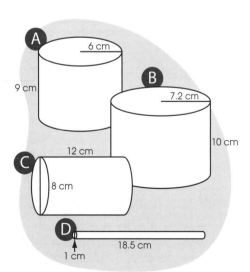

A 6 cm
9 cm
B 7.2 cm
10 cm
12 cm
C 8 cm
D 18.5 cm
1 cm

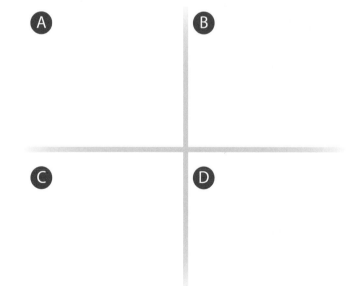

A   B

C   D

Find the capacity of each container in litres. Then answer the questions.

6.

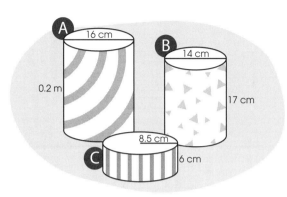

Hint

$1 \text{ cm}^3 = 1 \text{ mL}$

$1 \text{ L} = 1000 \text{ mL}$
$= 1000 \text{ cm}^3$

e.g. $45\ 800 \text{ cm}^3 = 45\ 800 \text{ mL}$
$= 45.8 \text{ L}$

A

B

C

7. Jason poured some water into **B** and the water level reached 12 cm. How much water did Jason pour?   _____

8. How much water can **C** hold if it is half full?   _____

9. One cup holds 450 mL of water. How many cups are needed to fill **A** and **C**?   _____

10. Philip filled up **B** with water and poured it into **C**. After filling up **C**, there is some water left in **B**. What is its water level?   _____

11.

I poured 3500 mL of water into **A**. What is its water level?

_____

Look at the net of a cylinder. Record the measurements. Then complete the formula for finding the surface area of a cylinder.

12.

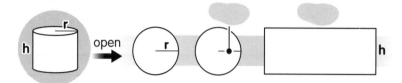

Surface Area of a Cylinder

$$= 2 \bigcirc + 1 \boxed{}$$

$$= 2\pi \underline{}^{2} + \underline{} \times h$$

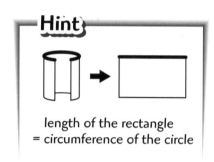

Hint

length of the rectangle
= circumference of the circle

Find the surface area of each cylinder.

13.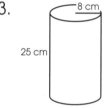

surface area =

8 cm

25 cm

14.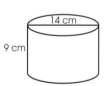

14 cm

9 cm

15.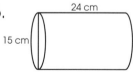

24 cm

15 cm

16.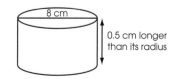

8 cm

0.5 cm longer
than its radius

Given the volume or surface area, find the height of the solids.

17. V = 706.5 cm³

5 cm

18. V = 1692.46 cm³

7 cm

19. S.A. = 979.68 cm²

8 cm

20.

Its surface area is 1215.18 cm².

254.34 cm²

Solve the problems.

21.

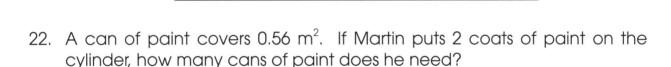

0.5 m   0.5 m

1.2 m

Martin the carpenter wants to make the largest cylinder possible from the block. What is the volume of the cylinder?

_____

22. A can of paint covers 0.56 m². If Martin puts 2 coats of paint on the cylinder, how many cans of paint does he need?

_____

23. If he cuts this cylinder into 3 identical small cylinders, what will be the surface area of each small cylinder?

_____

Write the numbers as a product of prime numbers. Then find the common factors of each set.

1.   12   12 = _____

   90   90 = _____

   Common factors: _____

2.   40
      60

   Common factors: _____

3.   30
   84
      126

   Common factors: _____

4.   75
   245
      315

   Common factors: _____

Estimate the square root of each number and solve the problems.

5. $\sqrt{14}$: between $\sqrt{9}$ and $\sqrt{16}$

   $\sqrt{9}$ = _____ $\sqrt{16}$ = _____

   So, $\sqrt{14}$ ≈ _____

6. $\sqrt{79}$:

7. $\sqrt{38}$:

8. $\sqrt{105}$:

9. The area of a square is 93 cm². What is its side length?   _____

10. Monica trims a square photo frame with ribbon. The area of the frame is 120 cm². How much ribbon does Monica need?   _____

Find the length of each missing side. Round the decimals to 2 decimal places.

11.
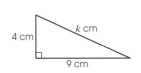

$k =$ _____

12.
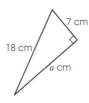

$a =$ _____

13.
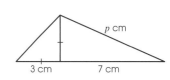

$p =$ _____

14.
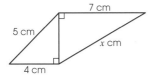

$x =$ _____

15.
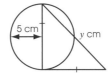

$y =$ _____

16.
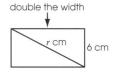

$r =$ _____

Find the answers.

17. $(2^3 + 5^2) - 3 \times 7$

18. $(3^2 + 5) \times 10 - 9^2$

19. $-3^3 + 7^2 + (-2)^4$

20. $(-3^2 - 2^2) \times (-5)$

21. $(3.5^2 - 10) \times 2^2 =$ _____

22. $2^3 \times (6.25 - 4.75)^2 - 3^2 =$ _____

23. $6^2 \div (2.7 + 3.3)^2 =$ _____

24. $7^2 \div (13 + 6^2) \times 0.1 =$ _____

25. $(-1.8 - 2.2)^2 + 1^{84} =$ _____

26. $(-9 + 10)^{25} \times (8^2 \div 2^2) =$ _____

Write the numbers in different forms.

27. **Expanded Form**

    a. $649 = 6 \times 10^{} + 4 \times 10^{} + 9$

    b. $40\ 685 =$ _____

    c. $308\ 250 =$ _____

28. **Scientific Notation**

    a. $71\ 000 =$ _____   b. $35.681 \times 10^3 =$ _____

    c. $0.047 \times 10^7 =$ _____   d. $300 \times 10^2 =$ _____

    e. $4 \times 10^5 + 2 \times 10^3 + 6 \times 10 =$ _____

    f. $3 \times 10^5 + 7 \times 10^4 + 3 \times 10^2 + 9 =$ _____

Answer the questions using proportion.

29. Jennifer and Elsa shared a jar of 240 candies in the ratio of 3:5.

    a. How many candies did Jennifer get?

    b. 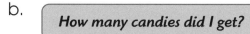 How many candies did I get?

    Elsa

    c. The ratio of red candies to yellow candies that Elsa got is 2:3. Elsa had 90 yellow candies. How many red candies did Elsa get?

    _____

Help Mrs. Collins find the unit price of each item. Check the best buy. Then answer the question.

30.
═══ **Steak** ═══

Ⓐ $6.75 for 1.5 kg   ($ /kg)

Ⓑ $9.70 for 2 kg   (   )

Ⓒ $10.50 for 2.5 kg (   )

═══ **Chicken Wings** ═══

Ⓐ $9.20 for 10 wings   (   )

Ⓑ $5.76 for 6 wings   (   )

Ⓒ $12.40 for a dozen wings (   )

31.

> I spent $16.42 on steak and chicken wings. If I spent $6.30 on steak, how many chicken wings did I buy?

_____

Complete the receipt and answer the question.

32.

Future Electronics		
Qty.	Item (Sales Price)	Cost
1	Toaster ($)	
2	Blenders ($)	
	Sub-Total	
	PST	
	GST	
	Total	

Future Electronics

*Get **25%** off regular price*

• $80.24

• $50.80

• $49.56

8% PST and 5% GST are applicable

33. James works at Future Electronics and he gets an employee discount of 30% on top of sales prices and before tax. How much did he need to pay for an iron?

_____

Find the answers.

34. $3\frac{5}{6} - 1\frac{1}{9}$

35. $2\frac{3}{4} + 1\frac{3}{10}$

36. $1\frac{1}{4} \times \frac{8}{15}$

37. $2\frac{1}{3} \times \frac{2}{21}$

38. $\frac{8}{9} \div \frac{4}{9}$

39. $2\frac{2}{7} \div \frac{8}{15}$

40. $(\frac{1}{8} + \frac{3}{4}) \times \frac{1}{21} =$ _____

41. $\frac{3}{8} + 2\frac{1}{2} \div 1\frac{1}{3} =$ _____

42. $\frac{3}{8} \times (3\frac{4}{5} - 1\frac{2}{3}) =$ _____

43. $2\frac{2}{11} \times \frac{7}{8} \div 1\frac{7}{11} =$ _____

44. $(4\frac{1}{3} - 1\frac{1}{8}) \div 11 =$ _____

45. $10 \div (4 - 1\frac{1}{2}) =$ _____

Draw the views of each solid. Then name the solids from the views.

46.

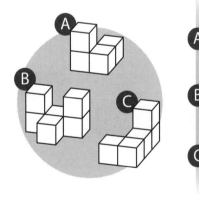

top   front   side

A

B

C

47.

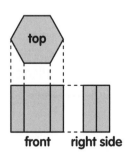

top

front   right side

_____

48.

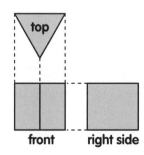

top

front   right side

_____

49.

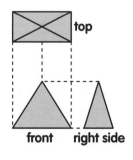

top

front   right side

_____

Draw the circles. Then find their circumferences and areas. (Use π = 3.14.)

50. **Circle A** (centre at A and with r = 4 cm)

area = _____

circumference = _____

Circle B (centre at B and with d = 6 cm)

area = _____

circumference = _____

•A

•B

•C

Circle C (centre at C and with d = 4 cm)

area = _____

circumference = _____

Find the information indicated for each cylinder. Then answer the questions.

51.   Volume: Surface area:

6 cm

15 cm

52.   **V = 310.86 cm³**   Radius: Surface area:

11 cm

53.   1 cm   Height: Volume:

S.A. = 50.24 cm³

54.   *What is the volume of the largest cylinder that I can cut out from this block of clay? How much clay will I have left?*

_____

11 cm

6 cm   7 cm

Volume and Surface Area of Solids (1)

- find the volume of solids
- find the surface area of solids
- solve problems involving volume and surface area of solids

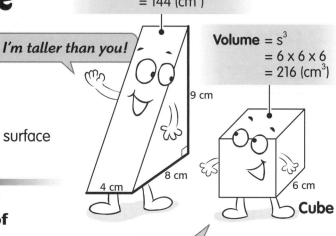

Volume = base x height
= (9 x 8 ÷ 2) x 4
= 144 (cm³)

I'm taller than you!

Volume = s³
= 6 x 6 x 6
= 216 (cm³)

9 cm

8 cm

4 cm

6 cm

Cube

But I have a greater volume.

Find the volume and surface area of each prism.

1.

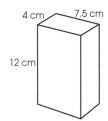

4 cm   7.5 cm

12 cm

2.

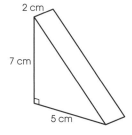

2 cm

7 cm

5 cm

Hint

Pythagorean Theorem

c   a

b

$c^2 = a^2 + b^2$

3.

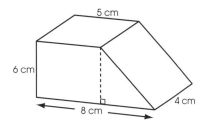

5 cm

6 cm

8 cm

4 cm

4.

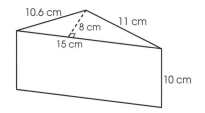

10.6 cm   11 cm

8 cm

15 cm

10 cm

Find the volume and surface area of each solid.

5.

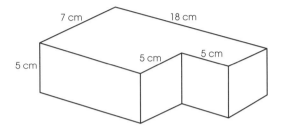

6.

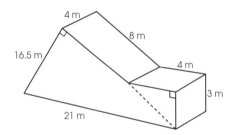

7.

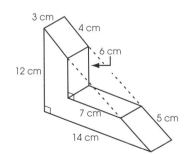

Look at the dimensions of the blocks that Justin uses to build the solids. Find the volume and surface area of each solid. Then fill in the blanks.

8.

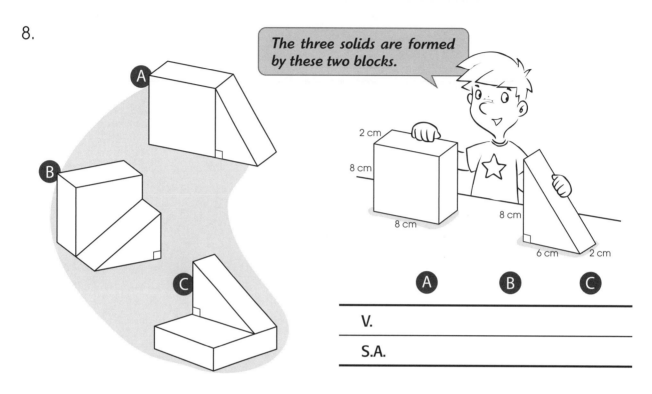

The three solids are formed by these two blocks.

	A	B	C
V.			
S.A.			

9. The volumes of the solids in different arrangement are _____ .

different / the same

10. The surface areas of the solids in different arrangement are _____.

different / the same

11. Justin stacks up some rectangular blocks to make the smallest possible cube. What is the volume of the cube?

_____

12. Justin makes a rectangular prism using 2 triangular blocks. What is the surface area of the rectangular prism?

_____

13. A rectangular prism that has a volume of 1024 cm^3 is made with some rectangular blocks. How many blocks were used?

_____

Solve the problems.

14. Connie paints the rectangular prism.

    a. What is the total surface area to be painted?

    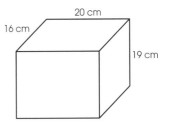

    _____

    b. If Connie removes a cube with the side length of 4 cm from each corner of the solid, what will be the volume of the solid?

    _____

15. A shoe box can hold 32 identical rectangular blocks. What is the total surface area of each block?

    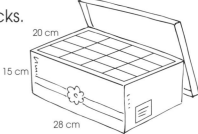

    _____

16

    > *I'm going to cut this loaf of cake into 10 equal pieces and coat each piece with icing.*

    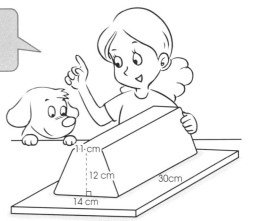

    a. What is the volume of each piece?

    _____

    b. One bag of icing covers an area of 980 cm². How many bags of icing does she need?

    _____

Volume and Surface Area of Solids (2)

- find volumes and surface areas of solids that have circular parts
- solve word problems involving volume and surface area
- identify the relationship between a change of radius or height to volume

Volume $= \begin{matrix} \text{Vol. of the} \\ \text{1st layer} \end{matrix} + \begin{matrix} \text{Vol. of the} \\ \text{2nd layer} \end{matrix}$

$= \pi \times 8^2 \times 3 + \pi \times 15^2 \times 5$

$= 4137.48 \ (\text{cm}^3)$

15 cm

8 cm

5 cm

3 cm

Do you know the volume of this cake?

The volume is about 4000 cm³.

Find the volume and surface area of each solid.

1.

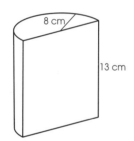

8 cm

13 cm

2.

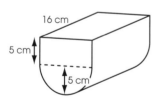

16 cm

5 cm

5 cm

3.

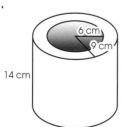

6 cm

9 cm

14 cm

Solve the problems.

4. Find the volumes and surface areas of the cylinder and the cube. Which one has a greater volume? Which one has a greater surface area?

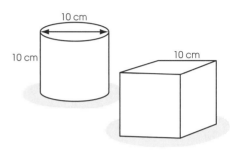

_____

5. Kenneth cuts out a cylinder with the greatest volume from a block of modelling clay. How much clay will be left?

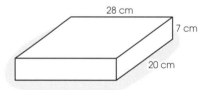

_____

6.

> *I want to paint two wooden blocks. Both have the same volume.*

a. What is the height of the rectangular prism?

_____

b. What is the total surface area to be painted?

_____

Draw cylinders to match the descriptions. Then find the volumes of the solids and answer the questions.

7. **cyclinder (A)**
    • radius: 3 cm
    • height: 5 cm

    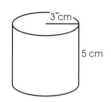

    3 cm
    5 cm

    $V = \pi r^2 h$

    =

cyclinder (B)
• radius: double of (A)
• height: 5 cm

cyclinder (C)
• radius: triple that of (A)
• height: 5 cm

8. If the heights of two cylinders are the same and the radius of the big cylinder doubles that of the small one, the volume of the big cylinder is _____ times that of the small one.

9. If the heights of two cylinders are the same and the height of the big cylinder triples that of the smaller one, the volume of the big cylinder is _____ times that of the small one.

10.

The heights of the cylinders are the same. The smallest cylinder has a volume of 450 cm^3.

• The radius of the medium-sized cylinder is 2 times that of the smallest one. Its volume is _____ .

• The radius of the largest cylinder is 3 times that of the smallest one. Its volume is _____ .

Draw cylinders to match the descriptions. Then find the volumes of the cylinders and answer the questions.

11. **cyclinder P**
    - radius: 5 cm
    - height: 2 cm

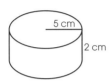

$V = \pi r^2 h$

$=$

cyclinder Q
    - radius: 5 cm
    - height: 4 cm

cyclinder R
    - radius: 5 cm
    - height: 6 cm

12. If the radii of two cylinders are the same and the height of the tall cylinder doubles that of the short one, the volume of the tall cylinder is _____ times that of the short one.

13. If the radii of two cylinders are the same and the height of the tall cylinder triples that of the short one, the volume of the tall cylinder is _____ times that of the short one.

14.

Our cylindrical containers have the same radius, but the height of my container is double that of yours. The volume of my container is 5400 cm³. What is the volume of your container?

_____

Angle Properties of Intersecting Lines

- Identify complementary angles, supplementary angles, and opposite angles
- Find measures of angles using angle properties

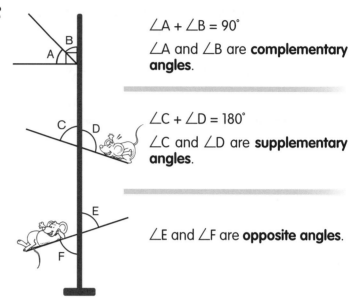

$\angle A + \angle B = 90°$

$\angle A$ and $\angle B$ are **complementary angles**.

$\angle C + \angle D = 180°$

$\angle C$ and $\angle D$ are **supplementary angles**.

$\angle E$ and $\angle F$ are **opposite angles**.

Circle the correct answer. Then use the given word to describe the relationship between each pair of angles.

complementary   supplementary   opposite

1.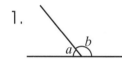

   The sum of $\angle a$ and $\angle b$ is   90° / 180° .

   $\angle a$ and $\angle b$ are _____ angles.

2.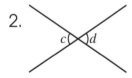

   The measures of $\angle c$ and $\angle d$ are   the same / not the same .

   $\angle c$ and $\angle d$ are _____ angles.

3.

   The sum of $\angle AOB$ and $\angle BOC$ is   90° / 180° .

   $\angle AOB$ and $\angle BOC$ are _____ angles.

4.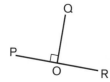

   The sum of $\angle POQ$ and $\angle QOR$ is   90° / 180° .

   $\angle POQ$ and $\angle QOR$ are _____ angles.

Name each pair of angles as "complementary", "supplementary", or "opposite".

5.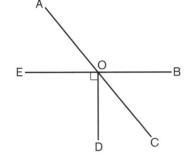

a. ∠BOC and ∠COD: _____ angles

b. ∠AOE and ∠AOB: _____ angles

c. ∠AOE and ∠BOC: _____ angles

d. ∠DOE and ∠DOB: _____ angles

6.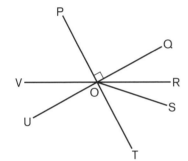

a. ∠VOP and ∠POR: _____ angles

b. ∠QOR and ∠ROT: _____ angles

c. ∠VOU and ∠QOR: _____ angles

d. ∠POV and ∠ROT: _____ angles

Name the angles.

7.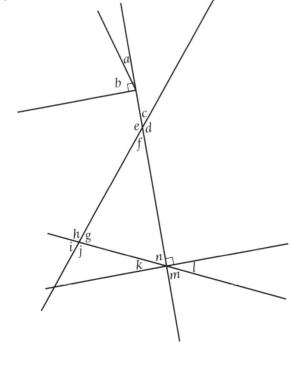

Complementary Angles

• ∠a and _____

• ∠n and _____

• ∠l and _____

Supplementary Angles

• ∠c and _____

• ∠i and _____

• ∠h and _____

Opposite Angles

• ∠d and _____

• ∠g and _____

• ∠k and _____

• ∠h and _____

Name the relationship between the angles. Then find the measure of each angle.

8. ∠AOB and ∠BOC are _____ angles.

   So, ∠AOB + ∠BOC = _____

   ∠BOC = _____ – ∠AOB

   = _____

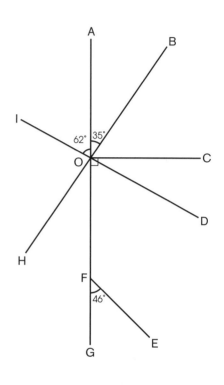

9. ∠DOF and ∠AOI are _____ angles.

   So, ∠DOF = ∠AOI

   = _____

10. ∠EFG and ∠OFE are _____ angles.

    So, ∠EFG and ∠OFE = _____

    ∠OFE = _____ – ∠EFG

    = _____

Look at the above diagram again. Find the measures of the angles. Show your work.

11. ∠FOH

12. ∠HOI

13. ∠DOF

14. ∠COD

Draw a pair of angles that match each of the following descriptions.

15. opposite angles each having an angle of 35°

16. supplementary angles that are congruent

17. complementary angles that are congruent

18. supplementary angles with the measure of one angle being 30°

Find the measures of the shaded angles. Give reasons and show your work.

19.

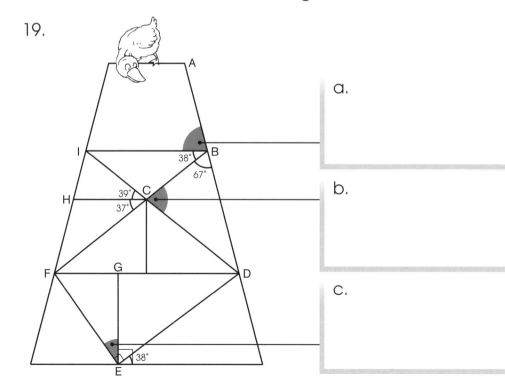

a.

b.

c.

Angle Properties in Parallel Lines

Joe, I've to climb up to find the measure of that angle.

- identify corresponding, alternate, and interior angles
- find the angles in parallel lines
- find the measure of angles and state reasons

Read the descriptions and draw the missing angles. Then fill in the blanks with the given words.

You don't need to do that, Sam. Since the ladder is a transversal of the two parallel horizontal lines, ∠a and the angle formed by the ladder to the ground are corresponding angles. So, the measure of ∠a is 62˚.

Interior	Corresponding	Alternate

1. _____ **angles**
   - two equal angles that are in matching corners

2. _____ **angles**
   - the two angles are inside the parallel lines and on the same side of the transversal where their sum is 180°

3. _____ **angles**
   - two equal angles that are either both inside or outside the parallel lines and on the opposite side of the transversal

4.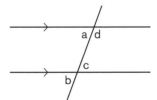
   ∠a and ∠b are _____ angles.
   ∠a and ∠c are _____ angles.
   ∠c and ∠d are _____ angles.

5.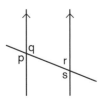
   ∠p and ∠s are _____ angles.
   ∠q and ∠s are _____ angles.
   ∠q and ∠r are _____ angles.

Fill in the blanks. Then find one more pair of angles of each kind from each diagram.

	alternate angles	corresponding angles	interior angles

6.

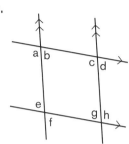

∠b and ＿＿＿   ∠a and ＿＿＿   ∠a and ＿＿＿

∠c and ＿＿＿   ∠b and ＿＿＿   ∠b and ＿＿＿

＿＿＿＿＿＿＿   ＿＿＿＿＿＿＿   ＿＿＿＿＿＿＿

7.

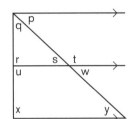

∠p and ＿＿＿   ∠p and ＿＿＿   ∠(p+q) and ＿＿＿

∠w and ＿＿＿   ∠r and ＿＿＿   ∠u and ＿＿＿

＿＿＿＿＿＿＿   ＿＿＿＿＿＿＿   ＿＿＿＿＿＿＿

Find the measures of the angles in each diagram.

8.

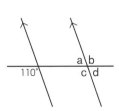

9.

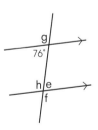

10.

11.

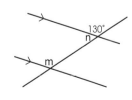

Find the measures of the angles in each diagram and state the reasons.

12.

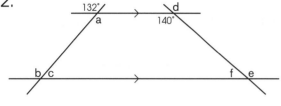

∠b = 132° (_____ angles)

∠a = ∠b (_____ angles)

　= _____

∠c + ∠b = _____

　　　　(_____ angles)

∠c = 180° – ∠b

　= _____

∠e = 140° (_____ angles)

∠d = ∠e (_____ angles)

∠f + ∠e = _____

　　　　(_____ angles)

∠f = 180° – ∠e

　　= _____

13.

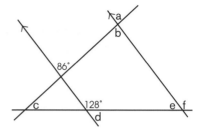

14.

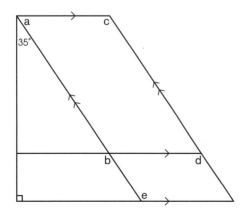

Check the correct answers and state the reasons.

15. If ∠ABD = 65°, then

    Ⓐ ∠CDG = 115° (_____ angles)

    Ⓑ ∠CDG = 65° (_____ angles)

16. If ∠DEF = 115°, then

    Ⓐ ∠CEF = 65° (_____ angles)

    Ⓑ ∠EDG = 75° (_____ angles)

17. If ∠CDG = 65°, then

    Ⓐ ∠ABD = 115° (_____ angles)

    Ⓑ ∠DEF = 115° (_____ angles)

18.

Angle AHG is 150°.

    Ⓐ ∠CIH = 30° (_____ angles)

    Ⓑ ∠CIG = 30° (_____ angles)

Draw a diagram to match what Tony says. Answer his question.

19.

The small angle of a pair of interior angle is 10° less than the big one. What are the measures of the two angles?

Angle Properties in a Triangle

- find the measures of angles in triangles
- identify the appropriate set of measures of angles in triangles
- sketch triangles with the given information and find the measures of the angles
- solve problems

$\angle a + \angle b + \angle c = 180°$

Jack, no matter how hard you pull, the sum of the angles in the triangle will still be 180°.

Find the measure of the angle in each triangle.

1.
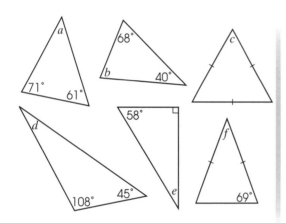

$\angle a =$ _____ $\angle b =$ _____

$\angle c =$ _____ $\angle d =$ _____

$\angle e =$ _____ $\angle f =$ _____

Check the appropriate set of measures of angles in each triangle.

2.
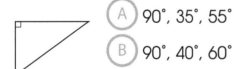
- (A) 90°, 35°, 55°
- (B) 90°, 40°, 60°

3.
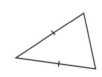
- (A) 65°, 65°, 70°
- (B) 70°, 40°, 70°

4.

- (A) 38°, 90°, 38°
- (B) 45°, 90°, 45°

5.
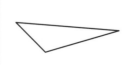
- (A) 20°, 120°, 40°
- (B) 30°, 150°, 0°

Find the measures of the angles. Show your work.

6.

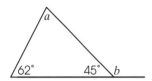

7.

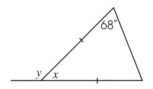

8.

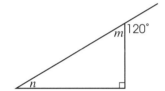

Find the measures of the shaded angles.

9.

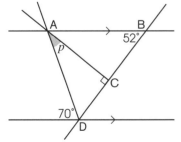

10.

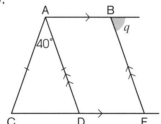

11.

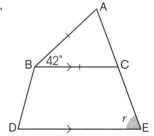

Draw the lines and find the measures of the angles.

12. Draw line $\overline{BD}$ so that $\angle ABD$ is 30°.

   • $\angle ABC =$ _____

   • $\angle ADB =$ _____

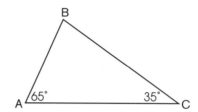

13. Draw line $\overline{FH}$ so that $\angle EFH$ is 20°.

   • $\angle GFH =$ _____

   • $\angle EHF =$ _____

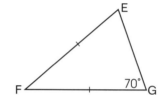

14. Connect points W and Y.

   • $\angle WYZ =$ _____

   • $\angle XYW =$ _____

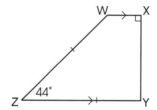

Sketch the diagrams and find the measures of the angles.

15. In $\triangle ABC$,

   • $\angle A = 35°$
   • $\angle B = 74°$

   The measure of the supplementary angle of $\angle C$ is _____ .

16. In isosceles $\triangle PQR$,

   • $\angle P$ is the vertex.
   • The supplementary angle of $\angle Q$ is 110°.

   The measure of $\angle P$ is _____ .

Solve the problems.

17. Sarah wants to make a regular pentagon with isosceles triangles. What are the measures of the angles in each triangle?

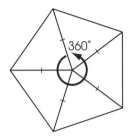

_____

18. The measures of the angles in a triangle are in the ratio of 1:3:6. Find the measures of the angles. (Hint: Let the measure of the smallest angle be x.)

_____

19. The vertex angle in an isosceles triangle is $y°$. If the measure of its base angle is 4 times that of the vertex, what are the measures of the angles?

_____

Prove that the sum of the angles in the trapezoid is 360°. Show your work.

20.

Draw a diagonal line in the trapezoid and think about the angle sum of triangles.

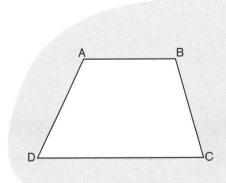

20

Constructing Bisectors

Let me have the compass. I'll show you how to bisect a slice of pizza.

- identify perpendicular bisectors and angle bisectors and their properties
- draw line bisectors and angle bisectors
- draw bisectors and find measures of the angles
- draw angles using only a ruler and a compass

Fill in the blanks to complete the sentences. Then highlight the perpendicular bisector of each line segment and the bisector of each angle.

1. The **perpendicular bisector** passes through the _____ of
   midpoint / endpoint

   the line segment. It meets the line segment at a _____
   acute / right

   angle(s).

   a.

   b.

2. The **angle bisector** passes through the _____ of an angle.
   arms / vertex

   It divides the angle into _____ equal parts.
   two / three

   a.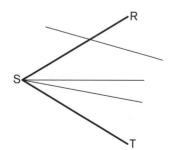

   b.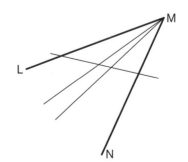

Draw the bisectors.

3.   Bisect the line segments.

4.   Bisect the angles.

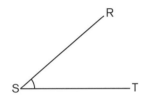 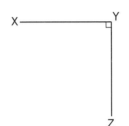 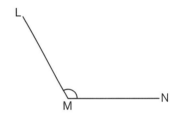

Draw the bisectors and find the measures of the angles without a protractor.

5.   • Bisect the lines $\overline{AC}$ and $\overline{BC}$.

   • Mark the intersection of the bisectors as X.

   • Mark the intersection of the bisector and $\overline{AC}$ as Y.

   The measure of ∠AXY is _____ .

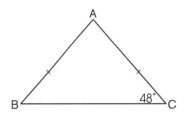

6.   • Bisect ∠P and ∠R.

   • Mark the intersection of the bisectors as M.

   The measure of ∠PMR is _____ .

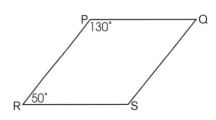

Bisect the two line segments and answer the questions.

7.

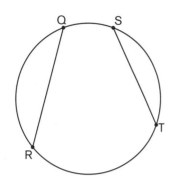

- Mark the intersection of the bisectors as X.
- Connect X to each point.

8. Find the lengths.

 a. $\overline{QX}$ = _____   b. $\overline{RX}$ = _____

 c. $\overline{SX}$ = _____   d. $\overline{TX}$ = _____

9.

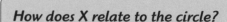

How does X relate to the circle?

_____

_____

_____

Follow the steps to construct a 45° angle from a 90° angle using only a ruler and a compass. Then fill in the blanks and do what the girl says.

10.

┌─── **45° and 90° Angle** ───┐
│   │
│   │
│   │
│   │
│   │
│   │
└─────────────────────────────┘

 a. Steps to draw a 45° angle:

 1st Draw a 90° angle by constructing a perpendicular bisector.

 2nd Bisect the 90° angle.

 b. To draw a 90° angle, construct a _____ bisector.

 c. To draw a 45° angle, bisect a _____ angle.

11.

Describe how you would draw a 135° using only a ruler and a compass. Then draw it in the box and mark the angle.

┌─── **135° Angle** ───┐
│   │
│   │
│   │
│   │
│   │
└──────────────────────┘

_____

_____

Steps to Draw an Equilateral Triangle

1st Draw a line.   **2nd** Draw an arc.   **3rd** Draw another arc.   **4th** Connect the intersection to the endpoints.

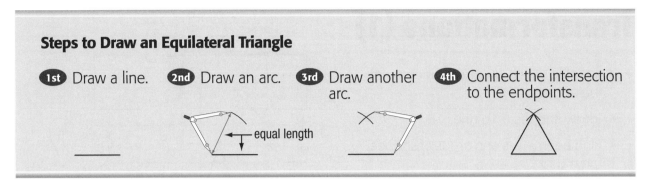

equal length

Make the drawings with only a ruler and a compass. Then fill in the blanks and do what the puppy says.

12. Draw an equilateral triangle.

13. Draw a 30° angle by bisecting one of the 60° angles.

14. To draw a 60° angle, construct an _____ triangle.

15. To draw a 30° angle, bisect a _____ angle.

┌────── 30° and 60° Angle ──────┐
│   │
│   │
│   │
│   │
└───────────────────────────────┘

16. *Describe how you would draw a 150° angle. Then draw it out and mark the angle.*

_____

_____

Draw the shape with the given information. Then answer the questions.

17. Parallelogram

Draw a parallelogram that has all these measurements.

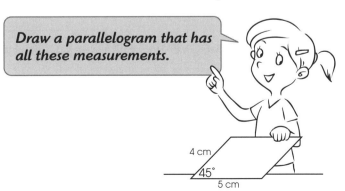

4 cm

45°

5 cm

Transformations (1)

- identify which quadrant each point belongs to
- draw shapes on a grid
- find perimeters and areas of shapes on a grid
- identify translation images
- understand the change of the value of coordinates in translation

Julie's Translation
2 units right & 3 units up

Look! Julie is the fastest one to show a translation image of A.

Look at the points on the grid. Fill in the blanks.

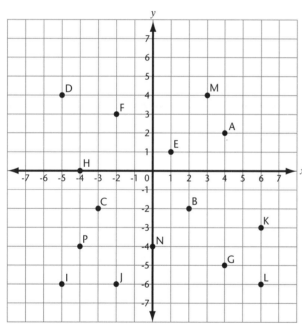

1. Points in each quadrant.

   Quadrant 1: _____

   Quadrant 2: _____

   Quadrant 3: _____

   Quadrant 4: _____

2. Points that do not belong to any quadrant:

   _____

3. Points that have the same x-coordinates: _____

4. Points that have the same y-coordinates: _____

5. Points that lie on the x-axis: _____

6. Points that have x-coordinate 0: _____

7. Points that have equal x- and y-coordinates: _____

8. Find the coordinates of each point.

A _____   B _____   C _____

D _____   E _____   F _____

G _____   H _____   I _____

J _____   K _____   L _____

M _____   N _____   P _____

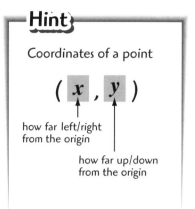

Hint

Coordinates of a point

(x , y)

how far left/right
from the origin

how far up/down
from the origin

9. Draw a line to join the points D and M.

   a. Is it a vertical or horizontal line?   _____

   b. Write the coordinates of any three points on the line. _____

   c. Do the points on a horizontal line have something in
       common? What is it?

   _____

10. Draw a line to join the points F and J.

   a. Is it a vertical or horizontal line?   _____

   b. Write the coordinates of any three points on the line. _____

   c. Do the points on a vertical line have something in common?
       What is it?

   _____

11. The points (6,3), (-1,3), and (-4,3) are on a line. Is it a
    vertical or horizontal line?

    _____

Plot the points and find the missing vertex of each shape. Join the points in order. Then find the area and perimeter of each shape.

12.

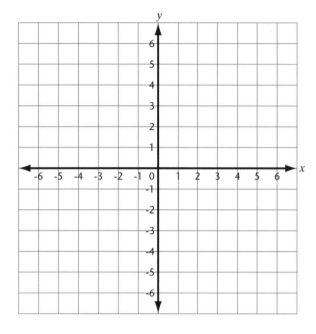

Square	(1,3)	(3,5)
	(5,3)	_____

Kite	(-3,4)	(-1,2)
	(-3,-2)	_____

Rectangle	(-1,-2)	(4,-2)
	(4,-4)	_____

13.

	Area (square units)	Perimeter (units)
Square		
Kite		
Rectangle		

Hint

Make use of Pythagorean Theorem to find the areas and perimeters.

$$a^2 + b^2 = c^2$$

Find the translation images of each shaded figure. Write the letters.

14.   **Translation Images**

triangle   _____

trapezoid   _____

L-shape   _____

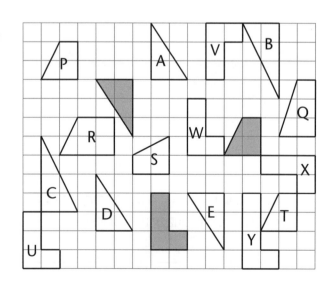

Check the correct translation.

15. Translate 2 units left and 3 units up.

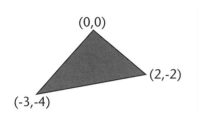

A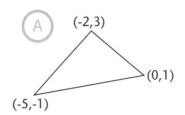

B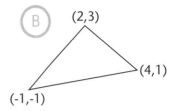

16. Translate 5 units right and 4 units down.

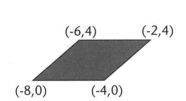

A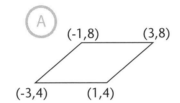

B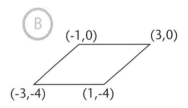

Write the coordinates of the vertices of the images after the translations. Then do what the boy says.

17. Translate trapezoid DEFG.

D(2,1)　　　　D'(-4,5)

E(4,1)　➔　E'(　　)

F(4,-1)　　　　F'(　　)

G(1,-1)　　　　G'(　　)

18. Translate kite IJKL.

I(-3,0)　　　　I'(3,-2)

J(-2,-1)　➔　J'(　　)

K(-3,-3)　　　　K'(　　)

L(-4,-1)　　　　L'(　　)

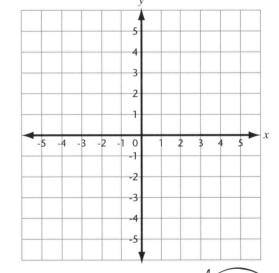

Describe each translation.

19. Trapezoid DEFG: _____

20. Kite IJKL: _____

Transformations (2)

- reflect the points and write their coordinates
- identify the change in the coordinates after reflections
- reflect shapes in the x- and y- axis
- rotate shapes
- identify the change in the coordinates after rotations

right eye (–2,2)
left eye (2,2)

> Your left eye is reflected in the y-axis. Its y-coordinate stays the same and its x-coordinate changes in sign.

Reflect and label the points. Write their coordinates. Then fill in the blanks with the given words.

1. **══ Reflect in x-axis ══**

    A (-4,4)   A' _____

    B _____   B' _____

    C _____   C' _____

    ══ Reflect in y-axis ══

    P _____   P' _____

    Q _____   Q' _____

    R _____   R' _____

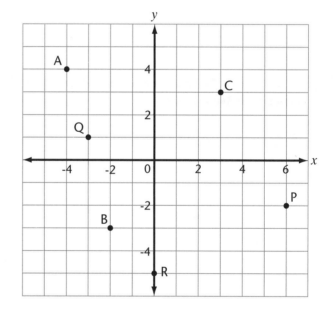

2. When a point is reflected in the x-axis,

    a.   the x-coordinate _____ .

    b.   the y-coordinate _____ .

3. When a point is reflected in the y-axis,

    a.   the x-coordinate _____ .

    b.   the y-coordinate _____ .

stays the same

changes in sign

Reflect each figure and write the coordinates. Then answer the question.

4. Reflect △ABC in the x-axis

△ABC _____

△A'B'C' _____

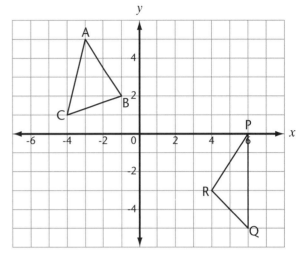

5. Reflect △PQR in the y-axis

△PQR _____

△P'Q'R' _____

6. The vertices of a trapezoid are (15,3), (18,3), (18,-1), and (13,-1). Find the vertices of the reflection image if the trapezoid is reflected in the y-axis.

_____

Reflect the shapes.

7.

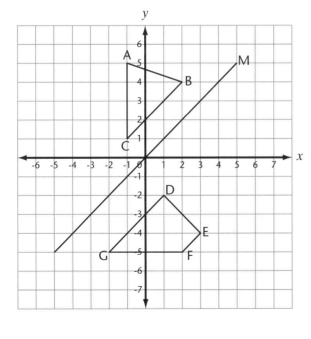

a. Reflect figure ABC in line M.

A(   )   A'(   )

B(   ) ➡ B'(   )

C(   )   C'(   )

b. Reflect figure DEFG in line M.

D(   )   D'(   )

E(   )   E'(   )

F(   ) ➡ F'(   )

G(   )   G'(   )

8. Describe what you observe in the coordinates of each point and its image.

_____

Draw the figure on the grid and do the rotations about the origin. Write the coordinates of the vertices of its image. Then read the descriptions to identify the rotations.

9.

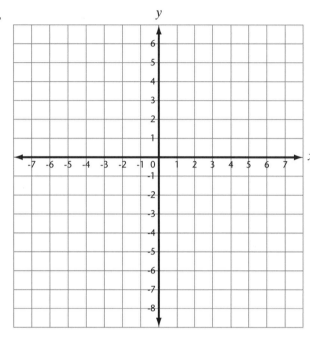

a. figure A

   (1,6)   (6,5)   (0,0)

b. rotate figure A 90° clockwise

_____

c. rotate figure A 180°

_____

d. rotate figure A 270° clockwise

_____

10.

Rotation	**Description**
 clockwise	Change the sign of the x-coordinate; then interchange the coordinates.
	Change the signs of both the x- and y-coordinates.
	Change the sign of the y-coordinate; then interchange the coordinates.

Write the coordinates of the vertices of the images after each rotation.

11.

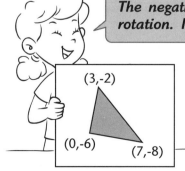

The negative sign denotes that it is a clockwise rotation. It is a counterclockwise turn otherwise.

(3,-2)

(0,-6)   (7,-8)

a. -270° turn   _____

b. -90° turn   _____

c. 180° turn   _____

Do the transformations and write the coordinates of the vertices of the images.

12. To get △I'J'K'
    - translate △IJK 2 units left and 1 unit up
    - reflect in x-axis

    Vertices: _____

13. To get △P'Q'R'
    - reflect △PQR in y-axis
    - make a 180° turn

    Vertices: _____

14. To get △A'B'C'
    - make △ABC a -270° turn
    - translate it 1 unit left and 2 units down

    Vertices: _____

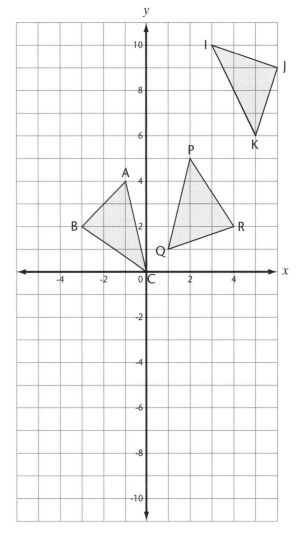

Find the vertices of the images.

15. a. *Translate the triangle 6 units right and 1 unit up.*

    _____

    b. Reflect the image in the y-axis.

    _____

16. a. Reflect the parallelogram in the x-axis.

    _____

    b. Make a 90° turn of the image.

    _____

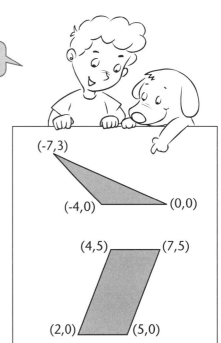

Number Patterns

- write algebraic expressions to describe patterns
- find the term value with the given term number
- find the term number with the given term value
- make graphs to represent patterns

Jacob, do you like my sombrero?

No. of Layers	No. of △
1	$1 (1^2)$
2	$4 (2^2)$
3	$9 (3^2)$
4	$16 (4^2)$

Yes, I do. I want to make one with 5 layers. I think I need 25 triangles, right?

Look at the number pattern. Write an algebraic expression to describe the pattern. Then answer the questions.

1.

Each term value increases by _____ . So, one of the terms in the pattern rule is _____ x n, where n is the term number. Compare the term values and the values of 3n.

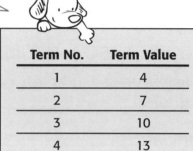

Term No.	Term Value
1	4
2	7
3	10
4	13

Term No.	Term Value	3n	
1	4	3 x 1 = 3	← 1 less
2	7	3 x 2 = 6	← 1 less
3	10		
4	13		

An expression for the *n*th term:

_____ x *n* + _____

2. Use the expression to find the value of each term.

a. the 10th term _____

b. the 14th term _____

c. the 26th term _____

d. the 35th term _____

Write an algebraic expression to describe each pattern. Then find the value of each term.

3.

Term No.	Term Value
1	3
2	7
3	11
4	15

a. an expression for the nth term: _____

b. the 10th term: _____   the 16th term: _____

    the 25th term: _____   the 30th term: _____

4.

Term No.	Term Value
1	1
2	4
3	7
4	10

a. an expression for the nth term: _____

b. the 9th term: _____   the 17th term: _____

    the 20th term: _____   the 33th term: _____

Look at the diagram. Complete the table and write an algebraic expression to describe the number pattern. Then find the value of each term.

5. Figure 1

Figure 2

Figure 3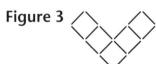

Figure 4

a.

Figure No.	1	2	3	4	5
No. of Lines					

b. an expression for the nth figure: _____

c. No. of lines in

   • figure 8   _____

   • figure 15   _____

   • figure 20   _____

d. Which figure is it if it has

   • 52 lines?   _____

   • 70 lines?   _____

   • 106 lines?   _____

Complete the chart and the graph.

6.

Figure 1   Figure 2   Figure 3   Figure 4

a.

Figure No.	No. of Sticks
1	
2	
3	
4	
5	
⋮	
k	
⋮	
30	

b.

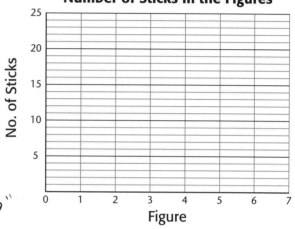

Number of Sticks in the Figures

7.

Figure 1

Figure 2

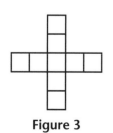

Figure 3

a.

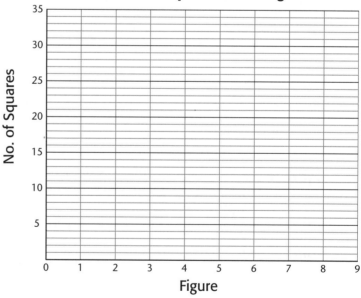

Number of Squares in the Figures

b.   The number of squares in

• figure n: _____   • figure 33: _____

c.   Which figure has 97 squares?   _____

Complete the chart. Then find the answers.

8.

Term No.	Term Value
1	1 ←
2	4 ←
3	9 ←
4	
5	
⋮	
k	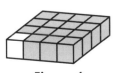

9. Find the term values.

   a. the 8th term   _____

   b. the 11th term   _____

   c. the 15th term   _____

10. Find the term number with the given term value.

   a. 400   _____

   b. 256   _____

   c. 361   _____

Complete the graph. Then answer the questions.

11.

Figure 1

Figure 2

Figure 3

Figure 4

a.

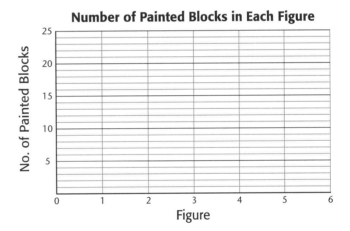

Number of Painted Blocks in Each Figure

b. Expression: _____

c. How many painted blocks are there in figure 20?

   _____

d. A figure has between 75 and 85 painted blocks. What is the number of this figure?

   _____

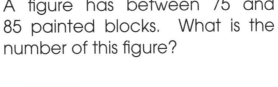

Algebraic Expressions

If you give me all your candies, I will have (4x + 2y) candies.

- match algebraic expressions to the correct statements
- write algebraic expressions for the statements
- Use algebraic expressions to describe different situations
- evaluate algebraic expressions
- solve word problems

$4x$ candies in all $2y$ candies in all

Match each algebraic expression with the correct statement.

1. the sum of 7 less than x and y •

    x divided by 7 plus y •

    6 times x and subtract y •

    x multiplied by $\frac{1}{7}$ plus 6 times y •

    the difference between x and y times 7 •

    x increased by 7 and subtract y •

• $6x - y$

• $x - 7y$

• $\frac{1}{7}x + 6y$

• $x + 7 - y$

• $x - 7 + y$

• $x \div 7 + y$

Write an algebraic expression for each statement.

2. add two different numbers _____

3. the product of two different numbers _____

4. subtract a number from 4 times another number _____

5. multiply a number by 5 and add another number _____

6.

the sum of 2 times a number and $\frac{1}{3}$ of another number

_____

Write the expressions and answer the questions.

7. Find the total amount of

   a. *m* toonies: _____

   b. *n* quarters: _____

   c. *i* toonies and *j* $5 bills: _____

   d. *x* loonies and *y* pennies: _____

> **Hint**
>
> Each term in an expression must have the same unit.

8.

   I have $*c* in toonies and $*d* in quarters. How many coins do I have in all?

   _____

9. Find the costs.

   a. 8 cones _____

   b. *p* cups _____

   c. 5 cones and *n* cups _____

   d. 9 cones and *k* cups _____

Ice Cream Parlour
$*m*
$3

10. Lucy and her three sisters share the cost of 3 cones and *r* cups of ice cream. How much does each child need to pay? _____

11. Conrad spent $32 on ice cream cones and $*d* on ice cream cups. How many cones and cups of ice cream did he buy in total? _____

12. Alicia bought 9 cones and *p* cups of ice cream and got $12 for change. How much did Alicia pay for her treats? _____

Evaluate $2x + y$ where x is 5 and y is 3.

$2x + y = 2(5) + 3$ ← Substitute 5 for x and 3 for y.
$\quad\quad\quad = 10 + 3$ ← Follow the order of operation to find the answer.
$\quad\quad\quad = \underline{13}$

Evaluate each expression using substitution.

13. $m = 7 \quad n = 6$

    a. $\quad 4m + n$

    b. $\quad m - \dfrac{1}{6}n$

14. $x = 3 \quad y = 8$

    a. $\quad 5x - y \div 4$

    b. $\quad 3(x + y)$

15. $i = 10 \quad j = 5$

    a. $\quad 50 - ij$

    b. $\quad (i + 5) \div j$

Evaluate each expression.

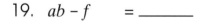

$$a = 8 \quad b = 6 \quad c = 15 \quad d = 7 \quad e = 12 \quad f = 10$$

16. $8a + 2c$

17. $\dfrac{1}{5}c + d$

18. $2b - e \div 6$

19. $ab - f \quad = \underline{\hspace{2cm}}$

20. $7(c - d) \quad = \underline{\hspace{2cm}}$

21. $2a - 3b \quad = \underline{\hspace{2cm}}$

22. $2c \div f \quad = \underline{\hspace{2cm}}$

23. $e - 2b \quad = \underline{\hspace{2cm}}$

24. $(a + b) \div d = \underline{\hspace{2cm}}$

25. $c - 2b + a = \underline{\hspace{2cm}}$

26. $(e \div b) + f = \underline{\hspace{2cm}}$

Evaluate the expressions to complete the chart and answer the question.

27.

x	y	$2(x + y)$	$2x + y$	$2x + 2y$
-2	0			
-1	1			
0	2			
1	3			
2	4			

28. Which two expressions are equivalent? _____

Write the expression for each problem. Then evaluate to find the answers.

29. Kate has 5 bags of x candies and 1 box of y candies. Find the total number of candies.

   (A) $5x + y$ (B) $5x - y$

   For $x = 10$ and $y = 3$, Kate has _____ candies.

30. Joe gives his sister y of the x dozens marbles he has. What is the number of marbles that he has left?

   (A) $12x - y$ (B) $x - y$

   For $x = 3$ and $y = 8$, Joe has _____ marbles.

31.

> The amount of frill that I needed to trim my pillow is y times that what you needed to trim yours, which is in the shape of an equilateral triangle.

Josie

x cm

x cm

How much frill did Josie need to trim each side of her pillow?

   (A) $\dfrac{4x + y}{3}$ (B) $\dfrac{4x}{3y}$

   For $x = 12$ cm and $y = 2$, the side length is _____ cm.

Equations

The number of marbles that I have is 6 times that of yours.

Sue's marbles:

6(5 + 30)
= 6 x 5 + 6 x 30
= 30 + 180
= 210

- evaluate expressions using the distributive property of multiplication
- expand expressions
- write expressions to describe the perimeters and areas of shapes
- solve equations
- solve word problems with equations

MARBLE

I can't believe she has so many marbles!

Find the answers using the distributive property of multiplication.

1. 2(35 + 9)

= 2(   ) + 2(   )

= _____ + _____

= _____

2. 3(9 + 7)

Hint

e.g. Evaluate 2(5 + 18) using the distributive property of multiplication.

multiply

$2(5 + 18) = 2 \times 5 + 2 \times 18$

multiply   = 10 + 36

= 46

3. 4(20 + 6 + 5)

4. 6(5 + 5 + 5)

Expand.

5. 4(3x + 2y)

= 4(   ) + 4(   )

= _____ + _____

6. 4(5 + 4p)

7. 9(2m + 3n)

8. 2(3p + 5q) = _____

9. 5(2a + 3b) = _____

Find the missing numbers.

10. $3(2a + \underline{\hspace{2cm}}) = 6a + 9b$

11. $6(a + \underline{\hspace{2cm}}) = 6a + 42$

12. $5(\underline{\hspace{2cm}} + 3n) = 20m + 15n$

13. $3(\underline{\hspace{2cm}} + q) = 3q + 21p$

14. $6(\underline{\hspace{2cm}} + y + 3z) = 12x + 6y + \underline{\hspace{2cm}}$

15. $7(i + \underline{\hspace{2cm}} + \underline{\hspace{2cm}}) = \underline{\hspace{2cm}} + 21j + 14k$

Write an expression for each situation. Then expand it.

16. 3 times the sum of 5 and $7a$

17. 2 times the sum of $4x$ and y

18. Find the perimeter of each shape.

a.
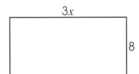

b.

c.
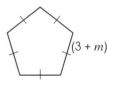

19. Find the area of the whole figures.

a.
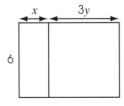

b.
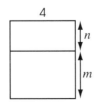

c.
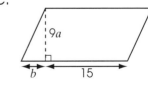

25

Solve the equations.

20. $x - 8 = 14$ 21. $2y = 30$ 22. $a \div 7 = 12$

23. $4y + 5 = 17$ $y =$ _____   24. $3j - 4 = 14$ $j =$ _____

25. $k \div 7 = 5 \times 3$ $k =$ _____   26. $10 = 2(3x + 2)$ $x =$ _____

27. $\dfrac{2b - 1}{7} = 9$ $b =$ _____   28. $4 = \dfrac{a - 6}{3}$ $a =$ _____

Solve each equation and check your answers.

29. $5x = 16 + x$

$5x -$ ____ $= 16 + x -$ ____

$\dfrac{4x}{} = \dfrac{16}{}$

$x =$ ____

Left side: **Right side:**

30. $2y - 4 = y + 8$

31. $4n - 5 = n + 13$

110

Solve the problems and check your answers.

32. Joseph rented a car at $27/day and he paid a total of $182 including $74 of gasoline. How many days did Joseph rent the car for?

    Let d be the number of days the car was rented.

    27(   ) + _____ = 182

    Joseph rented the car for _____ days.

33. Annie and Keith have a total of $(4n - 8)$ marbles. If Annie has n marbles and the number of Keith's marbles is 2 times that of Annie's, how many marbles does Annie have?

    _____

34. The height of a plant is 21 cm. If its growth rate stays unchanged, it will be twice as tall after 3 years. What is the growth rate of the plant?

    _____

35.
    Jack has *m* marbles and the number of marbles that I have is 3 times that of Jack's. If we have a total of 2(m + 13) marbles, how many marbles does Jack have?

    _____

26

Data Management (1)

- identify whether a situation is studied by census or sample
- make inferences about charts and graphs
- make a scatter plot and make inferences about it
- draw a circle graph and make inferences about it

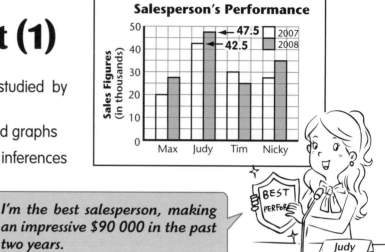

I'm the best salesperson, making an impressive $90 000 in the past two years.

Judy

Determine whether each situation is studied by "census" or "sample". Then check the one that is appropriate.

1.

   Find the names of the students in my school that start with "A".

   a. Obtain the name list of a Grade 8 class. _____ ◯

   b. Obtain the name lists of all classes. _____ ◯

   c. Find out the names of the students who get Grade A in English. _____ ◯

2.

   Find the highest temperature recorded this year.

   a. Find all temperatures recorded this year. _____ ◯

   b. Find all temperatures recorded in the summer this year. _____ ◯

   c. Pick out several temperatures recorded in the summer randomly. _____ ◯

3.

   Find the approximated mean of calories of 1000 lemons.

   a. Find the amount of calories of a lemon. _____ ◯

   b. Find the mean calories of 50 lemons. _____ ◯

   c. Find the mean calories of all lemons. _____ ◯

Look at the chart. Answer the question.

4.   Julie said that most people like "fantasy" movies.
     Do you agree with what Julie said? Explain.

     _____

     _____

Movie	No. of Votes
Comedy	11
Action	7
Romance	3
Mystery	8
Fantasy	12

5.   Write two inferences about the data.

     _____

     _____

Look at the graph and answer the questions.

6.   Check the sentence(s) that describe(s) the graph.

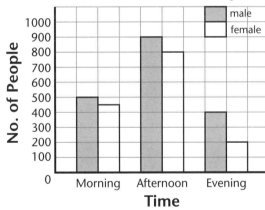

**Number of People at
Ski Resort Yesterday**

Ⓐ More people skiied in the evening
    than in the morning.

Ⓑ The greatest number of people
    skiied in the afternoon.

Ⓒ There are more male skiers.

7.   Make two inferences about the graph.

     _____

     _____

     _____

Look at the double line graph. Answer the questions.

8. What does the graph show?

_____

_____

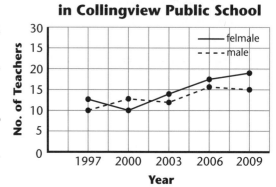

**No. of Teachers
in Collingview Public School**

9. Predict the number of teachers in 2012.

_____

10. Write two inferences about the graph.

_____

_____

_____

**Make a scatter plot to show the data.
Then answer the questions.**

11.

Years of Experience vs Income

Fashion Industry

Years of Experience	vs	Annual Income
0 yr – $21k		0 yr – $20k
1 yr – $25k		2 yr – $29k
4 yr – $34k		4 yr – $35k
4 yr – $34k		5 yr – $38k
6 yr – $39k		6 yr – $38k
7 yr – $39k		7 yr – $40k
7 yr – $42k		8 yr – $41k
9 yr – $42k		10 yr – $44k
10 yr – $45k		10 yr – $46k

"k" stands for 1000.

12. What relationship does the scatter plot show?

_____

13. Estimate the income of a person who has 12 years of experience.

_____

Look at the data that records the children's favourite superheroes. Complete the chart and make use of the data to draw a circle graph. Then answer the questions.

14.

Superhero	No. of Children	Sector Angle	Percent
Batman	17	$\frac{17}{65}$ x 360° ≈	$\frac{17}{65}$ x 100% =
Spiderman	15		
Superman	13		
X-men	9		
Ironman	11		
Total	_____	_____	_____

15. Draw a circle graph in the space provided to show the result.

16. There are 3500 children in the community of Tellington. Use the circle graph to predict how many children have Batman as their superhero.

_____

17.

Write two inferences about the circle graph.

_____

_____

115

Data Management (2)

- draw a histogram
- draw a circle graph
- make inferences about graphs
- determine which graph is suitable to represent a set of data
- identify outliers in a set of data

Dad, if not for the last two quizzes, I'd have got a mean score of 86.

Monica
Quiz Score
1 92
2 80
3 86
4 13
5 24
Mean: 59

mean score without the outliers (13 and 24):

$(92 + 80 + 86) \div 3 = 86$

The children recorded the heights of the plants they planted in their school garden. Make a histogram to show the data and answer the question.

1.

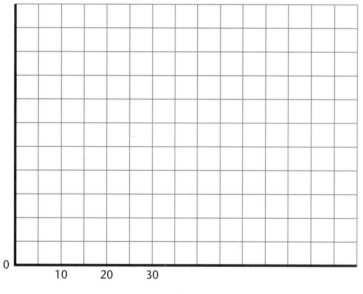

Height of the Plants

Height (cm)	No. of Plants
0-9	1
10-19	5
20-29	6
30-39	9
40-49	10
50-59	7
60-69	4

2.

Write two inferences you can make about the graph.

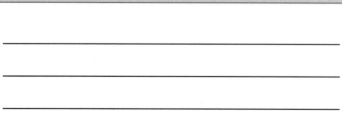

Types of Graphs

Circle graph:
to display part to whole relationship

Double bar graph:
to display 2 sets of discrete data

Double line graph:
to display 2 sets of continuous data

Scatter plot:
to represent 2 sets of related data

Histogram:
to display a set of data that can be grouped and arranged in numerical order

A histogram looks like a bar graph except that a histogram has no space between the bars.

Determine the most suitable graph for each situation.

3.   A sales manager wants to

a.   find out whether there is a relationship between the cost of an item and the quantity sold.

_____

b.   find out the number of two kinds of items sold from 12:00 p.m. to 4:00 p.m.

_____

c.   find out the popularity of different colours of an item.

_____

d.   compare the number of male and female customers who made purchases on Friday, Saturday, and Sunday.

_____

e.   find out the number of customers waiting for check-out from 10:00 a.m. to 8:00 p.m.

_____

f.   find out the relationship between the amount of discount of an item and the quantity sold.

_____

27

Mrs. Winter is planning a ski trip for the students. Look at the number of participants who skiied before. Present the data using the most suitable graph. Then answer the questions.

4.

Number of Participants at Each Age

Age	Skiied Before	Never Skiied
10	4	20
11	6	17
12	6	15
13	8	16
14	10	12

5. Which type of graph did you choose? Explain.

_____

_____

6. Write two inferences about the graph.

_____

_____

_____

7.

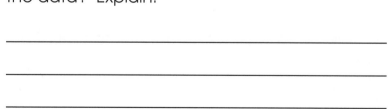

I want to compare the number of participants at each age to the whole group.

Which graph should Mrs. Winter use to display the data? Explain.

_____

_____

_____

Circle the outlier(s) in each set of data if applicable.

8. 2   28   29   29   32   33

9. 5   48   48   56   64   97

10. 3   7   32   43   47   53   59

11. 16   18   18   20   20   23   27   28

12. 5   33   39   40   45   46   102   180

> **Hint**
>
> An outlier is a number that is very different from other numbers in a set of data.
>
> e.g. ② 15   16   16   ㉝
>
> 2 and 33 are the outliers.

Circle the outliers and find the central tendency. Then answer the questions.

13.

Distances (km) Covered by 10 Cyclists
6   37   38
39   40   41
41   41
96   96

14.   **the central tendency**

with the outliners   without the outliners

mean: _____   mean: _____

median: _____   median: _____

mode: _____   mode: _____

15.   > *In general, would you use the mean to represent the data if ...*

a.   there are some outliers in the data?

_____

_____

b.   there are no outliers in the data?

_____

_____

Probability

- complete the formula for theoretical probability
- draw a tree diagram
- find probability from tree diagram
- identify the suitable model to do simulation
- find the odds in favour and odds against

Draw one ball, Sue. If the ball you picked is red, you'll do the dishes. Otherwise, I'll do them.

10 red
1 blue
1 yellow

2 favourable outcomes; 10 unfavourable outcomes

odds against drawing a red ball:
10 to 2 = 5 to 1

This is not fair. The probability that I need to do dishes is 5 times yours.

Complete the formula for theoretical probability. Then fill in the blanks.

1. Probability = $\dfrac{\text{No. of } \boxed{} \text{ outcomes}}{\text{No. of } \boxed{} \text{ outcomes}}$

numerator	equal
favourable	possible
0 1	5

e.g.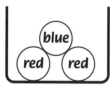

Draw a red ball from this box.

P(red ball) = $\dfrac{\boxed{}}{3}$

2. When all the outcomes of an event are favourable, the numerator and denominator are _____ , and the probability is _____ .

e.g.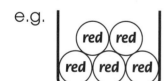

Draw a red ball from a box of 5 red balls.

P(red ball) = $\dfrac{\boxed{}}{5}$ = ____

3. When no outcomes of an event are favourable, the _____ equals 0, and the probability is _____ .

e.g.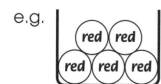

Draw a blue ball from a box of 5 red balls.

P(blue ball) = $\dfrac{\boxed{}}{5}$ = ____

Draw a tree diagram to show all the possible combinations. Then answer the questions.

4.

Blouse

• plain
• with ruffles
• with lace

Skirt

• black
• grey

Mrs. Nelly's Boutique

5. Find the probability that a customer will choose each of the following.

    a. P(a blouse with ruffles and a black skirt)   _____

    b. P(a plain blouse or a blouse with lace and a grey skirt)   _____

    c. P(not a plain blouse)   _____

    d. P(not a black skirt)   _____

6. Which simulation model below could Mrs. Nelly use to simulate the combinations that her customers could buy?

    Ⓐ a number cube labelled from 1 to 6 and a coin

    Ⓑ a spinner divided into 3 equal parts and a coin

    Ⓒ a spinner divided into 5 equal parts

Find the probability of each event in percent.

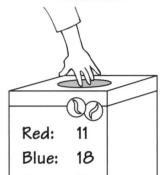

Draw a Marble

7. P(red marble) = _____

8. P(brown marble) = _____

9. P(green or blue marble) = _____

10. P(red or blue marble) = _____

11. P(red, blue, or green marble) = _____

Red: 11
Blue: 18
Green: 7

Loretta spins a wheel and tosses a dice. Find the probability and answer the question.

12. **Spin the wheel.**

a. P(getting "A") = _____

b. P(getting "C" or "D") = _____

c. P(not getting "A") = _____

d. P(not getting "E") = _____

Hint

Find the probability of not getting a "2" in a toss.

$P(\text{not } 2) = 1 - P(2)$

$= 1 - \dfrac{1}{6}$

$= \dfrac{5}{6}$

13. **Toss a dice.**

a. P(getting "1") = _____

b. P(not getting "3") = _____

c. P(not getting an odd number) = _____

d. P(not getting a prime number) = _____

14.

Is there a higher probability of not getting a vowel in a spin than not getting a composite number in a toss?

_____

Odds For and Against:

"Odds" refers to the likelihood that an event will occur.

odds in favour – the ratio of the number of favourable outcomes to the number of unfavourable outcomes

odds against – the ratio of the number of unfavourable outcomes to the number of favourable outcomes

e.g. The odds in favour of spinning "C": **1 to 5**
(no. of favourable outcomes: 1 ; no. of unfavourable outcomes: 5)

The odds against spinning a vowel: **4 to 2**
(no. of unfavourable outcomes: 4 ; no. of favourable outcomes: 2)

Joshua draws a card from his deck. Find the answers.

15.

Joshua's Cards

3 4 U 11
C 7 B ▲
5 E 2 A
★ E ♥

Picking a ...	Odds in Favour	Odds Against
a. "5"	_____	_____
b. a number	_____	_____
c. vowel	_____	_____
d. letter	_____	_____
e. prime number or vowel	_____	_____

16. Find the odds in favour of the "Toronto Tigers" winning.

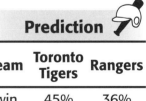

- probability of favourable outcomes: _____

- probability of unfavourable outcomes: _____

- odds in favour: _____
(write as a ratio in simplest form)

Prediction		
Team	Toronto Tigers	Rangers
win	45%	36%
lose	18%	24%
tie	37%	40%

17. What are the odds against the "Rangers" losing? _____

Review 2

Find the volume and surface area of each solid.

1.

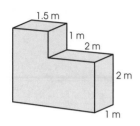

V = _____

S.A. = _____

2.

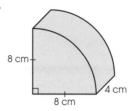

V = _____

S.A. = _____

3.

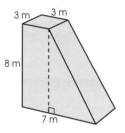

V = _____

S.A. = _____

4.

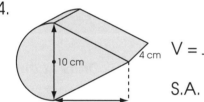

V = _____

S.A. = _____

5.

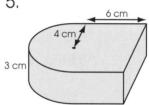

V = _____

S.A. = _____

Find the measures of the angles. Give reasons.

6.

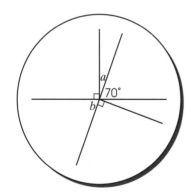

∠a = _____ – 70° (_____ angles)

= _____

∠b =

7.

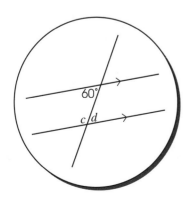

∠c =

∠d =

Find the measures of the angles. Show your work.

8.

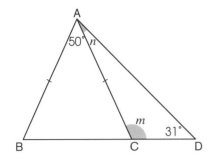

9.

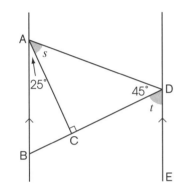

Draw each angle with only a ruler and a compass. Then mark the angle.

10. **105°**

11. **75°**

12. **120°**

13. **150°**

Do the transformations of the figure in the grid. Write the coordinates of the images.

14.

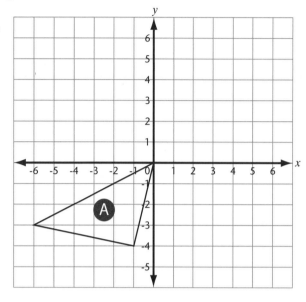

a. vertices of (A): _____

b. Translate (A) 6 units right and 5 units up.

   vertices: _____

c. Reflect (A) in the y-axis.

   vertices: _____

d. Rotate (A) 90° clockwise at (0,0).

   vertices: _____

15. If the vertices of the image of (A) are

  a. (0,0), (-1,4), and (-6,3), then (A) was reflected in the _____ .

  b. (-2,-1), (-3,-5), and (-8,-4), then (A) was_____ .

  c. (0,0), (1,4), and (6,3), then (A) was _____ .

Write the coordinates of the vertices of the images.

16.

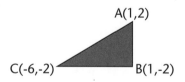

a. Translate △ABC 3 units left and 1 unit up.

   _____

b. Reflect △ABC in the x-axis.

   _____

c. Rotate △ABC 180° at (0,0).

   _____

17.

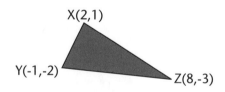

a. Translate △XYZ 2 units right and 2 units down.

   _____

b. Reflect △XYZ in the y-axis.

   _____

c. Make a -270° turn at (0,0).

   _____

Complete the charts and write the expressions to describe the patterns. Find the answers.

18.

Term No.	Term Value
1	0
2	4
3	8
4	
5	

a. Expression: _____

b. Find the term value of

• the 9th term: _____

• the 15th term: _____

c. What is the term number of 40? _____

19.

Term No.	Term Value
1	4
2	10
3	16
4	
5	

a. Expression: _____

b. Find the term value of

• the 10th term: _____

• the 20th term: _____

c. What is the term number of 88? _____

Evaluate the algebraic expressions and solve the problems.

20. $2a + 4b$

= 2(   ) + 4(   )

=

21. $3(a + d)$

22. $d^2(b - c)$

23. $b(e - 1)$

$a = 7$

$b = -2$

$c = -1$

$d = 3$

$e = 5$

24.

> I have 3 bags of e candies and I want to put all the candies equally into d jars. How many candies are there in each jar? Write an algebraic expression and evaluate.

_____

Solve the equations.

25. $4a - 2 = 14$

26. $\dfrac{10 + b}{3} = 7$

27. $2n + 9 = 12 - n$

28. $k - 6 = 4k - 36$

29. $3(m + 2) = 9$

30. $\dfrac{n - 4}{3} = 11$

31. $18 - 2c = 6$ $c = \underline{\hspace{1cm}}$

32. $5d + 4 = 29$ $d = \underline{\hspace{1cm}}$

33. $\dfrac{3p + 28}{p} = 7$ $p = \underline{\hspace{1cm}}$

34. $\dfrac{21 - 2r}{r} = 5$ $r = \underline{\hspace{1cm}}$

Jolie wants to find out if there is a relationship between the amount of time spent on studying and test scores. Make a scatter plot and answer the question.

35.

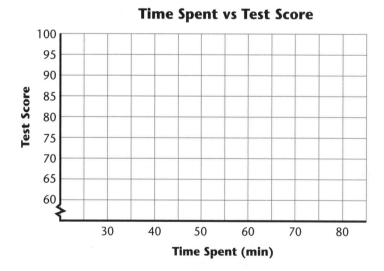

Time Spent vs Test Score

Time Spent vs Test Score	
30 min : 61	55 min : 75
30 min : 60	55 min : 74
35 min : 63	60 min : 78
35 min : 65	60 min : 70
40 min : 64	60 min : 80
40 min : 62	60 min : 79
40 min : 69	65 min : 81
45 min : 66	70 min : 82
45 min : 69	75 min : 84
50 min : 70	75 min : 90
50 min : 72	80 min : 89
50 min : 73	80 min : 91

36. What conclusion can you draw from the graph?

_____

_____

Determine the most suitable graph to display the information of each situation.

double bar graph

double line graph

pictograph

circle graph

scatter plot

histogram

37. the number of males and females who have learned to skate in each grade at a school

_____

38. the relationship between the age and height of plants

_____

39. the number of citizens in each age group in a city

_____

40.

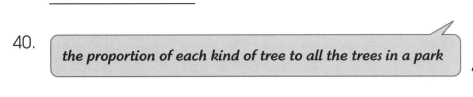

the proportion of each kind of tree to all the trees in a park

_____

Jason draws a ball from the box. Find the answers.

41.

16 Balls

2 K U
6 E 3 ▲
1 B ▲ 5
   4
3 8 P
   ▬

a. Find the odds in favour of drawing a

• number _____

• triangle _____

b. Find the odds against drawing a

• vowel _____

• rectangle _____

42.

What can I use to simulate the chance of drawing a number? Explain your choice.

_____

_____

_____

129

Polar Bears –
Did You Know?

Have you ever wondered what the most dangerous animal on Earth really is? It is generally agreed that bears are the most dangerous animals known to humans, and of all bear species, it is the large grizzly that inspires the most fear in us. However, it is the polar bear, and not the grizzly, that is in fact the most dangerous animal known to humans. The polar bear is as aggressive as the grizzly, but what makes it more dangerous is that it is more curious and less fearful of humans. This is partly due to the fact that most polar bears have had little interaction with humans, as the northern regions where they live are sparsely populated. Also, the polar bear's diet is almost entirely meat-based; they exist primarily on a diet of fish, seal, and walrus. However, these sea-borne food sources are becoming increasingly difficult to hunt down in northern climes, making the polar bear more prone to hunger.

Despite the fact that the polar bear has gained the title of "most dangerous animal", it has a lot to fear from people. Hunters are the polar bear's only predator, and other human activity threatens its existence to the same degree. This activity has led to global climate change, which is now believed to be a cause of significant shrinkage of the arctic ice cap. By now you have probably seen sad images of polar bears trapped on tiny ice floes as they try to hunt for food, or swimming in the sea up to 50 kilometres from land. Because of this, the polar bear has become a symbol of the reality of global climate change. They are an endangered species and may possibly become extinct within our lifetime.

Polar bears are actually descended from the brown bear species. During the Pleistocene period (when large swathes of Canada were covered in glaciers) some brown bears were isolated in northern regions. In order to adapt to the environment, these brown bears underwent a striking, and relatively rapid, evolutionary change. For example, a polar bear's fur differs from other bear species in an interesting way. The hairs on the outer coat of polar bears are actually hollow! These tube-like hairs, unique to polar bears, increase buoyancy and improve insulation. Polar bears also have thick coats of blubber. A polar bear's skin colour is black, another difference from other bear species, believed to be an adaptation to increase heat retention. The relatively long necks of polar bears make swimming easier, and their remarkably large stomachs can hold as much as 80 kilograms of food.

The habitat of the polar bear is the entire arctic polar region, covering Russia, Norway, Sweden, Greenland, Alaska, and Canada. Most polar bears live in Canada, in the arctic areas along the sea. But because of Hudson Bay, their habitat dips into the provinces of Manitoba, Ontario, and Quebec. It is not uncommon now for hungry polar bears to be found scavenging trash cans in the northern Manitoba town of Churchill. It seems a sad decline for the now endangered polar bear, the true "King of the Beasts".

A.   Check the best answer for each of the following questions.

1.   Which of the following is not true about the polar bear?

   A. It is more curious about humans than the grizzly.

   B. It is a carnivore.

   C. It avoids humans whenever possible.

2.   Polar bears are an endangered species because ____ .

   A. there are fewer and fewer sea-borne food sources for them

   B. global climate change has threatened their survival

   C. there is an increase in human activity in the northern regions

3.   Which two of the following statements are true?

   A. The arctic ice cap has almost vanished.

   B. Some brown bears evolved during the Pleistocene period to become polar bears.

   C. Canada was mostly covered in glaciers during the Pleistocene period.

4.   Which of the following is true about the polar bear?

   A. The hollow, tube-like hairs of the polar bear helps it float.

   B. The underlayer of short, fine black hair traps the heat.

   C. The polar bear's blubber helps conserve energy for the long winter.

Finite and Non-Finite Verbs

A **finite verb** is a verb that agrees with its subject, that is, it changes with the person or number of the subject. A **non-finite verb** or **verbal** is a verb that does not have to agree with the subject.

Examples: Polar bears <u>exist</u> primarily on a diet of fish, seal, and walrus. (finite)

The polar bear has a lot <u>to fear</u> from people. (non-finite)

There are three types of non-finite verbs:

- **Gerunds**: gerunds look like present participles but they function as nouns.
- **Participles**: both present and past participles function as adjectives.
- **Infinitives**: to-infinitives can function as nouns, adjectives, or adverbs. In some cases, an infinitive without "to" (**bare infinitive**) should be used.

B. **Look at the underlined verbs. Write "F" for finite verbs, "PRP" for present participles, "PP" for past participles, "G" for gerunds, "TI" for to-infinitives, and "BI" for bare infinitives.**

1. The shrinkage of the arctic ice cap makes people <u>realize</u> the destructive consequence of global warming. _____

2. A polar bear's fur differs from other bear species in an <u>interesting</u> way. _____

3. The relatively long neck of a polar bear makes <u>swimming</u> easier. _____

4. The polar bear <u>has</u> a keen sense of smell, so it can easily detect prey on land. _____

5. <u>To outrun</u> a polar bear is impossible as it can reach a speed of 40 kilometres per hour. _____

6. The polar bear is now on the long list of <u>endangered</u> animal species. _____

7. Let us all <u>do</u> something to help stop global warming so the polar bear will not become extinct. _____

C.   Make sentences of your own using the verb types given in parentheses.

1.   represent (finite verb)

_____

_____

2.   conserve (gerund)

_____

_____

3.   result (present participle)

_____

_____

4.   intensify (past participle)

_____

_____

5.   solve (to-infinitive as noun)

_____

_____

6.   trap (to-infinitive as adjective)

_____

_____

7.   understand (to-infinitive as adverb)

_____

_____

8.   help (bare infinitive)

_____

_____

Cambodia's **Angkor Wat:**
Endangered by **Tourism**

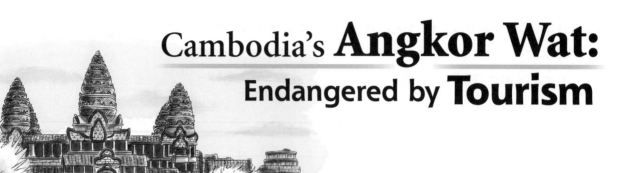

Angkor Wat is an ancient temple located just a few kilometres north of the town of Siem Reap in Cambodia. It was built in the early 12th century as a Hindu place of worship, but evolved into a revered Buddhist temple as the religion and inhabitants changed. In fact, it is part of a much larger complex of temples, which comprise the Angkor World Heritage Site under the auspices of UNESCO. Some of the structures and the grounds surrounding them are larger. Other temples are smaller and hidden away among the remarkable ancient trees that have grown in and around the ruins. (   )

The temples of Angkor were in ruin long before the first western explorers laid eyes on them, and it is a mystery as to why the ancient Khmer culture that built them allowed them to go to ruin. (   ) In more recent decades, rural poverty and demands in the illegal market for ancient Khmer artifacts meant that Cambodians themselves were participating in the destruction of the sites.

From 1976 to 1979, the country was under the control of Pol Pot, head of an organization called Khmer Rouge. He renamed the country Democratic Kampuchea and began a brutal campaign to force city-dwellers to live and work in the countryside. (   ) For this reason, while other countries in the region, such as Thailand and Malaysia, began to prosper and invite foreign tourists on a large scale, Cambodia, with little infrastructure, was still a place that outsiders knew little about.

However, over the last 20 years, international tourism to Cambodia has trickled in and is now, one could say, a torrent. (   ) Consequently, destruction of Cambodia's cultural heritage has increased. For example, the rapid urbanization of the Siem Reap area has led to a drop in the water table, resulting in the instability of the Angkor monuments. Moreover, the number of impoverished parents removing their children from school so that they can sell postcards and souvenirs to tourists has been increasing.

(   ) Cambodian businesses are encouraged to support the local economy by using Cambodian-made products where possible. Tourists are made aware that purchasing souvenirs from children causes social problems, and are invited to patronize businesses with the "Heritage-friendly" logo, to respect the temple sites and monuments, and to avoid purchasing ancient artifacts. Foreign governments are pitching in to help restore the Angkor site. These changes show that concerted efforts are finally being made to restore the ancient wonders of Angkor – and Cambodian society.

A. Each of the following statements goes with a paragraph of the preceding passage. Decide on the matching statements and paragraphs. Write the letters in the parentheses where the statements should go.

a. As a result, measures are now being taken to ensure that Cambodia's tourism industry is "heritage-friendly".

b. But of all the ruins, it is Angkor Wat that has become the symbol of Cambodia, appearing on that country's flag.

c. A few years ago (2004) over a million foreigners came to Cambodia, and more than half said they had come to visit Angkor Wat.

d. Ever since then, looting has persisted, as treasure-hunters from afar excavated ancient burial grounds, or simply walked off with chunks of the extraordinary architecture and stone carvings as souvenirs.

e. A state of anarchy ensued, and up to 1.7 million Cambodians died.

B. Answer the following questions.

1. Which sentence in the passage explains the evolution of Angkor Wat over the years?

_____

_____

2. Which sentence in the passage shows that there was little progress in Cambodia between 1976 and 1979?

_____

_____

3. Which sentence in the passage illustrates that international tourism to Angkor Wat has increased tremendously?

_____

_____

Non-Progressive Verbs

Some verbs are not normally used in progressive tenses. They are called **non-progressive verbs** or **non-action verbs**. They are verbs that describe sense perceptions, mental, emotional, or existing states, and possession. However, some of these verbs can be used in progressive tenses when they have meanings other than those mentioned above.

Examples: Many people <u>think</u> that the Cambodian government should put effort in restoring the Angkor site.
("think" here describes a mental state – non-progressive)

Foreign governments <u>are thinking</u> of ways to help restore the Angkor site.
("think" here means "consider" – can be progressive)

C. Put the following non-progressive verbs under the correct headings. Think of two more verbs that can be put under each heading if there are any.

appear   be   believe   belong   contain   fear   feel
hate   have   hear   know   like   mind   own
possess   remember   see   seem   taste   want

Sense	Mental State	Emotional State	Existence	Possession
_____	_____	_____	_____	_____
_____	_____	_____	_____	_____
_____	_____	_____	_____	_____
_____	_____	_____	_____	_____

D. Each of the verbs below can be used as both progressive and non-progressive verbs. Make a sentence with the verb in each form.

1. look

   Progressive _____

   Non-progressive _____

2. feel

   Progressive _____

   Non-progressive _____

3. have

   Progressive _____

   Non-progressive _____

4. be

   Progressive _____

   Non-progressive _____

5. smell

   Progressive _____

   Non-progressive _____

6. appear

   Progressive _____

   Non-progressive _____

7. weigh

   Progressive _____

   Non-progressive _____

8. see

   Progressive _____

   Non-progressive _____

The naming of the Nobel Prize winners is among the most eagerly anticipated awards ceremonies in the world. The Nobel Prizes were established at the bequest of Alfred Nobel (the inventor of dynamite) and first awarded in 1901, in the subject areas of physics, chemistry, physiology or medicine, literature, and peace. Sweden's central bank instituted a Prize in economics, first awarded in 1969, which is now identified with the Nobel Prizes. The "Nobels" are regarded as the most prestigious awards in the world. They consist of a medal, a personal diploma, and a money award (which increases in value annually and is more than a million dollars now). But the true value lies in the social prestige and worldwide attention brought to the subject associated with the winners.

Canada is well-placed among the countries that have Nobel laureates. There are 18 Canadian Nobel laureates, which is an impressive record. Most of our laureates are scientists: Bertram Brockhouse won the Prize in Physics in 1994 for his work on condensed matter; Michael Smith won the Prize in Chemistry in 1993 for site-directed mutagenesis; Rudolph Marcus won the Prize in Chemistry in 1992 for electron transfer reactions; Richard Taylor won the Prize in Physics in 1990 for verifying Quark Theory; Sidney Altman, a molecular biologist, won the Prize in Chemistry in 1989, sharing it with his colleague Thomas R. Cech, for their research into the catalytic properties of RNA; John Polanyi won the Prize in Chemistry in 1986 for chemi-luminescence; Henry Taube won the Prize

Canadian
Nobel Prize Laureates

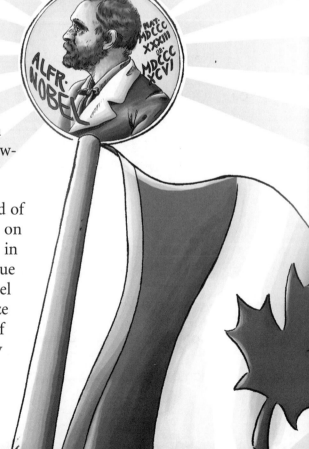

in Chemistry in 1983 for electron transfer reactions; David Hubel won the Prize in Medicine in 1981 for mapping the visual cortex; Gerhard Herzberg won the Prize in Chemistry in 1971 for his contributions to the knowledge of free radicals; William Giauque won the Prize in Chemistry in 1949 for research into the properties of matter at temperatures close to absolute zero; Sir Frederick Banting won the Prize in Medicine in 1923 for discovering insulin. He shared the prize with fellow-Canadian (Scotland-born) John Macleod.

The following Canadian Nobel laureates won in the field of economics: Robert Mundell won in 1999 for his work on currency areas and exchange rates; Myron Scholes won in 1997 for his work on a new method to determine the value of derivatives; William Spencer Vickrey won the Nobel Memorial Prize in Economics in 1996, sharing the prize with James Mirrlees for research into an economic theory of incentives under asymmetric information. Sadly, Vickrey passed away three days after the announcement.

Canada can also lay claim to two Nobel Peace Prize laureates – well...almost. Lester Pearson was a diplomat who won the Nobel Peace Prize in 1957 for his role in diffusing the Suez Crisis. He later became Prime Minister. And in 1995, a Nova Scotia-founded organization, The Pugwash Conferences on Science and World Affairs, shared the Nobel Peace Prize in 1995 with Polish physicist Joseph Rotblat (who co-founded the organization) for their efforts towards nuclear disarmament. Lastly, Saul Bellow, a Canadian-born American writer, won the Nobel Prize in Literature in 1976.

There are almost 800 Nobel Prize laureates now. They come from all over the world, are from various walks of life, and represent all faiths, social classes, and educational backgrounds. The stories of these people, and the 18 Canadians among them, are a testament to what can be achieved if you believe.

A. Complete the following with words from the passage.

Revered as the most 1._____ awards in the world, the Nobel Prizes were 2._____ in 1901 at the 3._____ of Alfred Nobel, who was the 4._____ of dynamite. The Nobel Prizes are awarded in these areas: physics, chemistry, physiology or medicine, literature, peace, and 5._____ . Apart from a medal, a 6._____ diploma, and a sum of money, a Nobel laureate enjoys social 7._____ and worldwide 8._____ .

Canada has an 9._____ record of 18 laureates, most of whom are distinguished 10._____ . The award of Nobel prizes is not confined to individuals; organizations can be recipients of Nobel Prizes, too. In 1995, for example, the Pugwash Conferences on Science and World Affairs, which was 11._____ in Nova Scotia, 12._____ the Nobel 13._____ Prize with Polish physicist Joseph Rotblat for their 14._____ towards nuclear disarmament.

Phrasal Verbs

A **phrasal verb** is a verb used with a preposition or an adverb. It usually has a meaning that is completely different from the verb itself.

Example: Vickrey <u>passed away</u> three days after the announcement.
                          (died)

B.   Fill in the blanks with the suitable phrasal verbs to complete the sentences. Use the correct form of the verbs.

> go through   break in   take down   keep to
> die down   carry on   get over   come about

1.   The interviewer asked the Nobel laureate in Literature how the idea for her winning book _____ .

2.   When the Nobel laureate was interviewed by the magazine, somebody _____ and asked for her autograph.

3.   The Nobel laureate's speech _____ for hours, but it was so amusing that no one wanted to leave. Some students even _____ what he said.

4.   The controversy about whether the Nobel Peace Prize laureate was justified in getting the award _____ as time went by.

5.   The candidate for the Nobel Prize found it hard to _____ his disappointment.

6.   The Nobel laureate in Physics _____ many ups and downs in his career.

7.   No matter how hard and impossible it may seem to achieve your dream, _____ it and one day it will be realized.

C. **Look up the definition of each phrasal verb below in the dictionary and write it on the given line. Then make a sentence with the phrasal verb.**

1. wear off

   Definition: _____

   Sentence: _____

2. draw up

   Definition: _____

   Sentence: _____

3. call on

   Definition: _____

   Sentence: _____

4. put off

   Definition: _____

   Sentence: _____

5. take after

   Definition: _____

   Sentence: _____

6. hand over

   Definition: _____

   Sentence: _____

7. iron out

   Definition: _____

   Sentence: _____

8. look into

   Definition: _____

   Sentence: _____

The Naming of a
Public Holiday

Winters are long and cold in Manitoba. And, what's more, February is one of the months in that province without a statutory public holiday. Slowly, the idea to pressure the Manitoba government to give Manitobans a holiday to help get rid of those "February Blahs" took hold in the local media. At first, the government officials scoffed at the idea, but eventually, after public pressure "snowballed", they began to give the idea serious consideration. And why not? After all, before the new holiday was proclaimed, Manitobans had only seven statutory holidays, less than Canada's national average. Moreover, Alberta has been enjoying a February holiday – called Family Day – since 1990, and Saskatchewan inaugurated its own Family Day on February 19, 2007.

But when you're a government leader, you need to be careful about how you do things. Of course, government leaders would be happy to give people this "gift", knowing that it could generate goodwill among the general public. But then you have to decide what to call it! A savvy political leader does not want to be seen to be spending precious time deciding on the name of a holiday when there are other important matters to discuss in the legislative assembly. So what do you do? You delegate. The government decided to give this important task to... Manitoba's young people! Certainly no one would argue with the decision to let the youth of the province have a role in government affairs – not even the Official Opposition!

And so it was that the students of the province decided on the name of Manitoba's newest statutory holiday. Schools were invited to submit names in a contest, and the MB4Youth Advisory Council (a committee of 15 young people between the ages of 15 and 24 selected on the basis of their community involvement, reporting to the Minister of Education, Citizenship and Youth) chose the winner from a shortlist. Some of the names offered up by schoolchildren included: Nellie McClung Day, Duff Roblin Day, Bison Break, Winnipeg Jets Day, and Spirited Energy Day. What was it going to be?

"It's very, very tough to make all of the people happy all of the time, but at the end of the day, this is the name that was chosen, and I think Manitobans will be happy with it," said Labour Minister Nancy Allan on September 25, 2007, when the winning name was announced. Manitoba's newest holiday was going to be called Louis Riel Day, in honour of the legendary – and controversial – Métis leader who led the Red River and Northwest Rebellions in a fight for Aboriginal rights. He was hanged for treason in 1885, but is considered by many to be the founder of Manitoba. Eleven schools had put his name forward and were each given a $1000 grant to buy library materials.

The Labour Minister was right; not everyone was pleased. Some felt it should have been called Family Day (since February is so cold you really can't do anything except stay at home with your family). Many businesspeople did not want a holiday at all, saying that it was unfair to expect businesses to pay for another public holiday for their staff. But many others also felt that these young people had done the adults proud by following their own lead, showing an appreciation of history and heritage, and being unafraid of the inevitable controversy. Manitobans celebrate Louis Riel Day on the third Monday of February.

A.   Check the best answer for each of the following questions.

1.   Which of the following statements is true?

   A. Manitobans pressured their government for a family day in February.

   B. Both Alberta and Saskatchewan have a holiday in February.

   C. Canadians on average enjoy seven statutory holidays.

2.   A savvy political leader is one who _____ .

   A. sticks to his or her principles

   B. is practical-minded

   C. is smart

3.   Which of the following is not true?

   A. Louis Riel was hanged for treason in 1885.

   B. Eleven schools took part in the naming contest.

   C. Louis Riel played a crucial role in fighting for Aboriginal rights.

B.   If you were asked to name a new holiday in June, what name would you give it? Why?

_____

_____

_____

Prepositional Verbs

Some verbs need to be used with particular prepositions. They are called **prepositional verbs**. A prepositional verb is different from a phrasal verb in that the adding of the preposition to the verb does not result in a complete change of its meaning.

Example: The students of the province <u>decided on</u> the name of Manitoba's newest statutory holiday.

C.   Write the preposition that goes with each of the following verbs.

1.   insist _____

2.   account _____

3.   borrow _____

4.   delight _____

5.   recover _____

6.   believe _____

7.   worry _____

8.   approve _____

9.   consent _____

10. vote _____

11. wrestle _____

12. substitute _____

D.   Fill in the blanks with the correct prepositions.

1.   The government officials of Manitoba scoffed _____ the idea of adding a statutory public holiday at first.

2.   The MB4Youth Advisory Council consists _____ 15 members between 15 and 24 years old.

3.   The committee members of MB4Youth Advisory Council agreed _____ naming the new holiday Louis Riel Day.

4.   Some businesses objected _____ adding one more public holiday. They were not happy about having to pay _____ another public holiday for their employees.

5.   Compared _____ some Canadian provinces or territories, Manitoba has fewer statutory holidays.

6.   Louis Riel was a Métis leader who fought _____ Aboriginal rights.

Prepositional Adjectives

There are some adjectives that must be used with prepositions, too. They are called **prepositional adjectives**.

Example: When you're a government leader, you need to be <u>careful about</u> how you do things.

E.   Write the preposition that goes with each of the following adjectives.

1. infamous _____
2. crazy _____
3. worried _____

4. curious _____
5. proud _____
6. popular _____

7. confident _____
8. guilty _____
9. capable _____

10. interested _____
11. fond _____
12. serious _____

F.   Make sentences of your own with the following prepositional adjectives.

1. angry with

_____

2. cautious about

_____

3. unafraid of

_____

4. quick at

_____

5. hesitant about

_____

6. competent in

_____

The Christmas tradition probably began in and around what is now Germany as far back as the 4th century! A man named Nicholas gave his inherited wealth to the poor and became a monk, travelling the countryside and helping those in need. Over the years, he became known as the protector of children and sailors, and was made a saint. By the 1500s, Saint Nick was the most popular saint in Europe. He would give gifts of fruits, nuts, and candies to good children and lumps of coal to naughty children, reminding us that even way back then children needed some help deciding whether to be "naughty or nice". The Christmas stocking tradition also seems to stem from Saint Nick: in attempting to help a poor girl who needed a wedding dowry, he threw a sack of gold coins through her window. The coins landed in one of her stockings, which had been hanging up to dry.

But the idea of gift-giving at Christmas stems from the Bible. The Book of Matthew tells us the story of the three wise men bringing gifts of gold, frankincense, and myrrh to baby Jesus. German advances in printing technology during the Middle Ages meant that the Bible was becoming more widely read, and this helps to explain how Santa became a central figure in the Christmas tradition.

The Christmas tree tradition also came from Germany, during the Middle Ages. To celebrate the feast day of Adam and Eve, which was on December 24, German families would set up a "Paradise Tree" in their homes representing the Garden of Eden. Originally, they hung wafers on the tree to symbolize the Holy Communion, but over time these were replaced by more delicious things: biscuits, sweets, nuts, fruits, and even popcorn strings. As years went by, the decorations became more ornamental: roses, barley sugar twists, gingerbread shapes, pretzels, paper flowers, and waxen figurines.

The History of
Christmas Giving

Victorian England took the Christmas tree custom to new heights. By the time it caught on in the mid-19th century, there were other decorations, including tinsel, silver wire ornaments, beads, and candles. But the British added their own touches from their Victorian-style crafts: finely embroidered pouches with secret gifts, delicate lace snowflakes, miniature paper baskets with sugared almonds, and glittery, beaded garlands. They also hung small toys on the tree. By the late 19th century, Christmas trees were jam-packed with ornaments, sweets, and toys! As the toys got bigger, they were placed under the tree. At the time, Victorian England was fascinated with moving things. In addition to wooden rocking horses, doll houses, and flip-books (the first motion pictures), mechanical toys such as kaleidoscopes, spinning tops, and jack-in-the-boxes were popular items.

Before the 1860s, Christmas was not widely celebrated in the United States, but by the close of the 19th century, Christmas had really taken off. The inventive Americans patented ornament hooks and the first electric Christmas tree lights. But this may not have come about if the big American department store Macy's had not seen the value of commercializing the holiday back in 1867. At that time, Macy's kept its doors open until midnight on Christmas Eve. In 1874, Macy's began enticing shoppers with Christmas-themed window displays. And so began Christmas as we know it. From teddy bears, board games (especially Monopoly), crayons, through to Barbie dolls, hula hoops, and G.I. Joe – these were just a few of our favourite toys of the last century. Toys are a reflection of the times and a reflection of our values, reminding us of who we once were, and what we are becoming.

A. Answer the following questions.

1. Who was Santa Claus?

    _____

    _____

2. "...even way back then children needed some help deciding whether to be 'naughty or nice'." How did Nicholas help children in that regard?

    _____

3. Describe how the stocking tradition came about.

    _____

    _____

4. How did Macy's commercialize Christmas?

    _____

    _____

5. Do you agree with the writer that "toys are a reflection of the times and a reflection of our values"? Why or why not?

    _____

    _____

Order of Adjectives

When we use more than one adjective before a noun, we need to put them in the right order according to the type of each adjective. Adjectives are usually put in this order: opinion, size, age, shape, colour, origin, material, purpose.

Opinion	great, terrifying, unforgettable
Size	tiny, big, enormous
Age	old, young
Shape	oval, square, triangular
Colour	green, beige, maroon
Origin	Canadian, American, French
Material	plastic, woollen, glass
Purpose	<u>dancing</u> shoes, <u>car</u> engine, <u>washing</u> machine

Example: Mom has bought a Christmas glittery beaded garland. (✗)
Mom has bought a glittery beaded Christmas garland. (✔)

B. **Put each of the following groups of adjectives in order before the noun they describe.**

1. a _____ tree
(tall, gorgeous, Christmas, green)

2. the _____ saint
(European, most, popular)

3. the _____ coins
(heavy, precious, gold)

4. a/an _____ tradition
(special, German, old)

5. the _____ ornaments
(long, wire, beautiful, silver)

6. the _____ baskets
(colourful, paper, miniature, interesting)

7. a/an _____ house
(expensive, doll, new, big)

8. the _____ store
(American, old, department, famous, big)

C. Rewrite each sentence by using at least three adjectives to describe the underlined noun.

1. We have put lots of <u>presents</u> under the Christmas tree.

   _____

   _____

2. All shopping malls around the country swarmed with <u>shoppers</u>.

   _____

   _____

3. Carl found a <u>jack-in-the-box</u> in the attic.

   _____

   _____

4. Wendy hung lots of <u>ornaments</u> on the Christmas tree.

   _____

   _____

5. We have <u>dinner</u> at Grandpa and Grandma's house every Christmas.

   _____

   _____

6. Grandma likes telling us a <u>story</u> after Christmas dinner.

   _____

   _____

7. My best friend Lisa bought me a <u>scarf</u> as a present.

   _____

   _____

8. Mom showed us the <u>toys</u> she had kept since she was a girl.

   _____

   _____

The Remarkable Journey of Al Gore

Albert Gore, Jr. was born in Washington, D.C. in 1948. He enjoyed his life in Washington, especially his summers working on the family farm in Tennessee. When he graduated from college, he enlisted to serve his country in Vietnam, even though he did not agree with the war. On his return, he began a career in journalism and later in politics. Just like his father, Gore became the congressional representative and then the senator of Tennessee. He eventually became the Vice President of the United States under Bill Clinton, a Democrat. In 2000, when Bill Clinton's eight-year term was complete, Gore ran for the presidency against the Republican candidate George W. Bush. People agreed it would be a close race, but no one ever expected what happened next.

Al Gore received about 500 000 more votes than George W. Bush, but those votes needed to be converted into delegates for the Electoral College, which decides the winner in this unique American system. The state of Florida was a close race, and there were reported irregularities in the way the election had been administered there. In the end, it was decided that all the delegates from that state were to come from the George W. Bush camp, effectively making him the next U.S. President. Many people wanted Al Gore to fight this outcome through legal action (and in fact legal action had already been started by both sides). After a lot of thought, Al Gore decided not to continue the legal battle. He did not want the country to be divided throughout a long court case. He pledged to support the new president, George W. Bush.

Shortly after, Al Gore and his wife, Tipper, went away to Europe for a while, to rethink their lives. When Gore returned, people asked if he would return to politics. Gore replied that he had "fallen out of love with politics". This response did not satisfy some people. The media did not treat him kindly; they made fun of his new beard and the fact that he had gained weight. Some said that U.S. vice president, not a particularly important job, would be his greatest achievement. But Gore continued to work quietly towards his long-held goals and beliefs. Long before Gore became U.S. vice president, he had created a slideshow about global warming. Now, with Tipper's encouragement, he dusted off the old slideshow. His children told him he needed to turn it into a PowerPoint presentation. Al Gore went back to the grassroots, imparting his message to small groups in places like schools and town halls. It was very different from the days when he could fill banquet halls with wealthy, powerful people and plenty of reporters to cover the event.

One day, a documentary filmmaker saw Gore's presentation and asked if he could turn it into a film. The result was *An Inconvenient Truth*. Not only was this documentary turned into a best-selling book (with a best-selling children's version following), but the film also won an Academy Award for Davis Guggenheim, the director. The film was shown around the world, making people everywhere take notice of the problem of global warming and climate change. As a result of this remarkable achievement, and along with all his other efforts, Gore was given the 2007 Nobel Peace Prize, sharing it with the scientists of the Intergovernmental Panel on Climate Change. People still ask Gore if he will ever run for the presidency again. Many hope that he will, as history has shown us that the best leaders are humble, wise, compassionate, and steadfast.

A. Read the following statements. Rewrite the ones that are not true.

1. George W. Bush beat Al Gore by 500 000 votes in the 2000 presidential race.

_____

2. Tipper encouraged Gore to make good use of his slideshow about global warming.

_____

3. The documentary *An Inconvenient Truth* was based on a best-selling book with the same title.

_____

4. Al Gore shared the 2007 Nobel Peace Prize with Davis Guggenheim for their efforts in addressing the problem of global warming and climate change.

_____

_____

B. Do you agree that Al Gore's defeat in the 2000 presidential race was in fact a blessing in disguise? Why or why not?

_____

_____

_____

_____

Interrogative Adverbs

"When", "why", "where", and "how" are **interrogative adverbs**. They are usually placed at the beginning of a question.

Examples: <u>When</u> was Albert Gore born?

<u>Why</u> did Al Gore serve the United States in Vietnam if he did not agree with the war?

<u>Where</u> did Al Gore and his wife go to rethink their lives?

<u>How</u> was his slideshow about global warming turned into a film?

C.   Write questions that elicit the given responses with interrogative adverbs.

1. _____

_____

Al Gore ran for the presidency against the Republican candidate George W. Bush in 2000.

2. _____

_____

Al Gore received about 500 000 more votes than George W. Bush.

3. _____

_____

Al Gore presented his message about global warming using PowerPoint.

4. _____

_____

The film *An Inconvenient Truth* was shown around the world.

5. _____

_____

Many people hope that Al Gore will run for the presidency again because he is humble, wise, compassionate, and steadfast.

Relative Adverbs

"When", "why", and "where" can also be used to join clauses as **relative adverbs**. They are often used to replace the more formal structure of "preposition + which" in a relative clause.

Examples: It was very different from the days <u>when</u> he could fill banquet halls with wealthy and powerful people.
("when" is used in place of "in which")

The media wanted to know <u>why</u> Gore gave up his pursuit of the presidency.
("why" is used in place of "the reason for")

Tennessee is the place <u>where</u> the Gores' family farm is located.
("where" is used in place of "at which")

D.   Join the sentences with the appropriate relative adverbs. Make any other necessary changes.

1.   Al Gore went to schools and town halls. He imparted his message about global warming.

_____

2.   1965 was the year. Gore enrolled in Harvard University in that year.

_____

3.   Gore enlisted in the U.S. military. The media wanted to know the reason.

_____

4.   There was a time. Gore struggled to make a decision about joining the U.S. military at that time.

_____

5.   This is the cathedral. Gore married Tipper here.

_____

6.   Gore gave a speech. He gave his reason for supporting the use of green energy in his speech.

_____

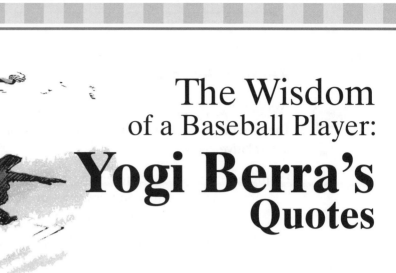

The Wisdom
of a Baseball Player:
Yogi Berra's
Quotes

The ability to amuse someone with clever witticisms is always appreciated, but not easy to do. Some people, such as stand-up comedians and writers of humour, make a career out of it – if they're good enough. But one of the English language's most quoted "humorists" is neither of those – but rather a retired professional baseball player who goes by the name of Yogi Berra.

Yogi was born Lawrence Peter Berra in St. Louis, Missouri in 1925. He quit school in the eighth grade and soon after served in the U.S. Navy during World War II. On his return to the United States, he began playing minor league baseball. In 1946, he began his remarkable career as a major league baseball player (with the New York Yankees) and later as a manager. He is known to many as the best baseball catcher of all time, was named the Most Valuable Player of the American League three times, and was one of only a handful of managers to lead teams from both the American and National Leagues to the World Series. He was inducted into the Baseball Hall of Fame in 1972.

Throughout his remarkable career, Yogi Berra was also well known for his unique sense of humour. He liked to offer his observations, often deceptively and cleverly simplistic on the one hand, yet quite meaningful, even profound, on the other. Some of his most quoted sayings are malapropisms. A malapropism is defined as an accidental misuse of a word in a sentence, usually with a comic effect – although in the case of Yogi Berra, one could easily assume he did it on purpose.

If this is not enough, Yogi is also a humanitarian. Throughout his life, he has given generously to worthy causes, in particular to organizations that support young people. His annual golf tournament has raised more than a million dollars for youth scholarships and educational programming. He founded the Yogi Berra Museum and Learning Centre in Little Falls, New Jersey, with the following mission statement: "...to preserve and promote the values of respect, sportsmanship, social justice and excellence through inclusive, culturally diverse, sports-based educational programs and exhibits."

For his many talents, Yogi Berra is a much-loved person. By now you are perhaps eager to read some of these great "one-liners". As you go down the list, think of how many you have already heard – and try not to smile!

- *When you come to a fork in the road, take it.*
- *Never answer an anonymous letter.*
- *I didn't really say everything I said.*
- *You can observe a lot by watching.*
- *We made too many wrong mistakes. (on why his team lost the 1960 World Series)*
- *I usually take a two-hour nap from one to four.*
- *It ain't over till it's over.*
- *If the world were perfect, it wouldn't be.*

A. Answer the following questions.

1. "But one of the English language's most quoted 'hurmorists' is neither of those..." What does "those" refer to?

    _____

2. Why is Yogi Berra revered as a humorist?

    _____

3. "...to preserve and promote the values of respect, sportsmanship, social justice and excellence through inclusive, culturally diverse, sports-based educational programs and exhibits." What does "inclusive" imply?

    _____

4. Which one of Yogi's quotes in the passage amuses you most? Why?

    _____

    _____

5. Search the Internet and find more of Yogi Berra's quotes. List them below, and share them with your friends.

    _____

    _____

    _____

    _____

Position of Adverbs

Adverbs can be placed at different positions in a sentence: at the beginning, in the middle, or at the end.

Generally, adverbs that modify adjectives or other adverbs go in the middle, right before the words they modify, with the exception of "enough" and "ago".

Examples: He liked to offer his observations, often <u>cleverly</u> simplistic on the one hand, yet quite meaningful on the other.

Some people can make a career out of their ability to amuse people – if they're good <u>enough</u>.

Adverbs of frequency go after the verb "to be" in both active and passive voice sentences, but with other verbs, they are put before them. However, if the main verb is preceded by a modal verb or an auxiliary verb, an adverb of frequency goes between them.

Examples: The ability to amuse someone with clever witticisms is <u>usually</u> appreciated.

In the case of Yogi Berra, one could <u>easily</u> assume he did it on purpose.

B. Check if the adverbs in the following sentences are put in the appropriate places. If not, rewrite the sentences to make them correct.

1. Stand-up comedy shows started to be popular ago long.

   _____

2. Yogi Berra is always ready to amuse others with his wit.

   _____

3. I find it never easy to be a person of humour.

   _____

4. It is amusing certainly to read Yogi Berra's one-liners.

   _____

5. Being humorous is different completely from being silly.

   _____

C. **Add the given adverbs in the appropriate places in the following sentences. Make any other necessary changes.**

1. never

   My brother finds it hard to make me laugh.

   _____

2. extremely

   The comedian is so famous that he drew a large audience to his show.

   _____

3. enough

   His performance is humorous to bring laughter to everyone throughout the two-hour show.

   _____

4. quite

   Lester commented casually on the controversial issue.

   _____

5. widely

   Yogi Berra is known for his sense of humour.

   _____

6. always

   He is quick at coming up with new one-liners.

   _____

7. usually

   You can discover great philosophy in what he says.

   _____

Too Much of a Good Thing: the "Law of Unintended Consequences"

Government leaders try hard to make the best decisions. Sometimes they canvass the general public or get expert advice, hold meetings, and set up committees and panels of inquiry. Of course, we already know the following from Aesop's fable "The Man, the Boy, and the Donkey": "Please all, and you will please none." These days, no policymaker – or member of the public – needs to be told that pleasing everyone is going to be impossible. But there are, perhaps more importantly, times when decisions made in good faith and with the best of intentions result in outcomes that are not what anyone could have foreseen. Good examples of this can be considered serendipitous, but sadly, there are cases where public policy decisions have resulted in injurious outcomes difficult to remedy.

In Australia – A large toad, known as the Giant Neotropical Toad or cane toad, native to the southern United States and Brazil, was introduced into Australia and certain countries in the South Pacific as a way to control the greyback cane beetle pests, which were devastating the sugar cane crops – those countries' main commodity crops at the time. This introduction of a foreign species was done after examining the case of the toad's introduction into several Caribbean islands, particularly into Puerto Rico, to curb the white grub population there. At that time, it was believed that the introduction of the toad had served its purpose. However, later studies concluded that it was wrong to attribute the reduction in the white grub population to the toad. The cane toad policy in Australia has obviously been a mistake: from 102 toads introduced in 1935 into northern Queensland, the population has now extended as far as the Northern Territory and New South Wales and numbers over 200 million. The cane toad's voracious appetite has caused considerable damage to the native Australian ecosystem, as well as to fauna and domestic animals that have been in contact with its poisonous skin. Concerted efforts are being made to eradicate what is now one of the country's biggest nuisances.

In Iceland – A lovely purple flower, the Alaskan Lupin (Lupinus nootkatensis) is a contentious issue in Iceland. The species was introduced into Iceland as a conservation measure to stabilize soil erosion. But it grew and spread like a weed, threatened the natural flora of the country, and slowed down, or got in the way of, forest rejuvenation. Iceland doesn't have much flora to begin with, and reforestation is a major undertaking there. But now the government of Iceland is embarking on a concerted effort to eradicate the Lupin. Summertime work projects have students from Iceland and abroad moving in to cut down the Lupin and, if possible, remove its seeds from the ground.

In Canada – Canadian Forest Service has become "too successful" with its fire-prevention initiatives. Fire is a natural part of the life cycle of forests, and the reduction of forest fires created new problems when, for example, large stands of mature trees, susceptible to pests and disease, were not killed off by fire. Moreover, accumulated matter on the forest floor remained longer, preventing new seedlings from sprouting and new trees from growing. The resulting forests of older trees are now seriously threatened by pests such as the pine beetle. They are now threatening to destroy the forests of British Columbia and Alberta.

A. Complete the following with reference to the passage.

1. Fact: 102 Giant Neotropical Toads were brought into Australia in 1935.

    Purpose: _____

    Consequence: _____

    _____

2. Fact: The Alaskan Lupin was introduced into Iceland around 2000.

    Purpose: _____

    Consequence: _____

    _____

3. Fact: Canadian Forest Service has launched many fire-prevention initiatives.

    Purpose: _____

    Consequence: _____

    _____

4. Describe another case of the "law of unintended consequences".

    _____

    _____

    _____

Viewpoint Adverbs

Viewpoint adverbs are used to help express our viewpoint or opinion about an action. They are placed at the beginning of a sentence.

Example: I feel sad that there are many cases where public policy decisions have resulted in injurious outcomes difficult to remedy.

<u>Sadly</u>, there are many cases where public policy decisions have resulted in injurious outcomes difficult to remedy.

B. **Rewrite each of the following sentences by starting it with a viewpoint adverb. Make any other necessary changes.**

1. I was surprised that the government did not do any research before introducing the species to the country.

    _____

    _____

2. According to theory, the cane toad can control the damage done by greyback cane beetles to the sugar cane.

    _____

    _____

3. In an ideal situation, the whole population of cane beetles could be wiped out from Australia.

    _____

    _____

4. To be honest with you, I don't think this policy will work without causing other problems.

    _____

    _____

5. It is now clear that the Australian government is facing another serious pest problem – the cane toad.

    _____

    _____

Commenting Adverbs

Commenting adverbs are similar to viewpoint adverbs. In many cases, they are the same words, but they go in a different position in the sentence – after the verb "to be" or before the main verb.

Example: The cane toad policy in Australia is a mistake.
The cane toad policy in Australia is <u>obviously</u> a mistake.

C.   Add an appropriate commenting adverb to each of the following sentences.

1.   Soil erosion has been a serious problem in Iceland.

2.   Reforestation is a major undertaking there, too.

3.   Cutting down the Lupin or removing its seeds from the ground is not an easy job.

4.   It is unwise to make public policy decisions hastily.

5.   It is not a problem that can be solved within the next decade.

6.   Matter accumulated on the forest floor prevents new seedlings from sprouting.

7.   Pine beetles will destroy all forests if the government takes no measures to control them.

No one wants to be out of style. The world of fashion changes all the time. What you say, as well as what you wear, tells people whether you are "in style" or not! So, let's look at the glossary of current style trends. There's plenty for you to dig (like) or dis (dislike, disdain, disregard).

Punk rock: The punk rock style usually consists of ripped jeans and T-shirts with the sleeves cut off and leather or denim jackets with punk rock band decals. For a more feminine look, girls wear fishnet stockings (with holes), black boots, and black leather miniskirts.

How to Talk Like a
Fashion Trendsetter

Goth glam: This is a dark, gothic style with a touch of glamour. For the gothic look, anything black works. Lots of makeup makes things more "glam", but the main colours are a pale face and large black-rimmed eyes. The goth glam look must include dyed black hair, too, if it isn't black already.

Boho chic: Boho chic is a mix of nice, old clothing updated by more fancy and trendy glamorous items. Boho is short for Bohemia, a place in Europe famous for the unique clothing of the gypsies that live there. Wide print skirts, especially with flower patterns, combined with neat T-shirts and string vests or denim and leather jackets, are good Boho chic choices. Lots of jewellery is important, too.

Bollywood: Bollywood is India's answer to Hollywood. In fact, more movies are made each year in Bollywood! This look borrows from the traditional Indian sari, a six-metre long piece of cotton or silk that women wrap around themselves to create a particular kind of dress. Bollywood fans will wrap themselves in bright colours to be beautiful!

Preppy chic: First found in American preparatory schools, this style consists of khaki pants or shorts, pastel-coloured polo shirts, and leather deck shoes. Sweater sets (short-sleeved sweater with matching knit jacket), pencil-skirts, and strings of pearls are what the girls wear when they want to dress up.

Hipster cool: This trend is about what the peace-loving hippies wore in the 1960s – bell-bottom trousers (striped is best!) and T-shirts with 1960s rockers like Joan Baez, the Beatles, or Bob Dylan on them. The peace-sign necklace is also an important part of the look. It's a look that borrows from the hippie saying, Feeling Groovy!

Classic: Some clothes are timeless. Sweater sets have been a favoured piece for more than 50 years. Regular blue jeans of almost any leg width can safely be called a "classic" item. A nice, simple woollen blazer can also last for ages, as long as it isn't in last season's "must-have" far-out print or doesn't have shoulder pads (that's so 1980s!). Neutral colours (tan, brown, black, navy) and simple lines are the key to buying classic pieces that outlast trends.

Remember that fashionistas (people who are passionate about clothes and keeping their own up-to-date) do not want to be out of style. If you like what you see, you can say to the person, "That's so fly!" But, if you need to tell your friend that what he or she has on is looking dated, you might want to whisper in his or her ear, "That's so last season!"

A. Name the styles that the following people are dressed in.

1. A man in his 30s in a T-shirt and a pair of striped bell-bottom pants _____

2. A teenage girl wearing black boots and a black leather miniskirt _____

3. A teenage boy in a polo shirt and a pair of khaki shorts _____

4. A young woman with a long piece of floral fabric wrapped around her _____

5. A girl wearing lots of makeup: blacked-rimmed eyes on her pale face _____

6. A woman in her 30s wearing a string vest and a wide print skirt _____

B. Which of the styles mentioned in the passage is your favourite? Why?

_____

_____

_____

_____

Conjunctions

A **coordinating conjunction** (and, or, but) is used to link independent clauses to form a compound sentence.

A **subordinating conjunction** is used to link a dependent clause to an independent clause to form a complex sentence.

Note that coordinating conjunctions and subordinating conjunctions are also used to join words and phrases in parallel structures.

Correlative conjunctions are used in pairs. Some common correlative conjunctions are "either...or", "neither...nor", "both...and", "whether...or", and "not only...but also".

C. **Circle the conjunctions in the sentences below. Write "C" for coordinating conjunctions, "S" for subordinating conjunctions, and "CR" for correlative conjunctions.**

1. A string of pearls is what the girls wear when they want to dress up. _____

2. Wide print skirts combined with neat T-shirts and string vests, or denim and leather jackets are some good Boho chic choices. _____

3. What you say, as well as what you wear, tells people whether you are "in style" or not. _____

4. If you find Boho chic too glamorous, you can try preppy chic. _____

5. Kate is a great follower of goth glam, and she stocks up her wardrobe with black clothing. _____

6. Both khaki pants and pastel-coloured polo shirts are the basics of preppy chic. _____

7. Would you like to buy this beige sweater, or would you like to get something brighter in colour? _____

8. Although this leather skirt looks great, it is way too expensive. _____

D. Rewrite each group of sentences below as one, using the appropriate conjunctions.

1. You can buy the belt. You can buy the necklace. You can't have both.

   _____

   _____

2. Try both jackets on. Then you decide which one to buy.

   _____

   _____

3. My friend, Sean, likes the punk rock style. I prefer the classic style.

   _____

   _____

4. Sharon has decided to wear something purple to the prom. Angela has decided to wear something purple to the prom, too.

   _____

   _____

5. Kenneth is saving up his allowance. He wants to buy a pair of leather gloves for his mom's birthday.

   _____

   _____

6. Jeans are a favourite for many young people. They have been popular since the 1950s.

   _____

   _____

Watch out for Those
Language Bloopers!

Everyone knows that public speaking is scary. However, even when speaking with friends, we can say the funniest things! And if you have some language "howlers", you are not alone. Former American president George W. Bush is well known for language bloopers in his speeches. There are all sorts of language errors that we may make from time to time. A few are listed below:

Metathesis – Have you ever transposed letters, sounds, or syllables within a word, such as in the case of "ossifer" for "officer" or "iern" instead of "iron"? Actually, metathesis is a common mistake, and many examples (like "aks" for "ask") have their roots in the evolution of the word: the word "ask" was pronounced as "aks" in Old English.

Spoonerisms – Have you ever said something like "keys and parrots" instead of "peas and carrots"? Such slips of the tongue are called spoonerisms – when the order of sounds is mixed up within a phrase. They are named after Reverend William Archibald Spooner, who lived at the turn of last century and apparently made these errors often. While some spoonerisms are unintentional, others are conscious plays on words, such as "Go and shake a tower" ("Go and take a shower"). Children's book author Shel Silverstein wrote a book called *Runny Babbit: a Billy Sook*, which is full of spoonerisms.

Mondegreens are mistakes of hearing, which happens often, particularly with song lyrics. For example, in the Christmas song "Rudolph the Red-Nosed Reindeer", some people heard the words "...All of the other reindeer..." as "Olive, the other reindeer". Eventually, a book was written about a dog named Olive who fills in for one of the reindeer. The word mondegreen was invented by a writer named Sylvia Wright who misheard a line from an old Scottish song: "They have slain the Earl of Murray, and laid him on the green." Wright thought she'd heard, "They have slain the Earl of Murray and Lady Mondegreen"!

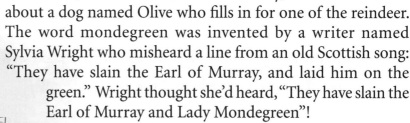

Eggcorns are examples of people saying new words because they are what they thought they heard, such as "eggcorn" for acorn and "duck tape" for duct tape. They are, in fact, homonyms of sorts.

A **malapropism** comes from the French phrase meaning "badly for the purpose". If you have heard someone accidentally substituting a

similar-sounding word for an obvious "other" word, you've heard a malapropism. These are named after Mrs. Malaprop, a character in Richard Sheridan's play *The Rivals*, who had a habit of mixing up her words. (In the play, Mrs. Malaprop says "He's the very pineapple of politeness", instead of "He's the very pinnacle of politeness".) George W. Bush said "nuclear power pants" instead of "nuclear power plants" in a 2003 speech.

Speaking of this former American president, there is another type of language blooper coined to categorize his unique gaffes – **Bushisms**. Of course, it's not nice to make fun of people's mistakes, but this is part and parcel of a public profile nowadays. Here are just a few of the many statements classified as Bushisms: "We need an energy bill that encourages consumption"; "Rarely is the question asked: is our children learning?"; "I know the human being and fish can coexist peacefully."

So, what does this tell us? No one ever needs to be afraid of public speaking! If you make a spoonerism, or a malapropism, or some other silly mistakes, you will be in good company – or, perhaps, "could gumpany"!

A.   Make up an example or two for each of the following language errors.

1.   metathesis: _____

2.   spoonerism: _____

3.   mondegreen: _____

4.   eggcorn: _____

5.   malapropism: _____

B.   Write the statements that the former U.S. President George W. Bush wanted to say.

1.   "We need an energy bill that encourages consumption."

    _____

2.   "Rarely is the question asked: is our children learning?"

    _____

Noun Phrases

A **noun phrase** is a group of words that functions as a single noun in a sentence. It can therefore be the subject, the object of a verb, the object of a preposition, a subject complement, an object complement, or an appositive in a sentence.

Examples: <u>Such slips of the tongue</u> are called spoonerisms. (subject)

When we speak with friends, we can say <u>the funniest things</u>. (object of the verb "say")

A malapropism comes from <u>the French phrase meaning "badly for the purpose"</u>. (object of the preposition "from")

Mondegreens are <u>mistakes of hearing</u>. (subject complement)

I consider this spoonerism of his <u>an intentional one</u>. (object complement)

Mrs. Malaprop, <u>a character in the play *The Rivals*</u>, has a habit of mixing up her words. (appositive)

C. Determine if each underlined noun phrase is the subject (S), object of a verb (OV), object of a preposition (OP), subject complement (SC), object complement (OC), or appositive (A) in the sentence.

1. *Runny Babbit: a Billy Sook* is <u>a book full of spoonerisms</u>. _____

2. Rudolph, <u>the red-nosed reindeer</u>, had a very shiny nose. _____

3. She considered him <u>the very pinnacle of politeness</u>. _____

4. Sometimes, spoonerisms are <u>conscious plays on words</u>. _____

5. Many examples of metathesis have roots in <u>the evolution of the word</u>. _____

6. A writer named Sylvia Wright invented <u>the word "mondegreen"</u>. _____

7. <u>"Keys and parrots" and "Go and shake a tower"</u> are examples of spoonerisms. _____

8. Reverend William Archibald Spooner lived at <u>the turn of last century</u>. _____

Other Phrases as Nouns

A **gerund phrase** or an **infinitive phrase** can also function as a noun and take the place of a noun in a sentence as a noun phrase does.

Examples: <u>Speaking with metathesis</u> is a common mistake.
(gerund phrase as subject)

A malapropism is <u>substituting a similar-sounding word for an obvious "other" word</u>.
(gerund phrase as subject complement)

<u>To make fun of people's mistakes</u> is not nice.
(infinitive phrase as subject)

Spoonerisms – <u>to mix up the order of sounds within a phrase</u> – are named after Reverend William Archibald Spooner.
(infinitive phrase as appositive)

D.   Make sentences of your own with the given phrases.

1.   making a silly mistake

_____
(Subject)

_____
(Object of Preposition)

_____
(Subject Complement)

_____
(Appositive)

2.   to speak publicly

_____
(Subject)

_____
(Subject Complement)

_____
(Appositive)

Don't Be a Dope:
Drugs
in Sports

Drugs are dangerous, and they are being abused more than ever these days. Decades ago, cigarettes (the main delivery system of nicotine, one of the world's most powerful and commonly used addictive drugs) used to be considered healthy and chic! They were often shown being smoked by beautiful women in films. They were given to soldiers during World Wars One and Two as part of their government rations. Some doctors even appeared in cigarette advertisements claiming that cigarettes had health benefits, such as providing extra protection against colds and boosting concentration. Of course, we all know now that smoking kills and that "second-hand" smoking can also kill by causing cancer, debilitating emphysema, and other terrible conditions. It is also, for many, the first step on the rough road to drug abuse.

Given these facts, it is surprising that drug abuse still goes on in the world of sports. The use of performance-enhancing drugs has been around for a long time and, in fact, during the earliest days of competitive sport, was not altogether frowned upon, in much the same way that cigarettes were thought to be "helpful". For example, it is alleged that the winner of the 1904 Olympic marathon was given an injection of strychnine and a dram of brandy to keep him going. An official race report noted, according to sports historian Dr. Jean-Pierre de Mondenard, that "The marathon has shown from a medical point of view how drugs can be very useful to athletes in long-distance races."

Doping in sports continued and was pushed into the realm of secret and illicit activity with both known and unknown risks and consequences. Soviet weightlifters were injected with the male hormone testosterone as early on as the 1950s. East Germany was notorious for plying its athletes with performance-enhancing drugs and illicit protocols. Females began to grow facial hair, and their voices became lower. Eventually, their menstrual cycles stopped. In some cases, they were told that the pills and injections were vitamins. Years later, when these women tried to have children, they suffered complications.

Doping in sports has ruined many promising athletic careers and reputations. Canadian Ben Johnson became the "World's Fastest Man" – the world-record holder and gold medalist for the 100-metre sprint at the 1988 Seoul Summer Olympics. But those accolades were taken away within days when he tested positive for anabolic steroid, and he admitted to using human growth hormone as well. Baseball star Barry Bonds and 2006 Tour de France winner Floyd Landis are some of the many other sporting "heroes" under the cloud of doping.

The formation of regulatory bodies and "watchdogs", such as the World Anti-Doping Agency (WADA – founded in 1999 in Switzerland and now headquartered in Montreal) helps keep a vigilant watch on sports cheats. Lists of banned substances are in place, making it very clear to all concerned which drugs will not be tolerated, and testing has become precise, as well as more frequent. However, new forms of illegal performance enhancement are being developed. The newest method of such illegal activity is called "gene doping". As the name suggests, it does not involve the use of drugs, but is something that many consider equally sinister. Gene doping activity involves the alteration of cells, genes, and other genetic material for the purpose of improving athletic performance. WADA has called on scientists and geneticists around the world to prevent gene doping from gaining ground.

A. Read the following statements. Check the true ones and rewrite the false ones, based on the information from the passage.

1. During the two world wars, soldiers were given cigarettes because cigarettes were said to be able to relieve pain. ☐

_____

_____

2. Cigarettes are regarded as one of the world's most powerful and commonly used addictive drugs. ☐

_____

_____

3. Performance-enhancing drugs have been banned from use in competitive sports right from the start. ☐

_____

_____

4. Gene doping refers to the activity of stimulating cells, genes, and other genetic material for the purpose of improving health conditions and muscle strength. ☐

_____

_____

Active Voice and Passive Voice

In the **active voice**, the subject performs the action of the verb; in the **passive voice**, the subject receives the action of the verb. While it is usually better to use the active voice since it is clearer and more forceful, the passive voice provides a shift of emphasis — from the doer to the thing or person being acted upon. We can leave out the "doer" if it is obvious, unimportant, or unknown.

Examples: Doping in sports has ruined many promising athletic careers and reputations. (active voice)

Many promising athletic careers and reputations have been ruined by doping in sports. (passive voice)

During the earliest days of competitive sport, the use of performance-enhancing drugs was not altogether frowned upon.
(passive voice with the "doer" left out)

B. Rewrite the following sentences using the passive voice.

1. The World Anti-Doping Agency has introduced some new drug-testing policies.

    _____

    _____

2. You can obtain the WADA Athlete Guide from their website.

    _____

    _____

3. One cannot dispute the hard evidence that some performance-enhancing drugs have resulted in long-term harmful consequences for those who took them.

    _____

    _____

4. Many people consider "gene doping" to be as sinister as drug doping.

    _____

    _____

Other Passive Forms

We can use "**get/have something done**" to focus on the result of an activity rather than the person or object that performs the activity.

Example: The International Olympic Committee banned the use of performance-enhancing drugs in Olympic Games.

The International Olympic Committee <u>had the use of performance-enhancing drugs banned</u> in Olympic Games.

We can also use "**need + v-ing**" to focus on the person or thing that will experience the action.

Example: The World Anti-Doping Code needed to be revised.

The World Anti-Doping Code <u>needed revising</u>.

C. Rewrite the following sentences using "get/have something done" or "need + v-ing".

1. The organizing committee needed to test all athletes for performance-enhancing drugs before the commencement of the competitions.

_____

_____

2. They want someone to examine the samples as soon as possible.

_____

_____

3. Methods of detecting various performance-enhancing drugs need to be improved.

_____

_____

4. People need to be educated about the harmful effects of doping.

_____

_____

12

One of the World's Most
Published Editorials

O ver one hundred years ago, an eight-year-old girl named Virginia O'Hanlon wrote a letter to the editor of *The New York Sun*. A response was printed as an unsigned editorial on September 21, 1897, and has become one of the most reprinted newspaper editorials in history.

The ☀ Sun.

TUESDAY SEPTEMBER 21 1897

DEAR EDITOR: I am 8 years old. Some of my little friends say there is no Santa Claus. Papa says, "If you see it in THE SUN it's so." Please tell me the truth; is there a Santa Claus? – Virginia O'Hanlon

VIRGINIA, your little friends are wrong. They have been affected by the skepticism of a skeptical age. They do not believe except they see. They think that nothing can be which is not comprehensible by their little minds. All minds, VIRGINIA, whether they be men's or children's, are little. In this great universe of ours man is a mere insect, an ant, in his intellect, as compared with the boundless world about him, as measured by the intelligence capable of grasping the whole of truth and knowledge.

Yes, VIRGINIA, there is a Santa Claus. He exists as certainly as love and generosity and devotion exist, and you know that they abound and give to your life its highest beauty and joy. Alas! How dreary would be the world if there were no Santa Claus. It would be as dreary as if there were no VIRGINIAS. There would be no childlike faith then, no poetry, no romance to make tolerable this existence. We should have no enjoyment, except in sense and sight. The eternal light with which childhood fills the world would be extinguished.

Not believe in Santa Claus! You might as well not believe in fairies! You might get your papa to hire men to watch in all the chimneys on Christmas Eve to catch Santa Claus, but even if they did not see Santa Claus coming down, what would that prove? Nobody sees Santa Claus, but that is no sign that there is no Santa Claus. The most real things in the world are those that neither children nor men can see. Did you ever see fairies dancing on the lawn? Of course not, but that's no proof that they are not there. Nobody can conceive or imagine all the wonders there are unseen and unseeable in the world.

You may tear apart the baby's rattle and see what makes the noise inside, but there is a veil covering the unseen world which not the strongest man, nor even the united strength of all the strongest men that ever lived, could tear apart. Only faith, fancy, poetry, love, romance, can push aside that curtain and view and picture the supernal beauty and glory beyond. Is it all real? Ah, VIRGINIA, in all this world there is nothing else real and abiding.

No Santa Claus! Thank GOD! He lives, and he lives forever. A thousand years from now, VIRGINIA, nay, ten times ten thousand years from now, he will continue to make glad the heart of childhood.

A. Explain in your own words what the following statements from the editorial imply.

1. They think that nothing can be which is not comprehensible by their little minds.

   _____

2. The eternal light with which childhood fills the world would be extinguished.

   _____

3. Only faith, fancy, poetry, love, romance, can push aside that curtain and view and picture the supernal beauty and glory beyond.

   _____

B. Answer the following questions.

1. How did the editorial explain the existence of Santa Claus to Virginia?

   _____

   _____

2. Why do you think The Sun's response to Virginia's letter to the editor has become one of the most reprinted newspaper editorials in history?

   _____

   _____

Mood

A verb can be in one of these moods: indicative, imperative, or subjunctive.

The **indicative mood** is the most common type used. It is used to make an objective statement.

Example: The response has become one of the most reprinted newspaper editorials in history.

A verb in the **imperative mood** expresses commands or requests.

Example: Please tell me the truth.

A verb in the **subjunctive mood** expresses a wish or something that is not true. The past or perfect tense is used.

Example: I wish I could see Santa Claus (but I cannot see him).

If Virginia's friends had seen Santa Claus (but they hadn't), they would have believed in his existence (they didn't believe in it).

C. Determine the mood in the following sentences. Write "IND" for indicative, "IMP" for imperative, and "SUB" for subjunctive.

1. Nobody sees Santa Claus, but that is no sign that there is no Santa Claus. _____

2. If I were Virginia, I would not have doubted the existence of Santa Claus. _____

3. How I wish I could see fairies in my backyard. _____

4. Don't forget to hang a Christmas stocking by your bed on Christmas Eve. _____

5. Children who believe in fairies and Santa Claus are more creative and imaginative than those who don't. _____

6. Please show this editorial to your friends who think there is no Santa Claus. _____

7. I would have told you if I knew the truth. _____

8. There are many things in the world that are beyond our imagination. _____

D. Rewrite the following sentences in the subjunctive mood.

1. Cindy has asked the silly question. She regrets that she has done so.

    _____

    _____

2. I don't think Keith should have turned down the offer.

    _____

    _____

3. Jan wanted to see fairies. Then she could take pictures of them.

    _____

    _____

4. Timothy thinks that Molly shouldn't have believed in that story.

    _____

    _____

E. Make sentences of your own using the three types of mood.

1. Indicative Mood

    _____

    _____

2. Imperative Mood

    _____

    _____

3. Subjunctive Mood

    _____

    _____

Steven **Fletcher,**
an Exceptional Public Servant

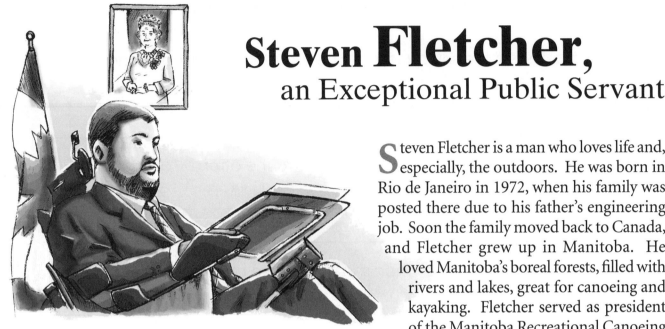

Steven Fletcher is a man who loves life and, especially, the outdoors. He was born in Rio de Janeiro in 1972, when his family was posted there due to his father's engineering job. Soon the family moved back to Canada, and Fletcher grew up in Manitoba. He loved Manitoba's boreal forests, filled with rivers and lakes, great for canoeing and kayaking. Fletcher served as president of the Manitoba Recreational Canoeing Association, and was twice the Manitoba kayak champion. He also decided to follow in his father's footsteps, earning a Bachelor of Science Degree in Geological Engineering from the University of Manitoba in 1995. He soon found work in his chosen profession in the environment he loved, and life was good.

A year later, while Fletcher was driving to a job site in northern Manitoba, his vehicle hit a moose. As a result of the collision, Fletcher became paralyzed from the neck down. Doctors told him he would be spending the rest of his life in an institution, but Fletcher decided things would be otherwise, and after a long and painful period of rehabilitation, during which time Fletcher regained the ability to speak, he returned to university to obtain a Master of Business Administration Degree. During this time, Fletcher got involved in student politics. He was twice elected president of the University of Manitoba Students' Union. He also served on the university's board of governors and the Canadian Alliance of Student Associations. It was only natural that Fletcher would want to continue this type of public service once his student career was completed.

Fletcher became involved in federal politics and was elected President of the Progressive Conservative Party of Manitoba. In 2004, he ran as a candidate for the Winnipeg riding of Charleswood–St. James–Assiniboia and won, becoming the first permanently disabled member of the House of Commons. He wasted no time becoming a busy Member of Parliament, taking up responsibilities as Official Opposition Critic for Health and member of the Standing Committee on Health, in addition to his duties to his constituents and his other community involvement. After his re-election in 2006, Fletcher was appointed Parliamentary Secretary to the Minister of Health.

Fletcher has worked hard to help people affected by Hepatitis C, mental illness, heart disease, and cancer, and has won numerous awards for his tireless endeavours, including the inaugural Award for Outstanding Individual Leadership, the Courage and Leadership Award from the Canadian Cancer Society, and the Champions of Mental Health Award. He was recently inducted into the Terry Fox Hall of Fame. Steven Fletcher's success shows us not only that mobility impairment does not mean an inactive and unsatisfying life, but also that a "catastrophic injury" does not have to define a person.

Fletcher still loves the outdoors. When his busy schedule allows, he likes visiting the Fort Whyte Centre. It is an environmental, educational, and recreational facility located at the edge of Winnipeg, on a man-made lake among aspen groves and nature trails, and it contains a 28-hectare prairie meadow supporting a herd of roaming bison.

A. Check the best answer for each of the following questions.

1. Steven Fletcher's father _____ .

    A. worked as an engineer in Rio de Janeiro

    B. moved to Rio de Janeiro before Steven Fletcher was born

    C. returned to Canada and took a job at the University of Manitoba

2. What made Fletcher consider going into public service?

    A. his long and painful period of rehabilitation after a serious accident

    B. his involvement in student politics while doing his MBA

    C. the influence of the board of governors at the University of Manitoba

3. Fletcher was _____ .

    A. the first President of the Progressive Conservative Party of Manitoba

    B. the parliamentary secretary to the Minister of Health

    C. the chairman of the Standing Committee on Health

4. Which one below was not one of Fletcher's achievements?

    A. He won the inaugural Award for Outstanding Individual Leadership.

    B. He was inducted into the Terry Fox Hall of Fame.

    C. He received an award from the Canadian Mental Health Society.

13

Types of Sentences by Structure

Sentences can be classified according to their structure.

- A **simple sentence** consists of a single independent clause with no dependent clauses.

- A **compound sentence** consists of two or more independent clauses with no dependent clauses. These independent clauses are joined together by coordinating conjunctions (and, or, but), punctuation, or both.

- A **complex sentence** consists of one independent clause with at least one dependent clause joined together by subordinating conjunctions like "if" and "although".

- A **compound-complex sentence** consists of two or more independent clauses, one of which has at least one dependent clause.

B. **Find examples of the following types of sentences from the passage "Steven Fletcher, an Exceptional Public Servant".**

Simple Sentence

1. _____

2. _____

Compound Sentence

3. _____

4. _____

Complex Sentence

5. _____

6. _____

Compound-Complex Sentence

7. _____

_____

C. Rewrite the following groups of sentences.

1. Fletcher has been inducted into the Terry Fox Hall of Fame. He has received the King Clancy Award. (Compound Sentence)

_____

_____

2. Fletcher won the Manitoba kayak competition two times. That was before the accident happened. (Complex Sentence)

_____

_____

3. Maybe you like the outdoors. You can visit the Fort Whyte Centre. You can hike along the pond. You can listen to the sounds of water foul there. (Compound-Complex Sentence)

_____

_____

D. Compose a paragraph that consists of the four types of sentences.

_____

_____

_____

_____

_____

_____

_____

_____

How can we become better people? From all the wisdom we can gather, there appears to be a strong overlap between cultures regarding certain ideas. Below is a list of what we consider the "Seven Sacred Teachings". This list is based on First Nations cultures and spirituality, but the concepts are found throughout cultures of the world, seen in the stories, actions, and beliefs of those different cultures. These seven sacred teachings are, in fact, what unify us, as they give us hope for the possibility of a better world, primarily through the betterment of ourselves. They can guide us in our relations with people, the natural world, and – more important now than ever – the planet itself.

Wisdom: Do you understand that your actions have consequences? If you took the time to think through the possible outcomes of your actions, would it change the way you do things? We all need to think before we act, and have a clearer idea in our minds about what is Good and Bad, or Right and Wrong. Wisdom is understanding that what we do and say is important because everything we do leads us to the next moment.

Love: Can you love someone unconditionally – give kindness without asking for or expecting anything in return? Try to understand that the best kind of love is the love given when it is needed the most, even though it may seem difficult to give our care and concern at that time.

The Seven Sacred Teachings

Wisdom
Love
Respect
Courage
Honesty
Humility
Truth

Respect: Just like love, respect is given without the expectation that it will be returned. And, just like love, the strongest respect is that which is given when the other person is not at their best, and may be showing disrespect, bitterness, or unjust behaviour towards you! Respect means you can honour people's sincere and healthy beliefs even if they are different from yours. And just as it is important to respect others, we must also respect ourselves.

Courage: Can you do the right thing even if you know it might have negative consequences for you? Do you have the courage to stand alone to do what you believe in? History is full of examples of people who did just this, from Laura Secord to Nelson Mandela. We can all show real bravery in our everyday lives by not entering a fight that someone wants to pick with us, or by deciding to do things differently because we've thought about it and decide the outcome would be better that way. And don't forget, asking for help when we need it is one of the bravest things we can do.

Honesty: Honesty comes in many forms, but it begins and ends with you, considering and formulating ideas about who you are, what you do, and why you do it. It is one thing to answer someone's question honestly, which we should always do, but that's the "easy" honesty. The more difficult kind is in trying to be honest with ourselves, about who we really are. Sometimes it may be easier to fool ourselves than others because we just don't want to know the honest answer! Try to say, think, and do only the things you really mean.

Humility: Can you admit you don't know everything? Can you show penitence when necessary, admitting mistakes? Can you accept success with pride and avoid slipping into arrogance? Can you step back and allow others the limelight, even if you could do just as well? Do you believe that it is a measure of your self worth to set aside what you want for the needs of another? If you say "yes" to all these questions, then you will do well in life, because life is full of times when personal setbacks will knock us down. People that have consciously practised humility in their lives will be better able to show resilience at such times.

Truth: Do you tell the truth even when you don't want to? Can you walk through life being truthful about yourself and others? Living with truth involves not only an ability to tell the truth, but a desire to be truthful because you believe that the truth is best no matter what.

What a wonderful world it would be if everyone followed the Seven Sacred Teachings!

A. Define in your own words the Seven Sacred Teachings described in the passage.

Sacred Teaching	How You Define It
Wisdom	
Love	
Respect	
Courage	
Honesty	
Humility	
Truth	

14

Types of Sentences by Purpose

Sentences can also be classified according to their purpose.

- A **declarative sentence** makes a statement.

  Example: The "Seven Sacred Teachings" is a list based on First Nations cultures and spirituality.

- An **interrogative sentence** requests information.

  Example: What are the common concepts found throughout the cultures of the world?

- An **exclamatory sentence** shows surprise and strong emotions.

  Example: How honest you are in admitting your weakness!

- An **imperative sentence** gives a command or makes a request.

  Example: Let's find more information about the "Seven Sacred Teachings" from the library.

B. **Find an example of each type of sentence from the passage, "The Seven Sacred Teachings".**

1. Declarative Sentence

   _____

   _____

2. Interrogative Sentence

   _____

   _____

3. Exclamatory Sentence

   _____

   _____

4. Imperative Sentence

   _____

   _____

C. Write sentences in the types specified based on the given situations.

1. Christine wants to know how she can improve herself.

   Interrogative: _____

   _____

2. The teacher explains what the "Seven Sacred Teachings" include.

   Declarative: _____

   _____

3. Ms. Deswell tells the class to hand in their project ideas on First Nations culture next Friday.

   Imperative: _____

   _____

4. Matthew's sister, Christine, will take part in a play at school. He wants to know what the play is about.

   Interrogative: _____

   _____

5. Christine asks Matthew to see her performance.

   Imperative: _____

   _____

6. Matthew is at Christine's school. He is asking someone where the school hall is.

   Interrogative: _____

   _____

7. Matthew exclaims that it is a great show.

   Exclamatory: _____

   _____

A. Read the passage. Write the underlined verbs in the correct places.

A vacation in Nova Scotia will never disappoint you. Whether you like <u>appreciating</u> the natural beauty or <u>engaging</u> in fun outdoor activities, Nova Scotia surely has something great <u>to offer</u> you.

At the Bay of Fundy, you can see the world's highest tides, and if you are lucky enough, you will also see an <u>endangered</u> finback whale <u>swim</u> in the distance. If you are an outdoors type, you can hike along the many <u>trodden</u> mountain trails in the Cape of Breton Highlands National Park, or bike around the Cabot Trail. You will be fascinated by the breathtaking coastal scenery on the way.

It is also a good idea <u>to explore</u> the colourful <u>fishing</u> town of Lunenburg, a UNESCO World Heritage Site, and cruise on Bluenose II, Nova Scotia's <u>sailing</u> ambassador and a replica of the original Bluenose.

If you <u>think</u> winter may seem too cold for these outdoor activities, why not visit the Alexander Graham Bell National Historic Site of Canada in Baddeck, and discover how Bell <u>invented</u> the telephone?

1. Finite Verb   _____   _____

2. Present Participle   _____   _____

3. Past Participle   _____   _____

4. Gerund   _____   _____

5. To-Infinitive   _____   _____

6. Bare Infinitive   _____

B. Fill in the blanks with appropriate prepositions.

1. If everyone pitches _____ , we can get all the preparations done by this Friday.

2. I'm still thinking of the best way to get my message _____ .

3. The poor little kitten curled _____ in a corner of the shabby shack, trembling _____ fear.

4. The police are looking _____ the case of the missing ship, but there has been little progress so far.

5. My mother is accustomed _____ sleeping just five hours a day.

6. Ian insisted _____ completing the jigsaw puzzle before going out.

C. Rewrite the following sentences to correct the order of adjectives or the position of adverbs.

1. No one dared to open the big, mysterious, wooden old chest in the attic.

   _____

2. The Canadian famous rock band will hold a concert this Saturday.

   _____

3. Jessica put the pink, small lovely shell carefully in the gift box.

   _____

4. Oh, completely I've forgotten my half-eaten pizza in the fridge.

   _____

5. The steps to making an origami crane are enough simple for everyone to follow.

   _____

D. Complete the sentences with the correct interrogative or relative adverbs.

1. _____ can you convince others if you don't believe it yourself?

2. This is the restaurant _____ I first tried deep-fried alligator.

3. Do you know _____ so many people like going on cruises?

4. _____ does Sharon keep asking you the same question?

5. I still remember the days _____ we had fun in the community centre every weekend.

6. _____ do the famous pianist's press conference and autograph session take place?

E. Fill in the blanks with the appropriate coordinating, subordinating, or correlative conjunctions.

The Miniature Schnauzer has long won the hearts of many pet owners. It has a bushy beard 1._____ eyebrows, 2._____ there is very little shedding.

Miniature Schnauzers are 3._____ intelligent 4._____ obedient. They are spirited and playful 5._____ can bring lots of laughter to their families. They make excellent companions 6._____ they are loyal and friendly, and like staying close to their owners. 7._____ their owners are too busy to play with them, they will invent their own fun.

8._____ Miniature Schnauzers are not aggressive by nature, they are alert and are enthusiastic barkers, 9._____ they are very good watchdogs.

10._____ you are thinking of getting a pet, why not get a Miniature Schnauzer?

F. Identify the underlined phrases. Write the letters in the parentheses.

A. noun phrase as subject

B. noun phrase as object of verb

C. noun phrase as object of preposition

D. noun phrase as subject complement

E. noun phrase as object complement

F. noun phrase as appositive

G. gerund phrase as subject

H. gerund phrase as object of preposition

I. infinitive phrase as subject

J. not functioning like a noun

Do you remember <u>the scary fish with a light hanging in front of it</u> (1.   ) in *Finding Nemo*? It is a deep sea anglerfish, <u>one of the ocean's most bizarre-looking fish</u> (2.   ). It is also <u>one of the best-known creatures of the deep</u> (3.   ). Because of its vicious-looking appearance with its big jaws lined with fang-like teeth, some people call the deep sea angler <u>"the common black devil"</u> (4.   ).

The deep sea angler you saw in *Finding Nemo* looked big but, in fact, it only reaches a length of about 12 centimetres. <u>To see a real deep sea angler in the sea</u> (5.   ) is nearly impossible. It is known for <u>inhabiting the world's oceans</u> (6.   ) at depths of more than 3000 feet. This fish is virtually invisible in the deep sea, but the female has a bioluminescent lure known as a photophore growing from its head. <u>This unique organ</u> (7.   ) can produce a bluish-green light. <u>To attract prey</u> (8.   ), the deep sea angler remains completely motionless in the dark water and waves its photophore back and forth. Once the prey gets close enough, it swallows it whole. <u>Swallowing prey larger than its body</u> (9.   ) is easy for a deep sea angler because it can extend both its jaws and its stomach to <u>an enormous size</u> (10.   ).

G. **Rewrite the following sentences using the passive voice.**

1. British and French cultures and traditions have influenced Canada's culture.

    _____

2. The teacher gave each of the children a sketchbook and some crayons.

    _____

3. Someone left a pair of mittens under the chair after the seminar.

    _____

4. No one will forget their excellent performance.

    _____

H. **Make passive sentences using the following structures.**

1. get something done

    _____

2. have something done

    _____

3. need + v-ing

    _____

I. **Determine the mood of the following sentences. Write "IND" for indicative, "IMP" for imperative, and "SUB" for subjunctive.**

1. I wish I could be there to give you support.   _____

2. Please tell Nicole that the meeting will start at two this afternoon.   _____

3. If there were no sun or water, nothing on Earth could survive.   _____

4. "Scrabble" was developed from a game called "Criss-Crosswords".   _____

5. Don't ever spend so much time playing video games again.   _____

J. Rewrite the following groups of sentences to the types specified in the parentheses.

1. After the Williams checked into the hotel, they met their friends in the lobby and the tour guide took them to different attractions in the city. (simple)

   _____

2. I can say that was the best clam chowder I've ever had. The price was reasonable. (compound)

   _____

3. The film has won many Oscars, including Best Picture and Best Director. Derek has no intention of seeing it. (complex)

   _____

4. We were watching television in the living room. All the lights went out. We were in complete darkness. (compound-complex)

   _____

5. Don't you know that Wilfred has been elected the Best Student of the Year? (declarative)

   _____

6. I want to know the fastest way to the airport. (interrogative)

   _____

7. Your show is amazing. (exclamatory)

   _____

8. Could you tell me what is going on? (imperative)

   _____

15

Twenty Thousand "Oskar Schindlers": the Holocaust Rescuers

Most Canadian students know who Oskar Schindler was, thanks in part to the movie *Schindler's List* directed by Steven Spielberg. Schindler was a German industrialist who saved the lives of over one thousand Jews during Hitler's era of Nazi atrocities in Europe. Schindler did this by persuading Nazi authorities to allow him to hire Jews for work in his enamelware and munitions factories, sparing them from the Nazi death camps.

What many may not know is that there were many "Schindlers" from different countries. Some of these rescuers were diplomats, posted in European countries at the time of the Holocaust. They did what they could, as diplomats do: they issued entry visas for Jewish refugees so that they could travel out of the danger zone. Most of these diplomats did so secretly, or even against the express orders of their own governments! Chiune Sugihara – the "Japanese Schindler" – saved the lives of over ten thousand Jews while serving as the Japanese Consul General in Lithuania, spending up to 20 hours a day filling out the necessary paperwork before the Japanese consulate was closed down. When he returned to Japan, his government asked him to resign. Other brave diplomats include: Raoul Wallenberg and Per Anger – the "Swedish Schindlers"; Ángel Sanz Briz – the "Spanish Schindler"; Carl Lutz – the "Swiss Schindler"; Giorgio Perlasca and Angelo Rotta – the "Italian Schindlers"; Aristides de Sousa Mendes – the "Portuguese Schindler"; Fengshan Ho – the "Chinese Schindler"; Constantin Karadja – the "Romanian Schindler"; Namik Kemal Yolga – the "Turkish Schindler". The list goes on.

Others rescuers, like journalist Varian Fry, the "American Schindler", risked their lives to run secret rescue networks. Jaap Penraat, the "Dutch Schindler", an architect, was able to save Jews by convincing the Nazis that the 406 people he was harbouring were slave labourers. He was later tortured for the ruse. Some rescuers were children, such as the German schoolgirl Sophie Scholl and her brother Hans, who started the "White Rose" resistance movement. It can also be said that the entire population of Denmark was a Holocaust "rescuer", a collective resistance, and it included an organized effort among Danish civil servants to evacuate about 8000 Danish Jews to Sweden. As a result, 99% of Danish Jews survived.

These are only a few of the more than 20 000 people on the List of Righteous Among the Nations, dedicated to those non-Jewish "rescuers" of the Holocaust, located at the Yad Vashem Holocaust memorial in Israel. But there are no native-Canadians on it. Is there a "Canadian Schindler"? Well, one couple Pauline and Georges Vanier can perhaps be so considered. Georges Vanier was Canada's top diplomat in France when World War II began, and he entreated his government to allow immigration for Jewish refugees, pointing out that "Canada has a wonderful opportunity to be generous and yet profit by accepting some of these people." The Vaniers returned to Canada in 1941 and spoke out about the plight of the Jews in Europe, but were often met with indifference and hostility. Immediately after the war's end in 1945, Georges Vanier and his wife returned to France. After viewing the Buchenwald concentration camp for himself, Georges said in a CBC radio broadcast: "How deaf we were then to cruelty and the cries of pain which came to our ears, grim forerunners of the mass torture and murders which were to follow." Pauline and Georges continued their efforts to help change Canadian immigration policy. Due in part to their efforts, along with those of humanitarian organizations, more than 186 000 European refugees settled in Canada between 1947 and 1953. Georges Vanier served as Governor General of Canada from 1959 to 1967, the year he died. Pauline then moved to France to live and work with their eldest son, Jean, who founded a humanitarian organization called "L'Arche" (The Ark), a worldwide movement to help people with mental handicaps live productive lives.

A. Answer the following questions.

1. What does the name "Schindler" stand for today?

    _____

    _____

2. Find a sentence that shows that some countries did not want to take in Jewish refugees in Paragraph Two.

    _____

    _____

3. What made the writer consider Georges Vanier a "Schindler"?

    _____

    _____

4. Georges Vanier pointed out that "Canada has a wonderful opportunity to be generous and yet profit by accepting some of these people." How do you think Canada might have benefited from accepting Jewish refugees?

    _____

    _____

Dependent Clauses

Some clauses cannot stand on their own as sentences. They are called **dependent clauses**. A dependent clause has to be attached to an independent clause to add information to that clause.

A **noun clause** is a dependent clause that acts as the subject or object of a verb or the object of a preposition.

Example: <u>What many may not know</u> is <u>that there were many "Schindlers"</u>.

An **adjective clause** modifies a noun or a pronoun.

Example: Schindler was a German industrialist <u>who saved the lives of over one thousand Jews</u>.

An **adverb clause** functions like an adverb and gives information about "when", "where", "why", and "how".

Example: Georges Vanier was Canada's top diplomat in France <u>when World War II began</u>.

B. **Underline the dependent clauses in the following sentences. Then write "N" for noun clauses, "ADJ" for adjective clauses, and "ADV" for adverb clauses.**

1. Some diplomats issued visas for Jewish refugees so that they could travel out of the danger zone. _____

2. Many Jews whom Schindler rescued were hired to work in his factories. _____

3. Chiune Sugihara saved over ten thousand Jews while he served as the Japanese Consul General in Lithuania. _____

4. He was asked by his government to resign when he returned to Japan. _____

5. "L'Arche" is a humanitarian organization which Georges Vanier's son, Jean, founded. _____

6. Exactly how many "Schindlers" there were is unknown. _____

7. Many people may not understand why someone risked his or her life to save others. _____

C. Complete the following sentences with the dependent clauses specified.

Noun Clause

1. _____

   _____ is still a mystery.

2. Many people believe _____

   _____ .

3. The students were sad to learn _____

   _____ .

Adjective Clause

4. The fact _____

   _____ is incontrovertible.

5. The journalist _____

   _____ was sent to the country to cover the event.

6. The story _____

   _____ is really touching.

Adverb Clause

7. A memorial has been put up _____

   _____ .

8. The students put the story on stage _____

   _____ .

9. *Schindler's List* is a great film _____

   _____ .

16

An Ancient Story about the *Sun* and *the Moon*

Every country and every culture has their own myths, legends, and folktales. For those who have spent time reading or researching these ageless stories, one thing becomes quite clear – there are a lot of similarities and "overlaps" among the legends and folktales of the world. For example, a great many folktales the world over have to do with the story of how the elements of the universe, our Earth, humans, and animals were created. Of course, this story is also in the Bible and other religious texts. Below is a folktale about the Sun and the Moon from the Philippines. Do you know which physical phenomena are being alluded to in this ancient folk story?

"The Sun and the Moon were happily married for a great many years. The Sun was always a little bit grouchy, but the gentle Moon was always there to cool down and placate the hot and fiery Sun. Even so, the Sun, over time, became ugly and quarrelsome in a way that not even the Moon could do anything about. One day, the hot-tempered Sun became enraged at the Moon and started to chase her around in circles. The Moon ran and ran, very fast, until she had created some distance between herself and the Sun, although there were times when she had grown tired and the Sun had almost caught her up. Ever since then, the hot and fiery Sun has been chasing the gentle, silvery Moon, at times almost reaching her, only to fall behind again and again.

The Sun and the Moon had a child, a large bright Star, and the object of the Moon's boundless maternal love. Over time, the Star grew larger and brighter, and became so large and bright that the Sun became jealous. Other heavenly bodies were attracted to the Star, and the Star returned their admiration with a pure love. Finally, one day, the hot-tempered Sun could take no more of this. He cut the Star up into small pieces and scattered the Star's body across the universe, just like a woman scatters rice in a field. Since that time, there have been many stars across the night sky, all pieces of the child borne of the Sun and the Moon.

The Sun and the Moon had another child, in the form of a giant Crab. The Crab lives with us still, and is such a powerful being here on Earth that he sends us flashes of lightning every time he opens and closes his eyes. He is the creator of the storms that roil the seas. This giant Crab lives at the bottom of the sea, in a huge dungeon-like lair. He spends half of his life in the lair and half out of it, prowling the seas. When he is in his lair, the waters are high; when he leaves his lair, the seas rush into the empty space he leaves behind, and the waters become low. His every move creates great waves – and dangers – for people on or near the water.

This giant Crab has inherited some of his father's, the Sun's, traits; he is quarrelsome and bad-tempered. He sometimes becomes so angry with his mother, the Moon, that he tries to eat her up. The people on Earth love their gentle silver Lady Moon, and so when they see the Crab going near her, they run out of their huts to shout and beat on their gongs until the giant Crab is frightened away, and the gentle Lady Moon is thus saved, until next time."

A. **Write about the physical phenomena described in the folktale *The Sun and the Moon.***

_____

_____

_____

_____

B. **Try illustrating the relationships among the sun, the moon, and the stars in another folktale way.**

_____

_____

_____

_____

_____

_____

_____

_____

_____

Reported Speech

In **reported speech** or **indirect speech**, we report what someone said without using the speaker's exact words.

Changing a sentence from direct speech to reported speech involves changes in verb tenses when the reporting verb (like "said") is in the past tense. Usually, the verb form is one step back into the past from the original. Note that pronouns need to be changed too.

Example: "<u>You</u> <u>will</u> be doing a project on folktales from around the world," Mrs. Wright said to the class.

Mrs. Wright told the class that <u>they</u> <u>would</u> be doing a project on folktales from around the world.

However, when the reporting verb is in the present tense, or when the reported subject is a general truth, the present tense is retained.

Examples: "Reading legends is my favourite pastime," Ida <u>says</u>.

Ida <u>says</u> that reading legends <u>is</u> her favourite pastime.

Tim said, "Different cultures <u>have</u> their own folktales."

Tim said that different cultures <u>have</u> their own folktales.

C.   Rewrite the following sentences in reported speech.

1.   Linda said to Julie, "The Star and the Crab are children of the Sun and the Moon."

_____

2.   "There are a lot of similarities among the folktales of different countries around the world," Timothy says.

_____

3.   Ginny said to Kingsley, "My mom has bought me a set of books on Greek mythology."

_____

4.   "I will tell you an interesting folktale before you go to bed," Mom said.

_____

Reported Questions and Commands

When we report a yes/no question, "whether" or "if" is used. If the question begins with a question word, the question word is retained.

Examples: Lily asked me, "Have you read the legend before?"

Lily asked me <u>whether</u> I had read the legend before.

The students asked Mrs. Wright, "When do we have to hand in the project?"

The students asked Mrs. Wright <u>when</u> they had to hand in the project.

When we report a command, we simply add "to" before the verb if it is positive; add "not to" if it is negative.

Examples: "Do some research in the library," the teacher told us.

The teacher told us <u>to do</u> some research in the library.

"Don't hand in your work late," she told the class.

She told the class <u>not to hand</u> in their work late.

D.   Rewrite the following as reported questions or commands.

1.   Jerry asked Shirley, "Who told you that there were ten suns in the past?"

_____

2.   The teacher asked the children, "Do you want to learn more about our country's legends?"

_____

3.   "Where can I find the illustrations of ancient heroes?" Cedric asked.

_____

4.   "Don't write or draw in the books," the librarian reminded us.

_____

5.   Mr. Willis told me, "Create another story about the sun and the moon."

_____

Do Aliens Exist?

Do you think alien beings exist somewhere in the universe? The idea has inspired the whole genre of science fiction – in the forms of film, literature, and even radio drama. Perhaps you have heard of *The War of the Worlds*. Orson Welles directed a radio drama adapted from a classic novel by the same name written by famed writer H. G. Wells and published in 1898. This novel was one of the first examples of science fiction, and was a story about aliens from Mars invading England. When Orson Welles adapted it for radio in 1938, it was said to have caused mass hysteria because some people, who had switched on their radios during the broadcast, actually believed that Earth was being invaded by aliens from Mars! It is believed that some people committed suicide over this.

It seems like Mars, our closest neighbour, has inspired the most science fiction as the place where aliens are most likely to come from. But *The War of the Worlds* is fiction, and recent Mars probes have shown us that there is no life on that planet – at least not now. But that does not mean that life does not exist elsewhere – after all, the universe is really big. A lot of scientific research is going on in the search for "extraterrestrial life" – life originating outside of Earth.

Think about it – why should the six billion people on this little planet be the only sentient beings in the universe? It would, in fact, seem logical that this is not the case. So scientific research in this matter is based around the idea of finding other planets that have environments that can support life – environments similar to Earth. The search is on for the evidence of the existence, or prior existence, of life: from sapient beings (beings with judgment) to simple organisms, such as bacteria.

So far, there have been a number of theories as to which planetary bodies may have an atmosphere that can support such life and therefore warrant closer attention. As for places within our own Milky Way Galaxy, it has been hypothesized over the decades that Mars and Venus, as well as some of the moons of Jupiter and Saturn, may have been hosts for life (or may continue to be!). Now, as technologies have improved and we can obtain measurements of the composition of the atmosphere on extra-solar planets (planets outside of our own Milky Way Galaxy, also called "exoplanets"), the chances of finding "alien" life forms are increasing.

Recently, there has been speculation that some of the planets in the habitable zone of the red dwarf star Gliese 581, the brightest star in the constellation Libra, may be able to support life as we know it to be. In 2007, scientists discovered exoplanet Gliese 581c – and felt that its atmosphere was most amenable to supporting life. But further research revealed that it would not. Now, attention has been turned to Gliese 581d, at the outer edge of the star's habitable zone. The main criteria for deciding whether a planetary body can be life-supporting are atmospheric conditions which allow the existence of water. Gliese 581 is about 20.4 light years away from Earth, so even if life does exist there, the distance would mean that communication would be unlikely.

Having said this – who says alien life forms (if they exist) need water?

A. Check the best answer for each question.

1. *The War of the Worlds* was _____ .

    A. written by Orson Welles

    B. adapted from a radio drama

    C. a novel published in 1898

2. Some people committed suicide because _____ .

    A. they believed that aliens from Mars were invading Earth

    B. they had been tortured by aliens

    C. they were worried that aliens would attack Earth

3. Scientists believe that _____ .

    A. the six billion people on Earth are the only living organisms in the universe

    B. simple organisms can be found on other planets

    C. there may be forms of life on other planets in the universe

4. Which of the following statements is not true?

    A. Gliese 581c was discovered in 2007.

    B. Gliese 581d is far away from Earth.

    C. Libra is the brightest star that is about 20.4 light years away from Earth.

More on Reported Speech

Changing sentences from direct speech to reported speech requires changes in place and time expressions too. Even certain verbs need to be changed.

Examples: "Did you see the DVD of *The War of the Worlds* I left <u>here</u> <u>yesterday</u>?" David asked Sue.

David asked Sue if she had seen the DVD of *The War of the Worlds* he had left <u>there</u> <u>the day before</u>.

Mr. Jamieson told Eric, "<u>Come</u> over <u>here</u> and take a look at <u>this</u> picture of Mars."

Mr. Jamieson told Eric to <u>go</u> over <u>there</u> and take a look at <u>that</u> picture of Mars.

B.   Change the given words or phrases to the reported form.

Direct Speech	Indirect Speech
1. now	_____
2. today	_____
3. tonight	_____
4. tomorrow	_____
5. last year	_____
6. next Monday	_____
7. eight years ago	_____
8. in five days	_____
9. next month	_____
10. three weeks ago	_____
11. last weekend	_____
12. next Christmas	_____
13. this afternoon	_____

C. **Rewrite the following sentences in reported speech.**

1. "I borrowed this book from the library last week," said Jenny.

   _____

2. Sandra asked Dave, "Do you believe there really are aliens now?"

   _____

3. Mr. and Mrs. Hayes said, "We saw a UFO hover over our house six years ago."

   _____

4. "We can go to the Ontario Science Centre next weekend," Anna said.

   _____

5. "A seminar about the existence of life on other planets will be held here next Friday," Emily told Sam.

   _____

D. **Rewrite the following sentences in direct speech.**

1. Nelson asked me if I would watch the program about aliens on the Discovery Channel the following day.

   _____

2. The astronomer explained to us that research into the atmospheric conditions of different planetary bodies had started some years before.

   _____

3. Tammy said her uncle had bought her those cute alien dolls the previous summer when he had gone to visit.

   _____

4. Ricky's sister told him that she had to hand in a book report on a science fiction book two weeks from then.

   _____

Saving Lake Winnipeg

ALGAE BLOOMS! STOP

- Avoid swimming or other contact with the water.
- Prevent pets or livestock from drinking the water.
- Do not eat fish from this lake that appear unhealthy.

If you look at a satellite image of Canada, you will see that the natural physical landscape is quite distinctive; different parts of the country look very different from one another. The Canadian Shield is comprised of millions of waterways and lakes – most are referred to as "finger" lakes, but some are large, such as the Great Lakes of Southern Ontario and the USA, and Lakes Winnipeg and Manitoba in the province of Manitoba.

Lake Winnipeg has often been referred to as one of Canada's "Great Lakes". In fact, it is the 10th largest fresh-water body in the world. Because of this lake and its neighbouring lakes, along with all the rivers that connect them to the sea, Manitoba can lay claim to the highest concentration of cottage owners in the world! Yes, Manitoba, with its lakes and rivers, its boreal forests, its gentle grassy prairie, and vast prairie skies, is a lovely place to live and play.

But Lake Winnipeg is now in deep trouble. Large blue-green algae blooms are occurring in the lake with increasing frequency, covering hundreds of square kilometres with a thick goo. They have occurred in summer almost every year for a decade now. The toxins in them can kill livestock, and they have caused the closures of many beaches in recent years as well. And what is perhaps most disturbing is that most of these algae blooms are happening in Lake Winnipeg's large, north basin, where there is considerably less human activity. This means that the whole body of water is on the verge of becoming a "dead" lake because the algae blooms can deplete the oxygen in the water and kill off plankton – the main food source of lake fish.

These algae blooms form when the water contains much more phosphorous than nitrogen. The phosphorous comes from different sources. Lake Winnipeg is a drainage basin for many of the rivers that cross the prairie. Fertilizers, rich in phosphates, are used by farmers growing crops in the watershed area. The phosphates leach into the soil and eventually into these rivers. Animal and municipal waste (sewage) is another source in the phosphate cycle.

Yet another source of the phosphates that end up in Lake Winnipeg is the wastewater effluent from the Red River. The Red River is an important waterway originating in the United States. It runs through, or alongside, many cities, such as Fargo, Grand Forks, Moorhead, and of course, Winnipeg. Water laden with phosphates, primarily from household detergents, is discharged into the river, exacerbating an already dangerous situation.

In 2003, the Government of Manitoba set up the Lake Winnipeg Stewardship Board to assist the government in formulating an action plan to save Lake Winnipeg. Positive steps are being taken, including campaigns to urge households to use phosphate-free detergents. Let's hope it is not too late!

A.   Check the main idea of each paragraph.

Paragraph 1

A.   Canada is a country with a distinctive natural physical landscape.

B.   The Canadian Shield comprises millions of waterways and lakes.

Paragraph 2

A.   Manitoba is a great place to live and play.

B.   Lake Winnipeg is one of Canada's "Great Lakes" and the 10th largest fresh-water body in the world.

Paragraph 3

A.   There is little human activity in Lake Winnipeg's large, north basin.

B.   Large blue-green algae blooms may cause Lake Winnipeg to become a "dead" lake.

Paragraph 4

A.   Phosphorous is the main cause for the blue-green algae blooms.

B.   Animal and municipal waste is the main source of phosphate.

Paragraph 5

A.   The use of household detergents is a primary cause for the blue-green algae blooms.

B.   Water laden with phosphates from the Red River flows into Lake Winnipeg.

Paragraph 6

A.   The Government of Manitoba has been taking steps to save Lake Winnipeg.

B.   Lake Winnipeg Stewardship Board is responsible for formulating an action plan to save Lake Winnipeg.

Conditional Clauses

Conditional clauses are clauses with "if" that are used to talk about a possible situation and its results. There are three types of conditional clauses.

- For something that may happen in the future, we use the present or present perfect tense in the conditional clause and the simple future tense in the main clause.

  Example: If you <u>look</u> at a satellite image of Canada, you <u>will see</u> that the natural physical landscape is quite distinctive.

- For something that is unlikely to happen, we use the past tense in the conditional clause and "would" in the main clause. Note the use of "were" instead of "was" in the conditional clause.

  Example: If I <u>were</u> a farmer, I <u>would not use</u> fertilizers rich in phosphates.

- For something that could have happened in the past but did not actually happen, we use the past perfect tense in the conditional clause and "would have" with a past participle in the main clause.

  Example: The problem <u>would not have become</u> that serious if farmers <u>had used</u> phosphate-free fertilizers.

B.   Complete the following conditional sentences.

1.   If you ask me why I like Manitoba, _____

_____ .

2.   If George were a government official, _____

_____ .

3.   If the Red River did not run through so many cities, _____

_____ .

4.   Lake Winnipeg will become a "dead" lake if _____

_____ .

5.   Large algae blooms would not have formed if _____

_____ .

C. Check the correct sentences and rewrite the wrong ones.

1. If I owned a cottage in Manitoba, I will spend every summer there. ☐

———————————————————————————

2. You will see the beautiful prairie, lakes, and forests if you go to Manitoba. ☐

———————————————————————————

3. If Macy had been to Winnipeg before, she would know more about the city. ☐

———————————————————————————

4. If the pollution problem of Lake Winnipeg continues, all wildlife would have been adversely affected. ☐

———————————————————————————

5. Lake Winnipeg will recover if everyone started using phosphate-free detergents today. ☐

———————————————————————————

6. If you swallow the lake water accidentally, you will probably suffer from gastrointestinal illnesses. ☐

———————————————————————————

7. I would teach everyone how to make phosphate-free detergent if I have the formula. ☐

———————————————————————————

8. If I was a citizen of Manitoba, I would do everything I could to help save Lake Winnipeg. ☐

———————————————————————————

Depression
in Teenagers: a Very Treatable Condition

Depression is more common than many people think. Each year, about one in ten adults experience a major bout of depression. In the past, not much was said about this common ailment, and sufferers were reluctant to talk about it or even to seek help, and this took a toll on families as well. Thankfully, people, and society in general, are more open about depression and other mental illnesses now. We know more about them and no longer attach a stigma to the conditions. And depression is not just a condition affecting adults. About one out of every 25 teens are affected by depression each year. Studies in other countries, such as Japan, have figures that are higher. In fact, studies there reveal that as many as one in 10 students have experienced a bout of depression within the previous year.

So what exactly is depression? Of course, everyone gets upset and sad and down-in-the-dumps from time to time – life is full of all kinds of problems, some of which we can control and some we can't. But for some people, these sad feelings last longer and affect them in serious ways. Depression can occur for many reasons. It can come about as a reaction to a stressful situation, a big disappointment, or a loss of a loved one. Sometimes it may appear to come about for no particular reason. Depression can also be the result of a chemical imbalance in the brain, and there is a hereditary link in some cases. Depression, if left untreated, can be very disruptive, affecting relationships with family and friends, work and school life, as well as physical well-being. The good news is that a variety of things can be done to treat the condition, ranging from a change in diet and exercise, to counselling, to group therapy, to medication – or a combination of these methods.

The Canadian Mental Health Association has advice for parents who are worried that their children may be experiencing a form of depression. If you think you may be depressed, ask yourself if any of these apply to you:

- *Changes in feelings – showing signs of being unhappy, worried, guilty, angry, fearful, helpless, hopeless, lonely, or rejected*

- *Physical changes – complaining of headaches or general aches and pains; having a lack of energy; sleeping or eating problems; feeling tired all the time*

- *Changes in thinking – saying things that indicate low self-esteem, self-dislike, or self-blame; having difficulty concentrating; frequently experiencing negative thoughts; thinking about suicide*

- *Changes in behaviour – withdrawing from others; crying easily or showing less interest in sports, games, or other fun activities that you normally like; over-reacting and having sudden outbursts of anger or tears over fairly small incidents*

People who are dealing with depression may try to hide it and may not want to talk about it, thinking, perhaps, that no one will understand them. But it is very important to talk about it. If the lines of communication in your family are not open, professional help is available. Your school guidance counsellor can refer you to an appropriate caregiver. You can also visit your family doctor in the first instance. Other community organizations, such as the Canadian Mental Health Association, can also offer assistance. The most important thing to remember is that you are not alone, and that there are people waiting to help you. Depression is a treatable condition.

A. Read the statements below. Check the ones that are true, and rewrite those that are not true.

1. Depression is a common ailment affecting 25% of the teens each year.

   _____

2. People suffering from depression did not want to talk about it or seek help.

   _____

3. Depression can be caused by an imbalance in hormones.

   _____

4. Depression cannot be treated with medication.

   _____

5. If you show changes in thinking, such as disliking yourself and having difficulty concentrating, you may be suffering from depression.

   _____

6. People suffering from depression may be saddened by fairly small incidents.

   _____

Use of Modals in Conditional Clauses

Modals like "can", "may", and "must" can sometimes be used in conditional clauses or main clauses.

Examples: If you <u>can</u> let people help you, depression will not be a problem.

If depression is left untreated, it <u>can</u> be very disruptive.

B.   Complete the following conditional sentences that involve the use of modals.

1.   You may give me a call anytime _____

_____ .

2.   Depression can be easily treated _____

_____ .

3.   We should always think positively _____

_____ .

4.   You must pay attention to mental health _____

_____ .

5.   If Sarah could talk more with her friends, _____

_____ .

6.   If a change in diet can help, _____

_____ .

7.   If you think you may be depressed, _____

_____ .

8.   If you cannot solve the problem on your own, _____

_____ .

212

Omitting "If" in Conditional Clauses

Some other expressions, such as "unless", "only if", and "as long as" can be used to begin conditional clauses to indicate that one event only happens or is true if another event happens or is true.

Example: We can be healthy both physically and mentally <u>as long as</u> we work out regularly.

C.   Make conditional sentences using the following expressions.

1.   unless

_____

_____

2.   only if

_____

_____

3.   even if

_____

_____

4.   provided that

_____

_____

5.   so long as

_____

_____

6.   as long as

_____

_____

Norway is a small country with a small population – and a long history. There are many myths and legends about the people and the place itself, and some of these stories constitute some of the world's oldest written legends – the sagas. The word "saga" originates from the Icelandic language, and is the word from which the English word "say" is derived. Present day Icelandic is actually a version of Old Norse. After all, it was the Vikings, from the region that today we call Norway, who made their way to Iceland and settled it about a thousand years ago. From that time on, the language of the people who lived on that island remained the same, while the language of the people back on the European continent continued to evolve.

Most sagas are long sweeping tales of fantastical adventures and heroic acts, and the litany of characters includes Scandinavian kings, an assortment of gods, strong women (the Valkyries), and mortals with human qualities and frailties. Many of the stories chronicle family feuds, Viking voyages, and even romance, and most were written in long prose, often with poems and stanzas included within the text. Alliterative verse was also a common literary device used in sagas.

One of the greatest writers of these sagas was the Icelandic poet and historian Snorri Sturluson. He wrote some of the best-known sagas, including the Prose Edda (meaning Younger Edda) and the King's Sagas (Heimskringla) about the lives of Norwegian kings of the day. He is also believed to be the author of another most popular work, Egils Saga. The Laxdœla Saga is another of the most popular sagas and is still widely read today; it is believed to have been written by a woman.

The Start of the
Sagas

There are numerous sagas, and the cast of characters is large. They contain a pantheon of gods in much the same manner as the legendary stories from the Greek civilization. The chief god in Norse mythology is Odin – the god of wisdom, war, and death. Loki is another popular god, or giant, and a member of Odin's family. Dagur was the god of the daylight. Delling was the god of dawn. But who begot them all? The progenitor of all gods in Norse Mythology is Búri. He did not have a mother or father but was borne, in effect, from a giant frozen cow. The cow, named Audhumla, licked a salt block in a place called Ginnungagap, between the barren land of snow and ice called Niflheim and a fiery vastness called Múspell. From the salt block Búri emerged. Búri means "the producer". He married an ice giantess and had a son named Borr. Borr started a family with a woman named Bestla and had three sons: Odin, Vili, and Ve. And from them, one could say, the adventures of Norse Mythology begin.

Much of the written record of these sagas originated in Iceland, but the original manuscripts were, over the ages, taken back to Norway and Denmark, which took turns ruling over the island until the mid-20th century. Now, however, the ancient written records of these legends are being returned, placed in special museums under special, sealed display cases.

A. **Read the descriptions and match them with the names of the sagas, characters, or places.**

Laxdœla   Niflheim   Odin   Loki   Dagur   Delling

Búri   Bestla   Heimskringla   Borr   Valkyries   Múspell

Name of saga/character/place	Description
1.	god of the daylight
2.	son of Búri and a giantess
3.	believed to be a saga written by a woman
4.	strong women
5.	about the lives of Norwegian kings
6.	god of wisdom, war, and death
7.	a giant god and a member of Odin's family
8.	a barren land of snow and ice
9.	mother of Odin, Vili, and Ve
10.	borne from a giant frozen cow
11.	god of dawn
12.	a vast land of fire

Paraphrasing

To **paraphrase** is to express someone's ideas in your own words.

Example: The sagas contain a pantheon of gods in much the same manner as the legendary stories from the Greek civilization. (original)

Like the legendary stories from the Greek civilization, the sagas have a pantheon of gods. (paraphrase)

B.   Paraphrase the following statements from the passage.

1.   There are many myths and legends about the people and the place itself, and some of these stories constitute some of the world's oldest written legends – the sagas.

_____

_____

_____

_____

2.   It was the Vikings, from the region that today we call Norway, who made their way to Iceland and settled it about a thousand years ago.

_____

_____

_____

_____

3.   From that time on, the language of the people who lived on that island remained the same, while the language of the people back on the European continent continued to evolve.

_____

_____

_____

_____

Summarizing

To **summarize** is to reduce a text to its bare essentials: the gist, the key ideas, and the main points that are worth noting and remembering.

In summarizing, we:

- read the original and understand the main subject
- pull out the main ideas
- focus on key details
- use key words and phrases
- break down the larger ideas
- leave out examples and illustrations

C. Write a summary of "The Start of the Sagas" in no more than 100 words.

_____

_____

_____

_____

_____

_____

_____

_____

_____

_____

_____

_____

_____

_____

_____

Green Iceland:
a Letter from Uncle Josh

Dear Sammy,

You have probably learned about Vikings in school. These rough and tough men travelled from Norway over 1000 years ago – stopped off in Ireland for some wives – then landed in Iceland. Later they travelled farther. In order to get more people to follow them and settle in these faraway places, they called the iciest places "Greenland" and "Vineland" (which is today's USA northeast seaboard). When I was a kid, my teacher told me to remember the place names by thinking: "Greenland is ice and Iceland is green". After coming here to Iceland this summer, I can tell you it's true: Iceland is green in more ways than one!

The capital city, Reykjavik, is filled with parks and gardens, and the air smells like flowers at the moment – honeysuckles and violets especially! The people of Iceland are very environmentally friendly. They are lucky: the country was founded on land that has a lot of volcanoes. They can trap the heat energy and use it to provide electricity and hot water. We call this energy geothermal energy. Almost 90% of homes in Iceland are heated this way. There are bicycle paths all through the city. You can even ride your bike in winter because some of the paths are geothermally heated. Some city buses and other government vehicles run on hydrogen fuel or biogas, such as methane. Icelanders are proud of their effort to live with a low carbon footprint.

Swimming is the national sport of Iceland, and there are seven geothermally heated outdoor pools in the capital city. The most famous "pool" of all is The Blue Lagoon. It is located in the middle of an old lava field, next to a geothermal power plant, about 50 kilometres from the city. The water is hot and full of minerals that are supposed to be good for the skin. Some people will tell you it smells like egg sandwiches because of the sulfur in it. You can also dig up white silica sand from the bottom of this outdoor pool and put it on your face. It really does make your skin feel smoother.

Tomorrow I plan to go on a special bus ride called "The Golden Circle Tour". It will take us to a great waterfall called Gulfoss, as important to Iceland as Niagara Falls is to Canada. We will also visit a place called Geysir, where there are a lot of colourful bubbling mud pots and steam vents and, of course, a few geysers. Then the bus will pass through Thingvellir National Park, to a place that is the site of the world's oldest parliament. Icelandic people call this the Althing, and it began more than 1000 years ago! We will also stop at the Nesjavellir geothermal plant nearby. I am really looking forward to it!

I am enjoying my visit to Iceland: the land of fire (volcanoes) and ice (glaciers). It's an interesting place for a geologist like me, but I know you would love it, too. You should ask your parents to bring you here someday – then I'll have an excuse to come back!

Take care,

Uncle Josh

A. Complete the chart based on the information from Uncle Josh's letter.

Place	How is it special?
Reykjavik	
The Blue Lagoon	
Gulfoss	
Geysir	
Thingvellir National Park	

B. Answer the following questions.

1. Give an example to illustrate that the people of Iceland are environmentally friendly.

   _____

   _____

2. Explain why Uncle Josh says that "Icelanders are proud of their effort to live with a low carbon footprint."

   _____

   _____

Adding Emphasis

We can **add emphasis** to someone or something in a sentence in a number of ways.

The **passive voice** can be used to draw the reader's attention to the person or thing affected by an action rather than who or what brings about the action.

Example: The minerals in the water are supposed to be good for the skin.

We can also use "**do**", "**does**", or "**did**" in a positive sentence to emphasize something we feel strongly about.

Example: It really <u>does</u> make your skin feel smoother.

C. Rewrite the following sentences in the passive voice to shift the emphasis.

1. The United Nations' Human Development Index ranked Iceland as the most developed country in the world in 2007.

    _____

2. Many restaurants in Iceland serve ocean-fresh seafood.

    _____

3. Icelanders still speak the ancient language of the Vikings.

    _____

D. Add emphasis to the sentences with "do", "does", or "did".

1. Many Icelanders believe in the existence of elves.

    _____

2. The hotel provides free shuttle services to many attractions around the city.

    _____

3. It's not usual to see polar bears in Iceland but I saw one on my trip there.

    _____

More on Adding Emphasis

Inversion is another way to add emphasis to a sentence. We can begin a sentence with expressions like "never", "seldom", "rarely", and "at no time", followed by inverted word order.

Example: <u>Never have I been</u> to a country where all citizens are so conscious about being environmentally friendly.

We can also use a clause introduced by "**what**" as the subject of a sentence to draw the reader's attention to this subject. This clause is followed by the verb "to be".

Example: <u>What Icelanders are proud of</u> is their effort to live with a low carbon footprint.

E. Rewrite the following sentences using inversion.

1. We did not expect to see the Northern Lights in Iceland.

    _____

2. Keith does not know much about Iceland.

    _____

3. Icelanders seldom add salt to their food.

    _____

4. The tourists had hardly arrived at the geyser when it erupted.

    _____

F. Rewrite the following sentences by using "What" to begin them.

1. We all must try the Icelandic skyr.

    _____

2. Some tourists to Iceland want to see the Northern Lights.

    _____

3. Many people do not know that it is not that cold in Iceland.

    _____

Countries that Are Younger than You

How many countries are there in the world? Do you know? You can be forgiven for not knowing this important number since – even in this era of global travel and instantaneous communication, when we have long since found the "final frontier" – it keeps getting bigger! In fact, over 30 new countries have been created since 1990, meaning that you may be older than some of them!

Of the 32 new countries created since 1990, 15 of them were the result of the dissolution of the USSR (Union of Soviet Socialist Republics) in 1991. When the Iron Curtain of Communism began to fall across Eastern Europe in 1989, many of these East European "satellite states" of the USSR broke free from their forced association with the USSR. But these countries (Yugoslavia, Czechoslovakia, Hungary, Poland, etc.) were already considered separate countries. More tightly affiliated with "Mother Russia" were 14 "republics" who were not considered independent states. They would compete in international events under the banner of the USSR. Building on the momentous events in Europe, most of these "Soviet Republics" declared independence from Russia in 1991, precipitating the final breakup of the once mighty Soviet Union. These new countries were: Armenia, Azerbaijan, Belarus, Estonia, Georgia, Kazakhstan, Kyrgyzstan, Latvia, Lithuania, Moldova (previously called Moldavia), Russia, Tajikistan, Turkmenistan, Ukraine, and Uzbekistan.

The European country of Yugoslavia, which had always been a country created by men in a conference room drawing lines on a map with little regard to the various ethnic makeups, began to experience civil unrest soon after. The regions of Slovenia and Croatia both declared independence peacefully on June 25, 1991. Macedonia declared independence in September 1991 although it was not recognized by the United Nations until 1993. The region called Bosnia and Herzegovina became independent in February 1992, and Serbia and Montenegro followed suit in April of that same year, forming the new "rump" state called Yugoslavia. In 2006, Montenegro became independent of Serbia. The region then became known only as Serbia (Yugoslavia ceased to be used) and a small region called Kosovo may someday soon gain its own independence. In 1993, another European country became divided when Czechoslovakia split into the Czech Republic and Slovakia.

Africa also experienced some re-alignment. In 1990, Namibia became independent of South Africa. Before 1990, it was called South West Africa, and was originally a German colony, later taken over by South Africa. Eritrea was seceded from Ethiopia in 1993. The islands of the Pacific had been colonies administered by larger countries for years and were also declaring independence in September 1991. The Marshall Islands, part of the Trust Territory of Pacific Islands, and Micronesia, previously known as the Caroline Islands, both declared independence from the United States. Palau, also part of the Trust Territory of Pacific Islands, declared independence in 1994. And in Asia, East Timor (Timor-Leste), part of an island in the Indonesian archipelago, declared independence from Portugal in 1975, but was then invaded by Indonesian forces. It became independent from Indonesia in 2002.

While most countries or unions were being torn up, a few countries were reuniting. Back in 1990, even before the USSR had fallen, East and West Germany reunited to become Germany once again, and in May 1990, North and South Yemen merged to form Yemen. Maybe someday, North and South Korea will do the same, becoming the newest "baby" of our world family.

A. Complete the chart based on the information from the passage.

Old Country	New Country
USSR	
Yugoslavia	
Czechoslovakia	

B. Choose one of the new countries mentioned in the passage. Find more information about the country and write some interesting facts about it.

_____

_____

_____

_____

Paragraphs

Almost all types of writing are made up of an introductory paragraph, body paragraphs, and a concluding paragraph.

An **introductory paragraph** lets the reader know what the piece is about. It contains a thesis statement that introduces the main idea. A well-written introductory paragraph should capture the reader's attention.

Body paragraphs give supporting details to the main idea. In writing body paragraphs, we should first list the points that develop the main idea, and then expand each point into its own paragraph, each consisting of a topic sentence, supporting facts, details, examples, and a concluding sentence.

A **concluding paragraph** restates or summarizes the main idea. We can also give our personal opinion or call for action.

C. **Search for information about the smallest countries in the world in the library or on the Internet. Compose an essay on this topic.**

Introductory Paragraph (thesis statement)

_____

_____

_____

_____

Body Paragraph 1 (topic sentence, supporting details, concluding sentence)

_____

_____

_____

_____

Body Paragraph 2 (topic sentence, supporting details, concluding sentence)

_____

_____

_____

_____

Body Paragraph 3 (topic sentence, supporting details, concluding sentence)

_____

_____

_____

_____

Body Paragraph 4 (topic sentence, supporting details, concluding sentence)

_____

_____

_____

_____

Concluding Paragraph (restate/summarize main idea, give personal opinion, etc.)

_____

_____

_____

_____

High Flight –
a Poem by
John Gillespie Magee, Jr.

When the American shuttle spacecraft Challenger exploded shortly after takeoff on January 28, 1986, U.S. President Ronald Reagan offered a moving memorial. Of that speech, written by presidential speechwriter Peggy Noonan, it is perhaps the last words which are the most memorable and still remembered and quoted today:

...The crew of the space shuttle Challenger honored us by the manner in which they lived their lives. We will never forget them, nor the last time we saw them, this morning, as they prepared for their journey and waved goodbye and "slipped the surly bonds of Earth" to "touch the face of God".

What is not well known is that President Reagan was, in fact, quoting from a poem written by a pilot-officer of the Royal Canadian Air Force named John Gillespie Magee, Jr. Although born in China to an American missionary father and a British mother, Magee joined the Royal Canadian Air Force at the age of 18, in 1940, before the U.S. entered World War II. He received his flight training and became a fighter pilot in Canada. He died a year later while on a flying exercise in England. The poem entitled "High Flight" is very evocative, clearly displaying Magee's infatuation with flight and his chosen career as a pilot (although not necessarily as a fighter pilot). Here is the poem in its entirety:

High Flight

Oh! I have slipped the surly bonds of Earth
And danced the skies on laughter-silvered wings;
Sunward I've climbed, and joined the tumbling mirth
Of sun-split clouds, – and done a hundred things
You have not dreamed of – wheeled and soared and swung
High in the sunlit silence. Hov'ring there,
I've chased the shouting wind along, and flung
My eager craft through footless halls of air...

Up, up the long, delirious burning blue
I've topped the wind-swept heights with easy grace
Where never lark, or ever eagle flew –
And, while with silent, lifting mind I've trod
The high untrespassed sanctity of space,
Put out my hand, and touched the face of God.

Peggy Noonan was a skilled speechwriter for President Reagan, penning some of his most memorable speeches. But she is actually a best-selling author, newspaper columnist, and essayist, writing mostly about politics, religion, and culture. One of the marks of a skilled writer is the ability to make references to other great works or issues, and to reinterpret them to achieve a desired effect. The reference to "High Flight" in President Reagan's speech is a good example of this. Can you think of others?

A. Answer the following questions.

1. Why do you think the writer has such a high regard for Peggy Noonan apart from Noonan's strong credentials as a writer?

   _____

   _____

2. How would you interpret "...slipped the surly bonds of Earth to touch the face of God"?

   _____

   _____

3. Why does the writer say that "...The poem entitled 'High Flight' is very evocative, clearly displaying Magee's infatuation with flight..."?

   _____

   _____

4. "Sunward I've climbed, and joined the tumbling mirth of sun-split clouds..." Check the best alternative for "tumbling mirth" below.
   A. the thrilling journey
   B. the merry acrobatic fall
   C. the slow movements
   D. the speedy descent

5. Which of the lines in "High Flight" impress you most? Explain why.

   _____

   _____

Words for Paragraphs that Explain

In writing a paragraph to explain a certain issue, words like "since...thus", "due to...hence", "because...therefore", and "as a result" are used to explore the causes and effects of certain events.

B. Compose short paragraphs with the following words and phrases.

1. since...thus

_____

_____

_____

_____

_____

2. due to...hence

_____

_____

_____

_____

_____

3. for this reason

_____

_____

_____

_____

_____

Words for Paragraphs that Compare and Contrast

In writing a paragraph to show the similarities and differences between people, things, places, or ideas, words like "similar to", "differs from", "in contrast", and "on the other hand" are used to compare and contrast.

C. Compose short paragraphs with the following words and phrases.

1. similarly

_____

_____

_____

_____

_____

2. in contrast

_____

_____

_____

_____

_____

3. on the contrary

_____

_____

_____

_____

_____

24

Hannah Taylor
and the Ladybug Foundation

Hannah Taylor is a schoolgirl from Manitoba. She was born in 1997. One day, when she was five years old, she was walking with her mother in downtown Winnipeg. They saw a man eating out of a garbage can. She asked her mother why he had to do that, and her mother said that the man was down on his luck, and was homeless and hungry. Hannah was very upset by this encounter. She couldn't understand why some people had to live their lives without shelter or enough food. Hannah started to think about how she could help, but – of course – there is not a lot one five-year-old can do to solve the large social problem of homelessness.

Later, when Hannah began attending school, she saw another homeless person on her way to school. It was a woman this time, shuffling along, pushing a battered, old shopping trolley. The trolley was piled with bags; it seemed that everything the woman owned was in those bags. This made Hannah very sad, and even more determined to do something. She had been talking to her mother about the lives of homeless people since that first time they saw the man eating out of the garbage can. Her mother told her that if she did something to change the problem that made her sad or worried, she wouldn't feel as bad. And this was the beginning of Hannah's remarkable journey.

Hannah began to speak out about the problem of homelessness in Manitoba and then in other provinces, spreading her message of hope and awareness further afield. She started the Ladybug Foundation, a charity organization dedicated to eradicating homelessness. She began to host "Big Bosses" lunches, where she would try to persuade local business leaders to help contribute to the cause, reminding them that it is certainly in their best interests to make sure that homeless people are not living on the streets. At her very first Big Bosses lunch, she drew pictures to sell at an auction, and two businessmen had a bidding war for a picture of a ladybug, which resulted in a $10 000 donation! She and the volunteers of the Ladybug Foundation also organized a fundraising drive in "Ladybug Jars" – household jars painted red and black to look like ladybugs and dispensed to schools and businesses across Canada to collect everyone's spare change during "Make Change" month. More recently, the foundation began another campaign called National Red Scarf Day – a day when people donate $20 and wear red scarves in support of Canada's hungry and homeless. For the inaugural National Red Scarf Day on January 31, 2008, Hannah went to Ottawa to speak to Members of Parliament and was congratulated in the House of Commons by Ontario MP Ruby Dhalla.

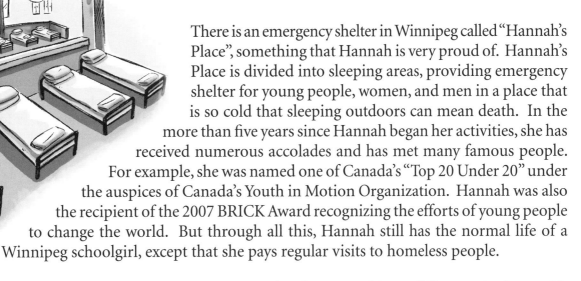

There is an emergency shelter in Winnipeg called "Hannah's Place", something that Hannah is very proud of. Hannah's Place is divided into sleeping areas, providing emergency shelter for young people, women, and men in a place that is so cold that sleeping outdoors can mean death. In the more than five years since Hannah began her activities, she has received numerous accolades and has met many famous people. For example, she was named one of Canada's "Top 20 Under 20" under the auspices of Canada's Youth in Motion Organization. Hannah was also the recipient of the 2007 BRICK Award recognizing the efforts of young people to change the world. But through all this, Hannah still has the normal life of a Winnipeg schoolgirl, except that she pays regular visits to homeless people.

Hannah is one of many examples of young people who are making a difference in the world. You can, too!

A. Answer the following questions.

1. "Hannah was very upset by this encounter." What incident does "this encounter" refer to?

_____

2. "And this was the beginning of Hannah's remarkable journey." What does "Hannah's remarkable journey" refer to?

_____

3. Why do you think Hannah met with Members of Parliament to kick-start National Red Scarf Day?

_____

_____

4. Hannah has been working for the welfare of the homeless. Describe another social problem that you think should be addressed, and how we could help address it.

_____

_____

_____

_____

Transitional Words and Phrases

Transitional words and phrases serve as the glue that holds ideas together in a piece of writing. They help clarify the relationships between ideas and ensure that sentences and paragraphs flow smoothly, making them easy for the reader to follow. Below are examples of some common transitional words and phrases for different relationships between ideas:

- Addition: besides, moreover, in addition
- Similarity: similarly, likewise, in like manner
- Contrast: although, however, on the contrary
- Example: for example, for instance, as an illustration
- Emphasis: in fact, surely, above all
- Sequence: afterwards, meanwhile, eventually
- Generalizing: generally, in general, as a rule
- Cause: since, because of, for this reason
- Consequence: thus, hence, as a result
- Exception: excluding, other than, with the exception of
- Summary: in short, to summarize, in conclusion

B. Think of three more words or phrases for each of the relationships specified below.

1. Addition _____ _____ _____
2. Similarity _____ _____ _____
3. Contrast _____ _____ _____
4. Example _____ _____ _____
5. Emphasis _____ _____ _____
6. Sequence _____ _____ _____
7. Generalizing _____ _____ _____
8. Cause _____ _____ _____
9. Consequence _____ _____ _____
10. Exception _____ _____ _____
11. Summary _____ _____ _____

C. **Improve the coherence of the following paragraph by using transitional words and phrases. Make any necessary changes to the sentences.**

Hannah Taylor was five years old. One day she saw a man eating out of a garbage can. She saw another homeless woman. The woman had everything she owned in a grocery cart. Hannah felt very sad. She thought everyone needed a home. She could not understand why some people were homeless and did not have enough to eat. She talked with her mother many times about homelessness. Her mother told her that if she could do something to change a problem, she would not feel as bad. Hannah founded the Ladybug Foundation in 2004. She wanted to raise the public's awareness of the needs of the homeless. She wanted to raise funds to provide food, shelter, and other necessities for them. Hannah has talked to many people about homelessness. More and more people know about this problem. More and more people want to help. Hannah hopes that everyone can share a little of what he or she has. She hopes that everyone can show his or her care, love, and support for the homeless. She hopes to eradicate homelessness and hunger from Canada.

_____

_____

_____

_____

_____

_____

_____

_____

_____

_____

25

Shania **Twain** –
More than a
"Rags to Riches" Story

S hania Twain is Canada's best-known singer-songwriter and one of the best-selling female music artists of all time. She has won numerous music awards, including five Grammys and 12 Juno Awards, American Music Awards, Academy of Country Music Awards, Billboard Awards, People's Choice Awards, and over 20 Broadcast Music Industry songwriter awards. Three of her albums have been certified as Diamond – meaning they have each sold over ten million units, and have sold more than 40 million records together. She is admired by fans of country music, but legions of pop and rock-and-roll devotees also love her music. On top of all this, she has been awarded Canada's top civilian honour, the Order of Canada, by the Governor-General.

This seems hard to believe for a girl from the small northern Ontario town of Timmins. But even more remarkable than the remote location of her upbringing is the reality of her family life. Shania was born Eilleen Regina Edwards in Windsor, Ontario, in 1965. Her parents divorced when Eilleen was young, and her mother moved back to her hometown of Timmins with her three young daughters. When Eilleen's mother remarried, the three girls were adopted by their stepfather, Jerry Twain, and two brothers soon followed. There was not a lot of money in the Twain household, and Shania began contributing to the family income at the age of eight by singing in bars around town. She had a passion for music, so much so that she skipped classes at the age of ten to find time to write her own songs!

As a teenager, Eilleen moved to Toronto, where she worked at a day job to make money for her family and sang in the evenings. Then one day, tragedy struck. Eilleen's parents were killed in a car accident. Eilleen moved back to Timmins to look after her four siblings. Those were lean times: there was so little money that Eillen could not afford real milk for her growing younger siblings, having instead to buy less expensive powdered milk. But things began to change when Eilleen moved the family to Huntsville, Ontario, and began a job as a singer at Deerhurst Resort. She changed her name to Shania in honour of her stepfather's Ojibway heritage, a word meaning "on my way". One day in 1991, Dick Frank, a music executive from Nashville, saw her at the resort and offered to produce a demo. Her first album was released in 1993. Shania was indeed on her way.

Legendary music producer Robert "Mutt" Lange saw her perform on television and wanted to work with her. They worked together on Shania's second album and fell in love along the way. They married in 1993, becoming one of the most successful artistic husband-and-wife teams in history. Her third album became the number one best-selling country album of all time and is tied for fifth best-selling record of all time. The Shania Twain Centre, a museum full of memorabilia, awards, and many personal items from the singer, was opened in 2001 in Timmins, Ontario. These days, Shania spends her time in Switzerland and on a New Zealand horse farm. She is busy focusing on her music and her perfume lines, eschewing the trappings of global celebrity. And she still makes sure her siblings are okay, like any good big sister.

Shania Twain's life is not so much marked by sadness and tragedy, but by resilience and creativity, by determination and generosity of spirit.

A. Answer the following questions.

1. Which sentence in Paragraph 1 shows that Shania has broad appeal?

    _____

    _____

2. Why does the writer think that "even more remarkable than the remote location of her upbringing is the reality of her family life"?

    _____

    _____

3. How does Shania honour her stepfather, Jerry Twain?

    _____

    _____

4. Why does the writer say that "Shania was indeed on her way"?

    _____

    _____

5. What does "eschewing the trappings of global celebrity" mean?

    _____

    _____

Chronological Order

Good and effective writing involves clear and logical organization. One way to achieve this is to arrange events in **chronological order**, that is, in the order in which they occur. Very often, the dates of the events are provided, and transitional words and phrases like "then", "after that", and "three years later" are used.

B. **Look at some facts about another Canadian celebrity, Avril Lavigne. Put them in chronological order and compose an article about her.**

Facts about Avril Lavigne

- moved to Manhattan and began work on her debut album at 16

- won 2005 Juno Award for "Artist of the Year"

- debut album, *Let Go*, released in 2002

- born in Belleville, Ontario

- won 2003 Juno Award for "New Artist of the Year"

- family moved to Napanee, Ontario when she was five

- discovered by Cliff Fabri when she was singing at a bookstore in Kingston in 1998

- born in 1984

- married to Deryck Whibley in 2006

- Cliff Fabri became her first manager

- *Let Go* certified six times platinum in the US

- the song "I'm With You" won the ASCAP Film and Television Music Award for the Most Performed Song from a Motion Picture (*Bruce Almighty*) in 2004

- won a contest to sing a duet with Shania Twain in 1998

- signed by Arista Records at the age of 16

- *Let Go* won 2003 Juno Awards for "Album of the Year" and "Pop Album of the Year"

Avril Lavigne

Yoga:
a Most Healthful Form of Exercise

Sports have always been a popular way to stay in shape. In more recent decades, the increased popularity of aerobic exercise routines has resulted in millions of gyms – equipped with devices such as rowing machines, elliptical trainers, stationary bicycles, treadmills, and "StairMasters" – being built all over the world, and even more millions of aerobic workout DVDs being sold to people who believe that, in order to be healthy, they need to move around a lot. This is not an incorrect assumption; physical movement gets the heart pumping, increasing the amount of oxygen in the blood and turning fat into needed energy. But now some people are turning to another form of exercise that seems quite the opposite of the frantic aerobic workout – but which provides just as many, if not more, health benefits: yoga.

Yoga originated in India centuries ago as a spiritual practice, a type of meditation that was meant to provide the practitioner with a deeper understanding or insight into the nature of our existence. The word "yoga" comes from the Sanskrit (a classical language of India) word yuj, meaning "yoke" – and we take this to mean the coming together of the mind, body, and spirit. To be able to achieve this, inner peace must first be realized, which means that the physical body and the spiritual and mental mind must be trained and disciplined. This used to be done through the practice of "asanas" or postures. These days, these postures form the basis of the exercise we know as yoga.

There are actually many different kinds of yoga. Hatha yoga is perhaps the most well-known and widely practised, with postures that cater to all levels of practitioners. Other yoga styles have developed from this one. Ashtanga yoga involves performing postures in a faster-paced, flowing sequence. Viniyoga involves gentler, synchronizing breathing techniques with the postures. The postures of Kundalini yoga are meant to unlock a powerful energy that is supposed to exist at the base of the spine. Ananda yoga involves hatha yoga poses and meditation, and is meant to promote self-awareness. Jivamukti yoga combines intensely physical postures with chanting and meditation. There are many other forms.

Some of these ancient forms have been adapted and marketed in yoga schools and studios, which are becoming as popular as all the fitness centres we now see, or have even become an integral part of them. For example, Bikram yoga, which is an ancient yoga practice in a heated room, has now been adapted for modern fitness buffs as "hot yoga". "Power yoga" is a step up from the rigorous Ashtanga postures, making sure you build up a sweat. "Forrest yoga" involves yoga sequences along with other core strengtheners based on a different type of workout called "Pilates".

Recently, people in the United States have started signing up for a new kind of yoga class: Happy Face Yoga. This yoga program consists of a series of 30 facial exercises such as sticking out your tongue, raising your eyebrows, pushing your nose up, and pressing your cheeks in, along with the usual deep breaths and relaxing moments in between. Of course, some people think Happy Face Yoga is just as silly as the faces of the people who are doing it, but let's not forget that just as our bodies have muscles, so do our faces – up to one hundred individual muscles in ten muscle groups.

Whether or not you believe in "facial yoga", the benefits of yoga cannot be disputed: it firms and tones muscles, builds self-esteem, and provides an understanding of anatomy as well as an avenue to personal spirituality, self-reflection, creativity, and imagination. Why not give it a try?

A. Complete the following charts on the different types of yoga.

Ancient Forms	
Type	**Feature**
Viniyoga	
Ashtanga yoga	
Kundalini yoga	
Jivamukti yoga	
Modern Forms	
Type	**Feature**
Power yoga	
Forrest yoga	
Happy Face yoga	

Argumentative Writing

In **argumentative writing**, we try to convince others to agree with us and adopt our way of thinking. We start by stating an argumentative proposition, which sets the tone of the argument and enables the reader to know our stand. In addition to explaining and supporting our proposition with details, evidence, and examples, we should also anticipate and overcome objections that the opposition might raise. Drawing up a chart to compare the two sides of the argument helps us consider how to refute the opposition's arguments.

B. **Below are some points about the harmful effects of yoga. Decide on an argumentative proposition related to yoga. Then draw up a chart to compare the two sides of the argument with the information from the passage and the points below. Add some points of your own.**

Harmful effects of yoga:

- common side effects include knee pains and backaches
- can harm muscles if body is not flexible
- may cause bone fractures or ruptures
- some experience adverse gastric or sleep problems after practising yoga
- may cause frustration for those who fail to do some poses
- has been reported that one may become more irritable and agitated
- Kundalini yoga poses done incorrectly can have adverse mental effects
- instructors might not be fully aware of the techniques

Proposition: _____

For   **Against**

C. **Based on the chart you developed in (B), write your argumentation.**

_____

_____

_____

_____

_____

_____

_____

_____

_____

_____

_____

_____

_____

_____

_____

_____

_____

_____

_____

_____

_____

Tips for **Effective** Public Speaking

It has been said that most people fear speaking in front of a large audience even more than death! Whether or not this is really the case, there are many things we can do to help make public speaking a less frightening ordeal for ourselves. Of course, not everyone will have a job or career that requires them to speak to large groups of people, but we can all benefit from feeling comfortable and confident when we speak in groups of any size. Let's not forget that students are required to give presentations in class from time to time, and being mindful of just a few tips for effective public speaking will mean that you can focus your attention on the research, without getting overly anxious about the speaking part to follow.

1. Do your research. (   ) Knowing that you have done your best to know your subject matter will give you the confidence that you know what you are talking about and can answer any questions. This confidence will be evident in the way you act.

2. Know how to organize your thoughts. Every good presentation or speech follows a logical sequence. Your presentation will need an introduction, in which you tell your audience your "thesis statement", possibly with an anecdote the audience can relate to. Next, the body of the speech will contain all the information (with each piece of information stated one at a time, without going back-and-forth) that supports your thesis statement. Last is the conclusion, explaining everything you have just said "in a nutshell". (   )

3. Know your audience. The type of audience you speak to will have an impact on what you say and how you say it. For example, you wouldn't want to give a speech about how you hated school to a group of students! (   ) Use humour when you can, but be careful that any jokes you tell are not rude in any way and are appropriate for your audience.

4. Use visual aids. Make use of visual aids such as PowerPoint to highlight crucial ideas or information. You should arrive early at your venue and, if possible, even run through the use of the equipment with the IT (Information Technology) person on hand – if you are lucky enough to have one. (   )

5. Throw in an element of drama. Understand that, as a public speaker, presenter, or debater, you are also an actor. You are not having an ordinary conversation. So, speak with conviction, and with a greater sense of yourself – and perhaps even a bit of drama. People want to hear someone who believes in what they are saying. You should speak clearly, with your chin held high, in order to project your voice out into the room. Understand the importance of pausing for effect. Sometimes a long silence gives people a chance to consider what you have just said. You must be mindful of body language. Make eye contact with your audience, all over the room, and maintain it. Learn how to move about, to walk and hold your arms and hands, and to gesticulate to emphasize a point. (   )

6. Know how to avoid "the jitters". Have you ever started speaking to an audience and then, after about a minute or so, your hands started to shake? This is a common reaction to nervousness, caused by adrenaline coursing through your body. That chemical is really a bodily reaction to stress, stemming from our days as cavemen – the "fight or flight" mechanism in action. Of course, you don't want to do either of these things at the lectern, so here is a tip to help reduce that flow of adrenaline: just before you go on stage, jump up and down very quickly, and open and close your hands very quickly many times, for about 30 seconds to a minute, until the muscles start to feel fatigued. (   )

A. Each of the following statements goes with a tip mentioned in the preceding passage. Decide on the matching statements and tips. Write the letters in the parentheses where the statements should go.

a. This will help to avoid any buildup of adrenaline as you start to get into your presentation.

b. And if the education levels of your audience vary, you may want to choose simpler, less nuanced ways of expressing yourself, and avoid idiomatic expressions.

c. As the old saying goes: "Say what you are going to say, say it in full, and then say it again."

d. When it comes to using machinery of any kind in your presentation – Be prepared!

e. There is no substitute for knowing your topic.

f. To do this well, you must practise in front of a mirror, or ask people to listen and give you some feedback.

27

Speech Writing

Before you start writing a speech, you have to determine the theme or message that you want to convey, and identify the occasion and audience. Stick to that theme throughout the speech and use the language appropriate for the occasion and audience.

A good speech follows a formal structure:

- Introduction - Explain clearly what the theme of your speech is. To get the audience's attention, you can raise a thought-provoking question or recite a relevant quotation.

- Body - Come up with a list of points that explain and support your theme. Group the points according to common topics, and organize them so that each point builds upon the previous one. Illustrate your points with relevant examples and personal stories.

- Closing - Reinforce the theme by summarizing the main points, and make a conclusion to your speech. You can also end it with another thought-provoking question or get your audience to act on your message.

B.   You are asked to deliver a speech at the opening ceremony of your school's "Share with Others Day". Complete the writing plan below in point form.

Theme: _____

Occasion: _____

Audience: _____

Introduction: _____

_____

Body: _____

_____

_____

_____

Closing: _____

_____

C. **Write a speech based on your writing plan in (B).**

A **Volunteer** and a **Tourist**?

What do a volunteer and a tourist have in common? Nothing. But can you be a volunteer and a tourist at the same time? Absolutely.

Voluntourism – a new trend combining volunteering and tourism – is catching on fast, with more and more people looking for opportunities to help others while visiting interesting places. Louis Palmer, a freshman from the University of Toronto, recently returned from a trip to Guizhou, China. It was not the usual sightseeing trip. Rather, Louis went on a one-week cycling trip through Guizhou organized by Protect the Earth, Protect Yourself (PEPY), a volunteer agency there to help improve the lives of rural children. Louis enjoyed the bike tour, but what was more, he had the chance to pitch in by teaching children at a rural elementary school. Louis's family and friends chipped in to sponsor his bike ride, and the funds collected were also used for building schools in rural areas in Guizhou and buying stationery for children.

Like PEPY, many organizations provide voluntouring projects. Earthwatch, for example, is a non-profit organization focusing on bringing science to life for those concerned about the Earth's future. It offers opportunities for people to join their teams of scientists on a diverse range of projects all over the world. It has also set up "teen teams" whereby young people aged 16 to 17 can work with, and learn from, leading scientists.

On the other hand, Habitat for Humanity, a voluntary agency well known for building houses for the poor and homeless, has developed a voluntouring package for participants to help out in their building projects across the world, mainly in developing countries. They provide affordable housing for the deprived. Jimmy Carter, the former president of the U.S.A., is a regular participant in Habitat for Humanity projects. You don't have to possess building skills to be part of its volunteering team; you can pitch in as long as you know how to hold a paintbrush or a hammer.

But just like in any other field, there are always black sheep that exploit the goodwill of voluntourists. They may come up with phoney schemes, like charging a voluntourist a premium just for a chance to hand out school supplies to children at a remote school. Would-be voluntourists should therefore be scrupulous and check out the organizations before taking part in their programs. Daniela Papi, founder of PEPY, advises anyone interested in voluntourism to do their homework beforehand. "Ask for a list of past participants and their contacts. Any reputable operator should be able to provide you with such a list."

It is not difficult, though, to figure out which organizations are genuine and which are phoney. Genuine voluntourism operators have long-term goals and they regularly assess the success of their projects. These are the ones that you can count on if you are thinking of a voluntour for your next vacation.

A. Check the main idea of each paragraph.

Paragraph 2

A. The definition of voluntourism

B. How Louis Palmer experienced voluntourism in Guizhou, China

Paragraph 3

A. The variety of voluntouring projects organized by Earthwatch

B. The mission of Earthwatch, another organization providing voluntouring projects

Paragraph 4

A. The projects developed by Habitat for Humanity for those interested in voluntouring

B. The projects offered by Habitat for Humanity to those who do not have building skills

Paragraph 5

A. Daniela Papi's advice to would-be voluntourists

B. Beware of phoney voluntouring schemes

B. If you had the chance to go voluntouring, which one of the three volunteer organizations – PEPY, Earthwatch, or Habitat for Humanity – would you join? Explain your choice.

_____

_____

_____

Editing

Editing is a very important process to ensure that our writing is the best that we can make it. In editing, we focus on the language (spelling, punctuation, subject-verb agreement, tenses, sentence structures, etc.) and organization of writing.

C.   Edit the following sentences for any language problems.

1.   Even breif periods of voluntouring gives everyone involved insight into the lifes of people in others countries.

2.   According to the travel industry association of America over 55 million American has participate in a voluntouring project.

3.   One-quarter of people planing for a vacation is considering a service-orient one.

4.   Some of the work voluntourists do on their trips include; teaching English, planting trees, build bridges, repairing trail.

5.   Jamie found two organizations who provide voluntouring projects on the internet but neither of them was non-profit organization.

D. Edit the following paragraph focusing on its organization.

> Make sure you have a topic sentence, supporting details, and a concluding sentence. Check if there are good transitions between sentences, and cut out redundancy.

PEPY organizes different programs in Cambodia to help foster and improve education of children in the country, especially those living in the rural areas. The average rural Cambodian is estimated to have 2.94 years of education. The Road-to-Literacy program (RTL) is one of the programs organized by PEPY. This program aims to increase literacy for children in rural Chanleas Dai, Siem Reap Province. As Kofi Annan said, "Literacy is, finally, the road to human progress and the means through which every man, woman, and child can realize his or her full potential." Kofi Annan was the seventh Secretary-General of the United Nations. RTL decided to create a school-based library for students of the Poverty Reduction Strategy (PRS) of Cambodia. A group of volunteers cleaned up and renovated a room with books originally donated by Room to Read, a non-governmental organization. This room was previously locked most of the time in fear that the books might get ruined or stolen. The library is now brightened and more donated books have been added. It opens during school hours. Teachers can arrange library classes to incorporate more books into their curriculum. Students are encouraged to read more. Library use has largely increased since the renovation.

_____

_____

_____

_____

_____

_____

_____

A. Underline the dependent clauses in the following sentences. Then write "N" for noun clauses, "ADJ" for adjective clauses, and "ADV" for adverb clauses.

1. How the plane went missing in such good weather conditions is still a mystery. _____

2. This software won't work unless you follow all the steps of installation. _____

3. The consultant whom Mrs. Mitchell requested to see was out for lunch. _____

4. Is there anyone here who can tell me why the meeting has been cancelled? _____

5. Although there have not been many reported sightings of the Ogopogo, this lake monster attracts many visitors to Lake Okanagan in British Columbia. _____

6. The cottage where we used to stay every summer was seriously damaged in the storm. _____

7. Not many people know that Olivia was the actual writer of the book. _____

8. Whoever comes onto the political scene will bring changes to the country. _____

9. Don't forget to ask your parents' permission before you sign up for the outing. _____

10. Lunenburg in Nova Scotia has been inscribed on the World Heritage List because it is the best surviving example of a planned British colonial settlement in North America. _____

B. Rewrite the following in reported speech.

1. "Meet me here at noon tomorrow," Jane told her friend.

   _____

2. "Do you think you can draw up a new plan in a week?" Mr. Ward asked Heather.

   _____

3. Mom says, "I have always had a great liking for country music."

   _____

4. "We will probably stay in Old Quebec City for two days," Mrs. Cooper told her daughter.

   _____

5. "Paris is the capital city of France," the teacher told her students.

   _____

C. Rewrite the following in direct speech.

1. Mark said he had seen that stranger outside his house a number of times that week.

   _____

2. Kelly asked her mother why she could not get a video game for her birthday.

   _____

3. Ned told Raymond that he did walk his dog after school every day.

   _____

4. The twin sisters said that they had taken a course in interior design together the previous year.

   _____

Review 2

D. Check the correct conditional sentences and rewrite the wrong ones.

1. If I were a government leader, I will try every way to help children in poor countries.

   _____

2. Ryan would not make this kind of mistake if he had had enough sleep the night before.

   _____

3. You will be notified within next week if you are selected for the role.

   _____

4. If Jimmy had not put on his seat belt, he could be more seriously injured.

   _____

5. You must answer at least three questions correctly if you wanted to join the club.

   _____

6. If I had a brother or sister, I would surely share my toys with him or her.

   _____

7. If Helen was Leona, she would not have agreed to wear that weird costume.

   _____

8. Mom will let me sleep over at your place if I could get all my work done this afternoon.

   _____

E.   Paraphrase the following statements.

1.   Figure skating is a sport in which skaters perform graceful but challenging moves on ice, and it requires years of hard training and practice to become a professional figure skater.

   _____

   _____

   _____

2.   The Parthenon is a temple in Athens, Greece, built more than 2400 years ago to worship Athena, the Greek goddess of wisdom.

   _____

   _____

   _____

F.   Rewrite the following sentences in the passive voice to shift the emphasis.

1.   The Montgolfier brothers built the first hot air balloon capable of carrying passengers.

   _____

2.   People in many Asian countries have used the soybean as food for thousands of years.

   _____

3.   Someone has donated a large sum of money to World Wildlife Fund Canada.

   _____

4.   Robert Lewis May wrote the famous Christmas song "Rudolph the Red-Nosed Reindeer".

   _____

G. Add emphasis to the following sentences by using inversion, adding "do", "does", or "did", or beginning them with "What".

1. There is not much we can do to solve the problem at this stage.

   _____

2. We have never seen anything as strange and unimaginable as this.

   _____

3. I met the famous author J.K. Rowling on my trip to England.

   _____

4. We have a member to take care of the registration of new members.

   _____

5. Rita bought a beautiful crystal brooch for her grandmother.

   _____

H. Underline the transitional words and phrases in the following sentences. Write what relationship between ideas they show on the lines.

1. My sister devoted her whole summer vacation last year to volunteer work. I have decided to do likewise this summer. _____

2. There are many Canadian Olympic gold medalists. Adam van Koeverden, for instance, won the gold medal in Men's K-1 500 m canoeing race in the 2004 Athens Olympics. _____

3. Derek got caught in the traffic congestion on his way home. As a result, he missed his favourite TV show. _____

4. Jeremy is a very generous person. In fact, he is the most generous person I've ever met. _____

I. **Choose one of the following argumentative propositions and write your argumentation.**

Don't forget to draw up a chart to compare the two sides of the argument.

- Fruit is the most healthful food.

- All dogs should be on a leash in public areas.

- Following fashion trends kills individuality.

- Animals should not be used in scientific research.

- Children learn best by observing the behaviour of adults.

_____

_____

_____

_____

_____

_____

_____

_____

_____

_____

_____

_____

_____

_____

_____

British North America: Before Confederation

By the mid-1800s, British North America was a land of colonies that spanned the width of the continent. Toward Confederation, there were still vast differences between them that could have divided rather than united them.

A. The shaded sections of the map are the colonies of British North America circa 1850. Colour and label them.

Colonies to Label:

- Vancouver Island
- British Columbia
- Canada West
- Newfoundland
- New Brunswick
- Nova Scotia
- Prince Edward Island
- Canada East

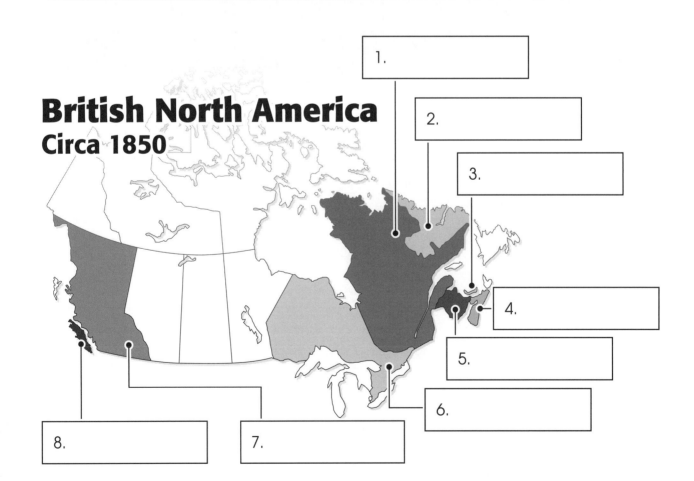

British North America
Circa 1850

1.

2.

3.

4.

5.

6.

7.

8.

B. Read the passages. Answer the questions.

British North America once traded exclusively with Great Britain. When trade with Britain began to decline, it flourished with the United States. The Reciprocity Treaty, signed in 1854, benefited both the United States and its northern neighbours.

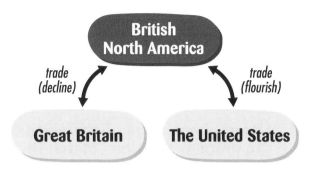

1. How did the economy of British North America in the 1850s differ from its earlier years?

_____

_____

_____

After the expense of previous wars and rebellions, Great Britain was reluctant to spend any more money defending its distant colonies. British North America would be more capable of defending itself if it was united, but some colonists were reluctant to unite.

2. In what ways did social differences make some colonists reluctant to unite?
    (Hint: What if your culture was in the minority?)

_____

_____

_____

2 Confederation

Early in the 1860s, some of the colonies in British North America had compelling reasons to unite. It took three conferences and three years to make the decision and work out the details of confederation.

A. **Read about some of the events that contributed to the colonies' decision to unite as a nation. Match the events with the descriptions and circle the correct words.**

Manifest Destiny	Reciprocity Treaty	Fenian Raids

1.

- a doctrine that promoted the expansion of the United States throughout the continent

- caused many British North American / Irish American colonists to feel unsafe

2.

- signed in 1854

- a free trade agreement between the United States and the colonies of British North America

- terminated in 1766 / 1866 by the United States

3.

- small attacks on British North American colonies by Irish Americans seeking to retaliate against Britain

Fenians
an Irish nationalist organization founded in the U.S.

- the colonists knew they would be safer from invasion if they were free / united

B.   Fill in the blanks with the given words.

Canada	Quebec	Nova Scotia	July
resolutions	Ontario	union	Dominion
September	1866	confederation	1864

> *These three formal meetings led to the formation of Canada the nation.*

Charlottetown Conference – 1._____ 1864

2._____ , New Brunswick, and Prince Edward Island planned the Charlottetown Conference to talk about the possibility of a Maritime union. Ontario and Quebec, known as the province of 3._____ at that time, had been considering a 4._____ of all the colonies, and asked to bring their proposal to the conference. The idea was enthusiastically received.

Quebec Conference – October 5._____

At this conference, attended by representatives of all concerned parties, 72 6._____ were drawn up in preparation for the London Conference. The 7._____ Resolutions were an important step to the final constitution of the new federation.

London Conference – December 8._____

Only Nova Scotia, New Brunswick, Canada East, and Canada West attended the London Conference, which resulted in the Royal Assent of the British North America Act. The new country was named the 9._____ of Canada, and it was made up of the provinces of 10._____ , Quebec, Nova Scotia, and New Brunswick. The conference attendees hurried home to prepare for 11._____ 1, 1867, the official date of 12._____ .

Growth of Canada

At the time of confederation, Canada was already a large country. It continued to grow to become what it is today: a diverse country of ten provinces and three territories.

A. Fill in the blanks to show the growth of Canada. Use the abbreviations to help with the provinces and territories.

| Dominion | gold rush | Britain | growth | referendum |
| Northwest Territories | | American | Ontario | province |

1867: Ontario, 1._____ (QC), 2._____ (NS), and New Brunswick

- four provinces join the confederation

1870: 3._____ (NT), Manitoba

- Canada buys land between 4._____ and British Columbia from the Hudson's Bay Company
- the Métis in the Red River area join Canada on their own terms, and a portion of the bought land is given to them with the status of a 5._____

1871: 6._____ (BC)

- many Americans settle there after the 7._____
- Canada promises a rail link to the rest of the 8._____ , and the people choose to become a part of Canada

1873: 9._____ (PEI)

- as part of the deal that brought PEI into the union, Canada buys the land back from landowners in 10._____ so Island residents can now own their land

1898: 11. _____ (YT)

  • 12. _____ prospectors come with the gold rush

  • fear of American take-over motivates Canada to give this part of the Northwest Territories its own name

1905: Alberta, 13. _____ (SK)

  • both provinces join confederation on the same date after breaking off from the Northwest Territories

  • both provinces need provincial status for further population and economic 14. _____

1949: 15. _____ (NL)

  • it is the last British colony to join Canada

  • people vote in a 16. _____ to join the Confederation, and it won by a very narrow margin

1999: 17. _____ (NU)

  • this section of the 18. _____ becomes a territory as a result of polls taken in the Northwest Territories, showing that the majority of residents were in favour of separation

B. Write the year that each map represents.

1.

Canada in _____

2.

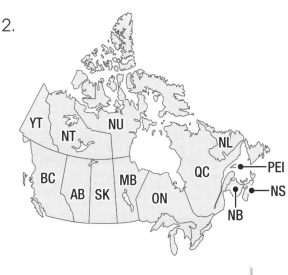

Canada in _____

People to Know

Besides the British monarch, the majority of personalities associated with the Canadian Confederation were wealthy men with British or French backgrounds. In spite of this, those without a voice or vote also helped make Canada what it is today.

A. Fill in the blanks to complete the descriptions of influential people who played a role in Canada's confederation.

prime minister   Sir John Alexander Macdonald   Fathers of Confederation
conferences   responsible government   George-Etienne Cartier
Canadiens   confederation   Royal Proclamation

1. A politician for Canada West (now Ontario), _____ argued for the unification of the colonies for many years. At the time of Confederation, he was named Canada's first _____ .

2. Joseph Howe, leader of Nova Scotia, brought _____ to that colony. He was such a persistent opponent of Confederation that the _____ appointed an individual to counter his published arguments.

3. _____ formed a strong alliance with John A. Macdonald in the promotion of _____ . As leader of Canada East (now Quebec), he made sure _____ kept their language, culture, and system of civil law.

4. The details of confederation were worked out at the three _____ . However, Canada could not become a union until Queen Victoria signed the _____ .

B. **Indicate which conditions belong to which group. Then unscramble the letters to fill in the blanks.**

> Read about the conditions of some groups who did not have input in the decisions that led to confederation.

| women | First Nations | Chinese |
| children | Black community | |

1. _____

   • often forced to work long hours for much less pay than their adult counterparts

   • were not given any special rights for their age; were denied many adult rights such as the _____ (tove) and property ownership

2. _____

   • represented about 50% of the population

   • were expected by society to attend to the care of their husbands and children rather than take _____ (elardehsip) roles in society

3. _____

   • many secretly made their way to Canada from the United States through the network known as the "Underground Railroad"

   • often living in separate communities, they faced a level of _____ (misidcirnaiotn) and persecution like no other groups of newcomers did

4. _____

   • forced off of their lands and onto reserves

   • were considered outsiders in the land they inhabited for thousands of years before the British and _____ (snrEueoap)

5. _____

   • brought over to Canada to finish building the Canadian Pacific Railway

   • faced discrimination by their employers and were paid _____ (sles) than their white counterparts

Into the West

Canada grew very quickly after confederation. All the land west of Ontario was gradually settled by people from places as close as eastern Canada and as far away as China and Europe.

A. **The map shows the different ways settlement in the West occurred. Fill in the shaded areas with the words on the map and the blanks with the given words to complete the sentences.**

CPR	rebellion	prairie
factories	smallpox	North
coal mining	buffalo

Map labels: Prairies, Dawson City, Alberta, Calgary, Winnipeg, Vancouver Island, Vancouver, Red River

1. _____ : Logging and _____ were very profitable for owners and provided plenty of jobs for people.

2. _____ : The Métis settled on the Hudson's Bay Company's land, and it was later sold to the Canadian government, triggering a _____ .

3. _____ : Industrialized Brits and Europeans did not fare as well as the old world farmers in the harsh climate and lonely expanse of the _____ .

4. _____ : These cities were home to much of the old world wealth, as well as the _____ that employed the less wealthy.

5. _____ : Located in the sparsely populated _____ , this was a lively city in the west during the Klondike gold rush.

6. ████████████ : Thousands of Chinese came to Canada to help
build the _____ or work in the mines.

7. ████████████ :

The disappearing _____ and being forced to move onto
reserves drastically changed the lives of Aboriginals. Numbers of First
Nations peoples dropped sharply, due mostly to _____ .

B. **Read the paragraph. Then create your own poster convincing people to move to "the last best west". Use the list of characteristics describing life in the west. Decide what to emphasize, or leave out, in your poster at your discretion.**

Canada offered 160 acres of free land per family to encourage Europeans and Americans to immigrate. The government advertised with posters. They promoted western Canada's good points and purposely left out the difficulties settlers might encounter.

Characteristics of Life in the West

- **productive farmland**
- **railway for travel**
- **protests**
- **loneliness**
- **clean air**
- **land ownership**
- **hard work**

Canadian Pacific Railway

There were many difficulties with building the Canadian Pacific Railway. In the end, however, the CPR was instrumental in building and uniting Canada.

A. **Identify the people by what they say. Write the names of the people on the lines. Write the letters associated with the functions of the CPR described below in the circles.**

Immigrants

Farmers

Chinese workers

Tourists

A enabled tourism industry to develop

B inadvertently increased immigration numbers as workers remained after completing the CPR

C carried immigrants past the difficult terrain of Lake Superior and across the vast prairies

D moved freight from the middle of the continent to world transportation routes

1. *How will we get from the ships we travelled on to our homesteads?*

_____ ; ◯

2. *We finished building the CPR, but we weren't paid enough to return to China.*

_____ ; ◯

3. *The prairies are far from the harbours and ships that can export wheat around the world.*

_____ ; ◯

4. *The Rocky Mountains are spectacular; I even saw workers building a hotel.*

_____ ; ◯

B. **Complete the sentences that describe the events that occurred during the building of the CPR.**

> Though there were many obstacles to overcome, the Canadian Pacific Railway was eventually completed.

workers   connect   **Rebellion**   immigrants
British   spike   leadership   **Shield**

Events during the Building of the CPR

1. British Columbia threatened to secede (leave Confederation) when the new government slowed the progress of building the railway that would _____ it to the rest of Canada.

2. The Canadian _____ proved to be some of the most difficult terrain to lay track across.

3. Despite heavy advertising, _____ were not arriving in the numbers expected.

4. When sufficient local _____ could not be found, Chinese workers were brought to work on the most dangerous section of the track: the Rocky and Selkirk Mountains.

5. There was little enthusiasm or financial support from the _____ government, who had its own financial concerns to worry about.

6. William Van Horne, the manager, provided the _____ needed to complete the transcontinental railway.

7. During the Riel _____ of 1885, the railway transported soldiers to quell the protest in a fraction of the time it would have taken without the railway.

8. Donald Smith, a major financial backer of the Canadian Pacific Railway, hammered the railway's last _____ at Craigellachie, BC in 1885.

7

The Riel and Northwest Rebellions

The Métis (descendants of First Nations and French Canadian people) settled in the west and north during Canada's expansion. Their presence and way of life were considered unacceptable and unseemly by the Canadian government.

A. **Read the series of events about the Riel Rebellions. Then number them from 1 to 3 to put them in order.**

The Riel Rebellions

Event 1

☐ Métis spokesperson Louis Riel and his followers stopped the land surveyors. They also prevented William McDougall, the new Canadian governor, from entering their land.

☐ The Hudson's Bay Company sold Rupert's Land to the Dominion of Canada on December 1, 1868. The Métis, settlers of the Red River Valley, were upset that they were not informed.

☐ Surveyors were sent from Ontario to divide the territory into square lots. The Métis had been using thin strips of land that gave all families access to the river.

Event 2

☐ Scott insulted the guards and threatened to shoot Riel if he got free. This prompted Riel to hold a court-martial hearing that led to Scott's execution.

☐ John Schultz was the leader of a group of Canadians who opposed Riel's ideas and attacked Riel and his men. During this attack, Riel captured several Canadians, including Thomas Scott.

☐ On December 8, 1869, Louis Riel set up a provisional government to negotiate with the Canadian government. A 14-point document outlining requests that addressed the colony's agricultural, religious, and language rights was presented.

Event 3

☐ On May 12, 1870, the Manitoba Act was passed, making the Red River Settlement a new province.

☐ Prime Minister Macdonald did not recognize the Red River people as having a government, but an agreement was made that saw the colony enter Confederation.

☐ Riel's position as the governor of the Red River was revoked. He fled to the United States and was later given amnesty.

B. **Fill in the blanks to complete the sentences that describe the Northwest Rebellion of 1885.**

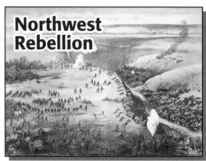

Northwest Rebellion

Poundmaker   provisional government
Parliament   Canadian Pacific Railway
Gabriel Dumont   Métis   treason

Location: present day Saskatchewan, Canada

Northwest Rebellion of 1885

1. In the 15 years after the Red River Settlement joined Confederation, the _____ had not seen their land claims recognized, witnessed a fulfillment of the Indian Treaty obligations, or been granted a local government with representation.

2. During this time, Louis Riel was elected twice to _____ , granted amnesty by the Canadian government, and grew to believe he was a messenger from God.

3. In March 1885, Riel set up a _____ after he sent a petition to the government stating the Métis demands but received no reply.

4. _____ , Riel's newly appointed leader, led an attack against the Northwest Mounted Police on March 26, 1885 at Duck Lake.

5. In support of the attack, Cree chiefs _____ and Big Bear led attacks on Battleford and Frog Lake respectively.

6. Prime Minister Macdonald sent troops on the not yet completed _____ to stop the rebellion. After three weeks of fighting, Riel was captured, Dumont fled to the United States, and Big Bear surrendered.

7. As a result of the uprising, several First Nations individuals were publicly hanged, and Louis Riel was charged with _____ and executed in November 1885.

8

Two Kinds of Gold

Western Canada saw remarkable growth after the building of the transcontinental railway. With the ease of transportation for both people and resources, two new industries flourished. One changed the prairie landscape to golden fields of wheat and the other removed gold from the cold, northern land.

A. Read the passage. Then fill in the blanks with the correct words from the passage to complete the sentences.

Gold and Growth

Miners and prospectors climbed the Chilkoot Trail during the Klondike gold rush.

The Klondike gold rush was an event that led to the immigration of thousands in a short period of time to a cold and harsh land that most people would normally avoid.

Although travel to the Klondike was difficult, economy-stimulating industries popped up nevertheless. Among them were outfitters along the route who equipped new prospectors for their trip, and skilled guides for muddy, steep trails and stormy waterways.

The population grew. The Canadian government worried Americans were becoming too interested in the area. So Canada created a new territory to bring into Confederation: the Yukon.

The gold rush did not last long, and it has been estimated that it took as much money from the people as they got out of it in gold. But it did have at least one lasting effect: the Canadian north had opened up to settlement.

1. The Klondike gold rush opened up the north to _____ .

2. Mass _____ occurred in a short period of time.

3. The gold rush stimulated the economy by creating new _____ .

4. The Klondike gold rush led to the creation of the _____ territory.

B. **Read what Maggie says. Then circle the correct words to indicate the circumstances that made wheat farming profitable in the early 1800s.**

> *With the opening of the west, the prairies transformed into family farms. The Industrial Revolution quickly produced new farm machinery; experimental farms developed new strains of wheat, and there was a high demand everywhere for this new Canadian product.*

- new, improved grains that did not require / require a long growing season

- new, improved / used farm machinery that came with advances in technology

- low / high wheat prices

C. **Match each of the following words with its meaning.**

agricultural economy   prospector

outfitters   Dawson City   Marquis

1. _____
   a person who searches for gold

2. _____
   a type of wheat developed for the short prairie growing season

3. _____
   merchants who profited from providing prospectors-to-be with supplies

4. _____
   the bustling city at the centre of the Klondike gold rush, and the original capital of the Yukon

5. _____
   a system that involves the exchange of agricultural goods, such as wheat

The Origins of the Royal Canadian Mounted Police

The Royal Canadian Mounted Police began as a small force under a different name shortly after Confederation. It was their efforts that enabled the opening of the west to both the CPR and settlement.

A. **Read the clues. Then place the correct initials on the timeline to show the various name changes of the RCMP.**

Changes in the name of the RCMP

1867: Confederation

1873: _____

1904: _____

1920: _____

- In 1904, they were renamed the **R**oyal **N**orth-**W**est **M**ounted **P**olice.

- In 1920, reorganization included the name change to the **R**oyal **C**anadian **M**ounted **P**olice, a title they have to this day.

- The **N**orth-**W**est **M**ounted **P**olice was established in 1873.

B. **Check the correct answers.**

The RCMP uniform, known as the Red Serge, is recognized around the world as a Canadian symbol. Few people know why the uniform is red. The scarlet tunic was chosen as part of the uniform because:

(A) the officers would be visible in the wide-open prairie.

(B) it was John A. Macdonald's favourite colour.

(C) it matched the Canadian flag.

(D) the officers would not be mistaken for U.S. soldiers, who were often in conflict with native groups.

(E) it was the style and colour of the British cavalry, which was where the first Mounties had begun their careers.

> There are three correct answers.

C. **Circle the correct answers to complete the sentences that describe the Mounties and their duties in the West.**

The Mounties and their Duties in the West

1. Once the new North-West Mounted Police were trained, they marched _____ to set up their first posts.

   A. north
   B. west
   C. east

2. The official duty of the North-West Mounted Police was to maintain _____ .

   A. law and order
   B. the education system
   C. the agricultural economy

3. The illegal _____ trade kept the Mounties busy during their early years.

   A. computer
   B. cigarette
   C. whiskey

4. The North-West Mounted Police found themselves keeping the peace between natives and _____ .

   A. fishermen
   B. settlers
   C. farmers

5. They also helped resolve conflicts between _____ and homesteaders.

   A. the government
   B. ranchers
   C. immigrants

6. During the gold rush, the North-West Mounted Police helped keep the peace but were also often needed as _____ .

   A. medical officers
   B. guides
   C. miners

7. _____ was one of the most common types of crime committed in the early years of western settlement.

   A. Bank robbery
   B. Assault
   C. Arson

8. Knowledgeable Mounties often assisted in treaty negotiations between _____ and the government.

   A. First Nations
   B. immigrants
   C. farmers

9. The _____ of the West happened in large part due to the efforts of the North-West Mounted Police.

   A. settlement
   B. sales
   C. trade

Changes in Canada: 1885–1914

There were many changes in Canada between the time of the Northwest Rebellion and the First World War. Immigration and the Industrial Revolution changed Canada and its relationship with the rest of the world significantly.

A. Match the events with the correct headings.

- Challenges of Increased Migration and Settlement
- Canada's Changing Role within the British Empire
- Canadian / American Relations
- Rapid Advances in Technology
- Rapid Industrialization

Read about some of the important Canadian events that occured between the time of the Northwest Rebellion and World War I.

1. _____

In 1899, Canada was asked to send troops to help Britain in the Boer War in South Africa. Some felt that Prime Minister Laurier did not send enough troops. French Canadians opposed any involvement in the distant war.

2. _____

In 1890, Canada was still dominated by the agricultural industry, but it also had more than 75 000 factories employing almost 400 000 workers. Labour issues arose as a result of industrialization.

3. _____

The United States and Canada could not agree on the boundary line between Alaska and British Columbia. Easy access to Klondike gold was at stake. In 1903, the dispute was settled in favour of the United States.

4. _____

The head tax on Chinese immigrants increased from $50 to $100. In 1903, the government raised it again to $500. This effectively ended Chinese immigration to Canada. Families were split up; many people were unable to join their family members in Canada as planned.

5. _____

At first, Canadians had mixed feelings about the automobile. In 1908, automobiles were banned in PEI. British Columbians embraced them, however, and opened Canada's first gas station that same year.

B. **Using the information in part A, add the missing events to the timeline.**

From
Northwest Rebellion

To
World War I

1885: Northwest Rebellion, Louis Riel executed, CPR's last spike

1890: manufacturing economy established

1896: first moving picture shown in Canada, Klondike gold rush, Wilfred Laurier elected as Prime Minister

1898: first automobiles imported to Canada from the U.S.

1899: 1._____

1901: first transatlantic wireless message received in Canada

1903: 2._____ ,

3._____

1905: Alberta and Saskatchewan become 8th and 9th provinces

1906: world's first public radio broadcast

1908: 4._____

5._____

1909: first airplane flight in Canada

1914: World War I begins

C. **There were many technological advances that had an impact on Canadians between 1885 and 1914. List the technological advances with the help of the timeline above.**

1._____   2._____

3._____   4._____   5._____

People Who Made a Difference: 1885–1914

1885 to 1914 saw many political and artistic achievements that made Canada what it is today.

A. Fill in the blanks to complete the description of each person's contribution to Canada.

> activist   landscape   Mohawk   compromise   novels   immigration
> vote   Prime Minister   native villages   Native Canadians

1. **Pauline Johnson**
She was the daughter of an English woman and a _____ chief. Her songs and poetry gave a voice to those not often heard: _____ and women.

2. **Sir Wilfred Laurier**
As the first French-speaking, Roman Catholic _____, he was known for finding _____ between the two major language and religious groups in Canada.

3. **Lucy Maude Montgomery**
She brought the _____ and life in PEI to the world in her widely read _____ about a young orphan, called *Anne of Green Gables*.

4. **Nellie McClung**
A writer and an _____ , she fought for the rights of women to _____ in elections and to own land; she also campaigned for human rights.

5. **Emily Carr**
Her art includes West Coast forests and _____ painted using a progressive and uniquely Canadian style.

6. **Clifford Sifton**
As Minister of the Interior, he set policies that encouraged the _____ of people from many countries and cultures.

B. **What impact did the people and their achievements introduced in part A have on Canadian society? Read what the people say. Then write about whom each person is talking. Choose from the people introduced in part A.**

We take it for granted now, but at one time we did not have the right to own property or to vote.

1.

The ancestors of most of this Ukrainian community would not have immigrated to Canada if it weren't for the encouragement and policies of this man.

2.

There is nothing like this: even the famous Group of Seven artists admired her work.

3.

French or English, Roman Catholic or Protestant, we are all Canadian.

4.

Canadian literature is not British nor French. In her poems, another voice is heard.

5.

I would like to visit Prince Edward Island – home to Anne.

6.

Living and Working in Canada

In Canada in the 1900s, people worked very hard and actively sought to improve life through new laws, organized labour, and societies to help children as well as the poor.

A. **Fill in the blanks to complete the sentences that describe common working conditions circa 1900.**

women	death	factory	children	mines	compensation

1. **Forestry** Injuries and _____ occurred fairly frequently in the forestry industry, and there was no _____ given to either the workers or their families.

2. **Mining** The small stature of _____ made them ideal workers for cramped, underground _____ .

3. **Factories** _____ employees worked twelve hours a day, six or seven days a week. _____ and children were often employed, as they required less pay than men.

B. **Unscramble the words to find out how people responded to the poor working conditions.**

The organization of 1._____ , while not
    ublaro   usnino
a new concept, was stepped up during this time,

and was followed by massive unrest and striking.

2._____ were put in place by the government to
    rbaLou   wlas
protect workers from exploitation.

280

C. **Read the sentences about living conditions in the early 1900s. Write sentences about today's living conditions. Then circle either "same" or "different" to compare the conditions.**

1. **homes**   same / different

In the early 1900s: With the exception of the upper class, homes did not have indoor toilets. Outhouses were common, even in the cities.

Now: _____

2. **health care**   same / different

In the early 1900s: People paid out of pocket for health care although churches often provided help for the poor.

Now: _____

3. **communication**   same / different

In the early 1900s: Postal delivery was expensive; people often relied on travelling immigrants to reach distant relatives and friends. With the invention of the telephone, telegraph, and other new technology, this was an area of rapid change.

Now: _____

4. **transportation**   same / different

In the early 1900s: A horse and carriage was commonplace. The newly invented bicycle was gaining popularity for local transportation and leisure, while train travel carried long-distance travellers over vast expanses of land.

Now: _____

Review

A. **Leah and Andrew are preparing a presentation for Canada Day. Help them complete the information about the sequence of events that led to Confederation by filling in the blanks.**

Canada East
conferences
Dominion
Manifest Destiny
Reciprocity Treaty

- Before it became the province of Quebec, this British North American colony was called _____ .

- Trade between British North America and the U.S. flourished with the _____ .

- _____ was a doctrine that promoted U.S. expansion throughout the continent.

- Three _____ were held in Charlottetown, Quebec, and London.

- On July 1, 1867, the _____ of Canada officially became a country.

Confederation

B. **Help Leah fill in the missing provinces and territories with the help of the circumstances given below.**

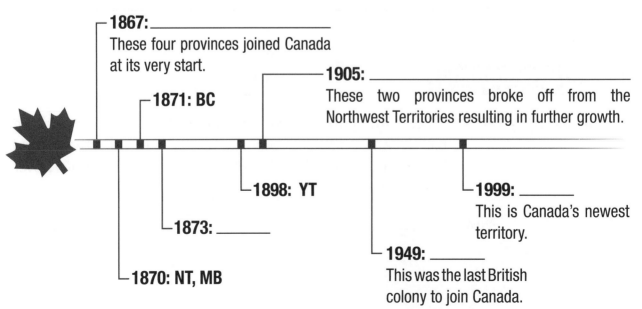

1867: _____
These four provinces joined Canada at its very start.

1871: BC

1905: _____
These two provinces broke off from the Northwest Territories resulting in further growth.

1898: YT

1873: _____

1870: NT, MB

1999: _____
This is Canada's newest territory.

1949: _____
This was the last British colony to join Canada.

C. **Leah wants to discuss important figures in Canada's confederation. Match the points with the influential characters by writing the letters in the boxes.**

A He brought responsible government to Nova Scotia.

B He was the leader of Canada East.

C He was Canada's first Prime Minister.

D He was once a Canada West politician.

E He was an opponent of confederation.

F He ensured the preservation of the French language, culture, and system of civil law.

John A. Macdonald

☐ ☐

Joseph Howe   George-Etienne Cartier

☐ ☐   ☐ ☐

D. **Help Andrew complete the passage about how settlement in the west occurred. Fill in the blanks.**

Settlement
in the West

Métis   cities
gold rush   Vancouver
smallpox   logging
First Nations   Chinese

The 1._____ settled near Red River before the Hudson's Bay Company sold the land to the Canadian government.

Many factories in the 2._____ employed the less well-off. In the North, Dawson City thrived due to the 3._____ .

Many 4._____ people settled in 5._____ after coming to Canada to build the CPR or work in mines.

Many people settled on Vancouver Island because the booming 6._____ and coal mining industries provided lots of jobs. 7._____ killed many 8._____ people in Alberta.

E.   Circle the correct answers to the quiz Andrew has prepared.

A Quiz on
Canada

1.   This province almost left confederation when progress on the Canadian Pacific Railway slowed down:

   A. British Columbia   B. Alberta   C. Nova Scotia

2.   Because there was a lack in local help to build the railway, these people were brought over:

   A. Ukrainians   B. Irish   C. Chinese

3.   This man was a spokesperson for the Métis:

   A. John Schultz   B. Louis Riel   C. Thomas Scott

4.   The railway allowed the government to send soldiers to help defuse this crisis in 1885:

   A. The gold rush

   B. Industrial Revolution

   C. The Northwest Rebellion

5.   This is what happened to Louis Riel after the Northwest Rebellion of 1885:

   A. He fled the country.

   B. He settled in Quebec.

   C. He was captured and executed.

How many questions have you answered correctly? Write the number in the circle.

/5

F. **Leah will be discussing the gold rush. Help her complete her speech by filling in the blanks.**

NWMP   terrain   immigrants   Yukon   guides

outfitters   prospectors   American   settlement

The Klondike gold rush brought many 1._____

to the north. The trip was difficult but 2._____

prepared new 3._____ for their route.

There were also 4._____ , who were

often 5._____ officers, to help people get across the harsh

6._____ . A new territory called the 7._____ was created

to protect the land from 8._____ interest. In the end, the gold rush

opened up the Canadian north to 9._____ .

G. **Match the people from 1885-1914 with the outcomes that have resulted from their contributions.**

Pauline Johnson, of both English and Native Canadian descent, published her poetry.

Nellie McClung, a writer and an activist, fought for the rights of women.

Clifford Sifton, a minister of the Interior, encouraged people from all over the world to immigrate.

Sir Wilfred Laurier became the first French-speaking, Roman-Catholic Prime Minister.

A Canada becomes a multi-cultural country.

B Women can vote and own property in Canada.

C A new voice is heard in Canadian literature, proving that there are more than just English and French voices in the country.

D Compromises start to be made between the two major language and religious groups in Canada.

285

Human Settlement Patterns

When people settle in a new environment, the physical geography and resources of that particular area shape their settlement patterns. These patterns can be classified into three main types: scattered, linear, and clustered.

A. **The pictures show two resort locations that possess very different geographical features. Sort the activities that could take place in the pictured locations.**

Types of Activities

downhill skiing   canoeing   water-skiing   cross-country skiing

swimming   archery   snowshoeing   camping   hiking   tobogganing

Lakeside Paradise

Mount Utopia

_____

_____

_____

_____

B. **The way that Canada has been settled forms patterns. Match the type of settlement pattern with its definition. Then use the words in bold to indicate the type of settlement each map shows.**

1.

Types of Settlement

scattered •

linear •

clustered •

• Patterns like this occur when a lot of people gather in a place that is rich in resources.

• The population is distributed along a line.

• These patterns occur when limited resources support a small number of people.

2.

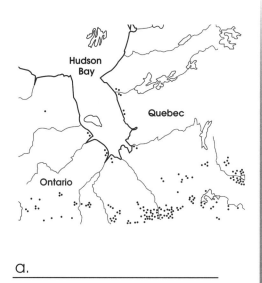

a. _____

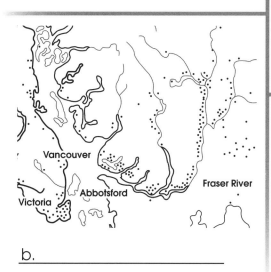

b. _____

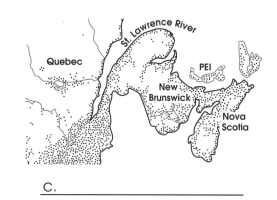

c. _____

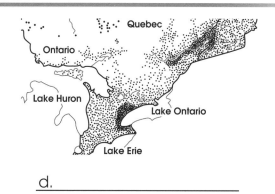

d. _____

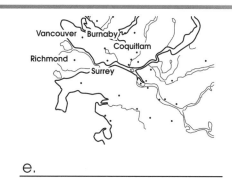

e. _____

Factors That Affect Settlement

Situation and site are factors that must be taken into consideration before settlement occurs.

A. Complete the passage with the given words.

crossroads	strategic	transportation	employment
site	harbour	climate	situation	natural resources

Geographically speaking, a 1._____ is the exact spot where a settlement is located. Factors considered when looking at a site include whether or not there is a body of water so that a 2._____ may be built, its access to 3._____ , whether it is a meeting place or at a 4._____ , and, in some instances, its 5._____ position.

6._____ describes the general location of a settlement in relation to other settlements and larger physical features around it. Landforms, 7._____ , waterways, and natural resources are physical factors that must be considered. Human situation factors include population, 8._____ , and 9._____ factors.

B. **Read what the children are saying. Write "site" or "situation" to identify the area they are referring to.**

1.

I know this answer! Fort Vermilion is Alberta's oldest settlement, established in 1788. Its main access to the trading community of the North West Company was by river.

_____

2. The high cliffs on this narrowing river would make this location easy to defend!

_____

3. Man, I have to move here! The music industry is growing quickly in this city. All the people here love music. This is where all the bands get their big break!

_____

4. We decided to choose this location for our solar-powered home because here in the Northern Hemisphere, slopes that face south receive the most sunlight.

_____

C. **Consider the area in which you live. Why did your family decide to live here? Make two site and two situation observations about your area.**

_____

_____

Site Factors: 1. _____

2. _____

Situation Factors: 1. _____

2. _____

3

Populations – High/Low Density

Population density is the measurement of the number of people settled per unit area. The formula used to derive population density is as follows:

$$\text{Population Density} = \frac{\text{number of people in an area}}{\text{area in square kilometres}}$$

A. **Find the population density of each province or city in 2006. Then answer the questions.**

1.

Province	No. of People	Land Area (km²)	Population Density (No. of People/km²)
New Brunswick	729 997	71 355.67	$\frac{729\,997}{71\,355.67} =$ _____
British Columbia	4 113 487	926 492.48	
Ontario	12 160 282	907 655.59	
Yukon Territory	30 372	474 706.97	
Prince Edward Island	135 851	5684.39	

2.

City	No. of People	Land Area (km²)	Population Density (No. of People/km²)
Fredericton	50 535	130.68	
Victoria	78 057	19.68	
Toronto	2 481 494	629.91	
Whitehorse	20 461	416.43	
Charlottetown	32 174	44.33	

3. Which province had the highest population density? _____

4. Which city had the lowest population density? _____

B. Write "valid" or "invalid" for each sentence by making use of the tables in part A.

Many statements can be made about population patterns. Some sort of data must validate them. Some are true, or valid, and are reflected in the data. Some are false, or invalid.

1. More than half of the Yukon's population is found in its capital city, Whitehorse.

   _____

2. The crime rate in Toronto is much higher than in Fredericton.

   _____

3. The harsh environment has a lot to do with the low population density of the Yukon.

   _____

4. Many people settle in cities because of the employment opportunities.

   _____

5. The larger the land area, the greater the population density.

   _____

C. Answer the questions.

1. Do you live in a region of high, moderate, or low population density?

   _____

   _____

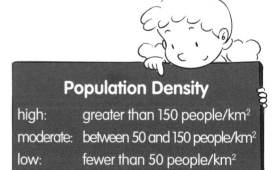

Population Density

high: greater than 150 people/km²
moderate: between 50 and 150 people/km²
low: fewer than 50 people/km²

2. List five things that you think are affected by the population density of a particular region or city, for example, hospitals.

   _____

   _____

293

How We Use Land

Communities make use of land in many different ways. Using land wisely helps the growth and development of communities.

A. Identify the type of land use being referred to. Write the answers on the lines.

Types of Land

Institutional	Industrial	Residential	Transportation
	Commercial	Park land/Open space	

1. Mrs. Cowan says, "From big mansions to high-rise apartments and everything in between, people have to live somewhere." _____

2. Mr. Patel says, "With a maximum of 14 lanes through Toronto, Ontario, Highway 401 is one of the widest highways in the world. It's time to make it even wider!" _____

3. "Schools, hospitals, public libraries, and places of worship fall into this kind of land use," says Dr. Allen. _____

4. Mr. Smith, a factory owner, is at a news conference. He says, "Land use of this type creates a lot of employment opportunities for the community. They are often located close to transportation routes. It is what brought me to this city." _____

5. Mrs. Brown says, "Park Royal, opened in West Vancouver, BC, is officially Canada's first covered shopping mall. It was opened in 1950." _____

6.  *It is important to ensure that this type of land use continues, as it helps to preserve the natural heritage of a community.* _____

B. **Complete the circle graphs to show the data of the two cities. Then answer the question.**

	Residential	Transportation	Institutional	Park Land	Industrial	Commercial
City A	50%	20%	10%	10%	5%	5%
City B	35%	30%	15%	5%	10%	5%

1.

Land Use in Two Canadian Cities

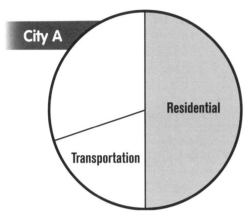
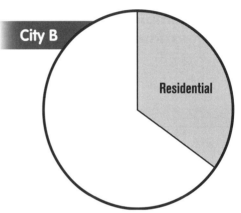

2. Which city do you think has greater employment opportunities? _____

C. **Answer the questions.**

> A **rural area** has a population of fewer than 1000 people.
> An **urban area** has a population of more than 1000 people.
> A **suburb** is a residential outlying district.

1. Do you live in an urban, a suburban, or a rural area? _____

2. The street patterns of older communities follow a grid pattern, where stores and other types of businesses or services are often located at intersections. Does your community have this type of street pattern? If not, how is it different?

_____

3. If you had to make one change in the land use of your community, what would it be? Why?

_____

What Is an Economic System?

Goods and services are produced and offered to people through what is known as an economic system. Economic systems provide answers to questions about the way goods and services will be produced and distributed.

A. Give examples of goods and services shown in the picture. Then answer the questions.

Beauty Hair Shop
A & B Wireless
ny's Shoes
Beethoven's House
Star Fashion
OPEN
Happy Tour

1.

Examples of	
Goods	**Services**

2. Name one thing that you paid for recently.

_____

3. What did you pay for: a product or a service?

_____

B. **Jason has some questions about economic systems. Read how the people answer his questions. Match the answers with the questions. Write the letters.**

A *We will produce jars with extra tight screw-top lids and offer a jar-opening service in every community.*

B Mr. Young says, "Jars will be distributed to all, but only those who can afford it will use our jar-opening service."

C "We will make them the way they've always been made because it works!" says Mrs. Clark.

1. **What** goods are produced? **What** services are offered? ◯

2. **How** are goods produced and services offered? ◯

3. **Who** receives the goods and services? ◯

C. **Match the words with their meanings.**

> consumers   goods   producers   competition
> services   industry   distribution   market

1. the makers or providers of goods and services   _____

2. producers of related goods and services   _____

3. the producers and consumers of an industry   _____

4. a product provided for consumers   _____

5. work or action provided for consumers   _____

6. the method of providing goods or services for consumers   _____

7. the receivers of goods or services   _____

8. the relationships between producers of similar goods or services   _____

Types of Economic Systems

Three major types of economic systems exist today, each with its own characteristics. All societies have a mixed economic system to some degree. That is, even though they may lean strongly toward one system, they also have characteristics of others.

A. **Match each type of economic system with its definition.**

1. _____ Economy

   An economic system in which the government controls all factors of production and distribution of goods and services.

2. _____ Economy

   An economic system that makes economic decisions based on how things were done in the past. Tradition and custom are highly regarded.

3. _____ Economy

   An economic system that allows individual ownership of business or industry and has a free relationship between producers and consumers. What happens in the market determines its success or failure.

Market

Traditional

Command

B. **Different economic systems have different answers to the questions below. Circle the correct words to complete the answers.**

Questions

1. What goods are produced? What services are offered?
2. How are goods produced and services offered?
3. Who receives the goods and services?

Command Economy

1. The government / mayor decides what goods will be produced.

2. The government controls all factors of production / exhibition .

3. The goods and services that are crucial / distributed to the people are decided by the government.

298

Traditional Economy

1. Whatever was produced in the past will `continue / stop` to be produced.

2. Goods will be produced in `a different / the same` way they were produced in the past.

3. People who received the goods and services in the `past / morning` , or their offspring, will continue to receive them.

Market Economy

1. What `consumers / customers` want will dictate what will be produced.

2. Producers will produce in ways that can be `modern / competitive` and profitable.

3. Whoever wants a product or service, and has the `money / luck` to buy it, may have it.

C. The following quotes are hints about the characteristics of economic systems. Put the sentences into the correct columns. Write the letters.

A "Her inventiveness has finally paid off! Everyone is buying her new SmartDrink!"

B "We exchanged our homemade pies for guitar lessons."

C "We are only allowed to produce 10 000 can openers this year, by order of the Ministry of Markets."

D "The grocers do not set food prices; the authority does."

E "We farmers own our land and all the machinery, too."

F *Only women may work as early childhood educators here.*

Traditional Economy	Command Economy	Market Economy
_____	_____	_____

Industry

Industry is an important part of an economic system. There are three main types of industry: Primary, which is concerned with the removal of raw materials; Secondary, which is the manufacturing industry; and Tertiary, which covers the service industry.

A. **Match the definitions of different types of industries on page 301 with the names given below. Then identify the types of industries that are pictured below and write the letters in the correct categories on page 301.**

Primary Industry   **Secondary Industry**   **Tertiary Industry**

A

B

C

D

E

F

G

H

I

1. _____: These industries remove the natural resources of an environment.

   Illustrated examples: _____

2. _____: Service industries such as food, health, personal and business, fall under this category.

   Illustrated examples: _____

3. _____: Industries in this category make use of the extracted natural resources.

   Illustrated examples: _____

B. **Name a secondary and a tertiary industry that may arise from each primary industry. Then give your own example starting with naming a primary industry.**

Primary Industry	Secondary Industry	Tertiary Industry
1. Logging	_____	_____
2. Sugar Plantation	_____	_____
3. Quarrying	_____	_____
4. Mining	_____	_____
5. Fishing	_____	_____

My Example

| 6. _____ | _____ | _____ |

Canadian Industry

Canada's industries have changed from being mostly resource-based at the time of confederation to mostly service-based today. Our land and water are still abundant natural resources, and they, as well as manufacturing industries, play an important role in the Canadian economy.

A. List Canada's major natural resources with the help of the map. Then answer the questions.

1.

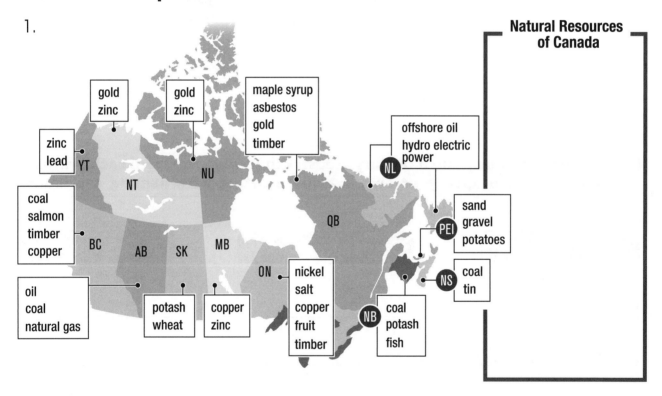

2. Where would be a good place to locate a new logging business?

_____

3. In which province would you likely find an oil refinery?

_____

4. Give two possible locations for the seafood industry.

_____

B. Use a circle graph to show what percentage of Canada's gross domestic product (GDP) each type of industry provides.

**Percentage of Canada's Gross Domestic Product
Each Type of Industry Provides**

Resources Industries

(oil well, farm, mine, logging camp)

about **7%**

Manufacturing and Construction Industries

(paper, textiles, shingles, cars)

about **28%**

Service Industries

(groceries, banking, courier, Internet service)

about **65%**

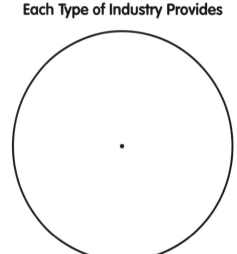

Percentage of Canada's GDP
Each Type of Industry Provides

C. Four resource industries were part of Canada's early existence. Some were even a reason for European settlement in Canada. Unscramble the words to discover the early Canadian industries.

Early Canadian Industries

1. _____
   rfu tared

2. _____
   turcuelagir

3. _____
   bremti

4. _____
   inming

D. Name two industries that are a major part of your community. Identify what types of industries they are.

Name: _____

Type: _____

Name: _____

Type: _____

303

Human Migration

People have always moved from one place to another when there is good reason to do so. This movement, or migration, can be within the same country or across the world. Reasons for migration are varied, and are called either push factors or pull factors.

A. Match each "human migration" word with its meaning. Write the word on the line.

Government of Canada

Immigration

---

migration   transportation   pull factors

barriers   accessibility   refugees   mobility

immigration   emigration   push factors

---

1. The means of moving people from one place to another _____

2. Things that prevent people from migrating _____

3. The permanent move into a new country _____

4. The openness of a place to new immigrants _____

5. The ability to move from one place to another _____

6. The movement from one area to another _____

7. The permanent exit out of one's country to another _____

8. The reasons people have for leaving a particular area _____

9. People who are forced to move from one place to another _____

10. The reasons people choose a particular new place of residence _____

B. **Identify each of the following as a push factor or pull factor for migration. Write "push" or "pull" on the line.**

═══════════════ **Factors for Migration** ═══════════════

1. drought _____

2. sold into slavery _____

3. banishment _____

4. natural disaster _____

5. persecution _____

6. religious tolerance _____

7. war _____

8. lack of freedom _____

9. climate of new place _____

10. discrimination _____

11. lack of security in old place _____

12. cost of living in new place _____

C. **Answer the questions.**

1. *During the Industrial Revolution, Great Britain transported criminals to the faraway land of Australia. Which push or pull factor does this historical event describe?*

_____

2. Find an example from the newspaper of a push or pull factor for migration. Explain how you identify it as a push or pull factor.

Newspaper: _____   Date: _____

Headline: _____

Comment: _____

_____

What Makes Migration Difficult?

Migration is a common, well-established part of human life. Even still, different barriers, such as government policies and financial concerns, occur which prevent it. At the same time, improved technology and transportation has made migration easier in many ways.

A. **Read the quotes below to discover factors that make migration difficult. Write the letters.**

1. "I can't afford the bus ticket!" _____

2. "Here I have a job. How do I know I will get work in a new country?" _____

3. "My government won't allow emigration." _____

4. "I cannot leave all my friends and family behind." _____

Factors

(A) **Physical barriers**

(B) **Financial/Economic**

(C) **Legal**

(D) **Political**

(E) **Emotional/Cultural adjustments**

5. "Since I cannot take everything I own with me, it is not worth emigrating." _____

6. "Immigration to this country is minimal; it is thousands of miles from most everywhere else." _____

7. "Even though I received most of my education here, the law makes it difficult to fully immigrate. It is time for me to go home." _____

8. "How can I move to a country if I don't speak its official language?" _____

9. *Concerns about terrorism have caused some countries to lower their immigration rate.* _____

B. **Mobility is the ability to migrate. Compare each pair of pictures. Decide which factor makes each of them less or more mobile. Write sentences describing each situation.**

Things to Be Considered When We Migrate

- Occupation
- Financial standing
- Family responsibilities
- Means of transportation
- Support in country of immigration
- Ability to connect with people through technology

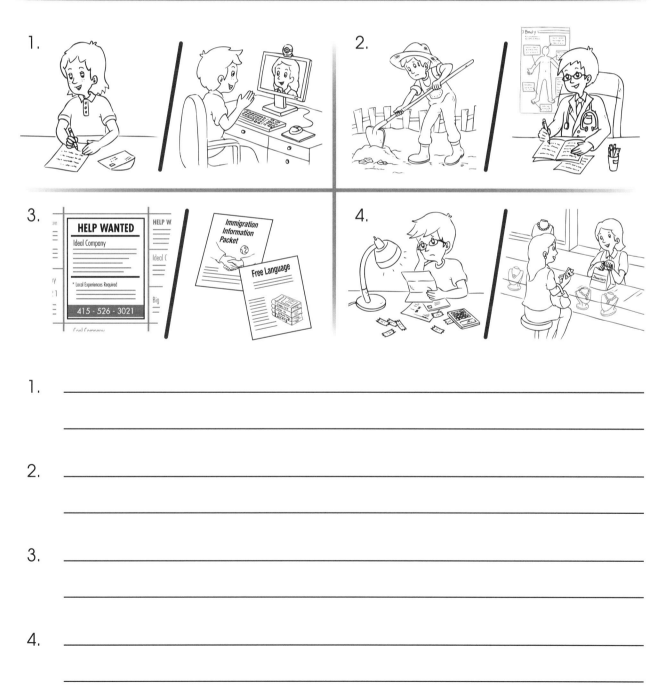

1. _____

_____

2. _____

_____

3. _____

_____

4. _____

_____

Migration and Culture

Human migration affects many aspects of culture. Though sometimes there is conflict, cultural diversity is the usual outcome of migration.

A. Give three examples of cultural diversity caused by human migration for each category. Then write about one of the listed examples you are interested in, and say why you like it the most.

1.

Cultural Diversity Caused by Human Migration

Food

- Southern fried chicken
- _____
- _____
- _____

Music

- Scottish bagpiper
- _____
- _____
- _____

Clothing

- Japanese Kimono
- _____
- _____
- _____

Art and Dance

- Inuit carving
- _____
- _____
- _____

Celebrations

- St. Patrick's Day
- _____
- _____
- _____

2. I am interested in _____

_____

_____

_____

_____

B. **The everyday words below come from another culture and language. Use a dictionary to find the etymology, or origin, of each word.**

> *Language is a component of culture that is highly susceptible to change due to human migration.*

1. karaoke _____
2. terra cotta _____
3. kayak _____
4. dachshund _____
5. confetti _____
6. rendezvous _____
7. cafeteria _____
8. wok _____

C. **Your community is celebrating its acceptance of others. Write the name of your community. Then complete the poster to show welcome to the many cultures that make up your community.**

Translate the word "WELCOME" into different languages to display and reflect your openness to other people's heritage.

Welcome!

_____
my community

_____
Afrikanns

_____
Danish

_____
French

_____
German

_____
Hawaiian

_____
Hindi

_____
Japanese

_____
Polish

_____
Thai

12

Migration and Canada

With the exception of Aboriginal Peoples, Canada is a land of immigrants. Different factors at play throughout history have determined who has wanted to migrate to Canada, who has needed to migrate to Canada, and who has been allowed to migrate to Canada.

A. Fill in the blanks with the given words to complete the sentences about early immigration to Canada.

Migration in Early Canada

persecution   Irish Potato Famine   French settlers   head tax

opening of the West   Russian Mennonites   Chinese Exclusion Act

Europeans and Americans

1. _____ were the first European immigrants to what was to become Canada. The British followed and conquered the French, even though they were outnumbered by the French for a few years to come.

2. Loyalists from the United States and African Americans escaping slavery through the Underground Railroad migrated North to Canada, hoping to leave behind _____ and oppression.

3. The failure of potato crops in Ireland, known as the _____ , initiated the migration of many Irish people to Canada; by 1871, they were outnumbered in Canadian society only by the French.

4. The Confederation of Canada and the _____ occurred when people in the British Isles were looking for relief from poverty and displacement caused by a newly industrialized society.

5. _____ , already accustomed to a harsh climate, were promised freedom to practise their religion upon immigration to Canada.

6. The Canadian government went to great expense trying to entice certain _____ to immigrate to the Canadian West.

7. Due to the large sum of money spent on advertisements encouraging immigration from other countries, the Canadian government collected a _____ from Chinese people wishing to immigrate.

8. The head tax was followed by the _____ , which excluded virtually all Chinese from immigrating to Canada.

B.   Re-read part A. Then answer the questions.

1. *Was Britain's Industrial Revolution a cause or an effect of British migration to Canada after Confederation?*

    _____

2. Was slavery in the United States an example of a push factor or a pull factor for migration to Canada?   _____

3. What was the cause of Irish migration to Canada around 1870?   _____

C.   Name the countries on the world map to show the origins of some of Canada's newest immigrants.

Top eight countries
(in order from greatest no. of immigrants)

Birthplaces of Canada's Immigrants

- China
- India
- Philippines
- Hong Kong
- Sri Lanka
- Pakistan
- Taiwan
- United States

A. **Write a definition for each type of settlement. Then identify the type of settlement each map shows.**

1. Types of Settlement

   • scattered: _____

   • linear   : _____

   • clustered : _____

2.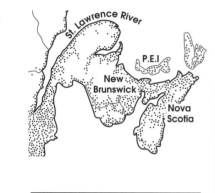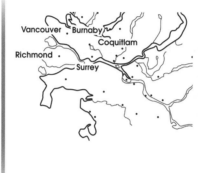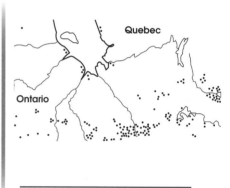

   _____   _____   _____

B. **Look at the circle graphs showing land use percentages in City Simcoe. Analyze the graphs and write about the development of City Simcoe in the past 30 years.**

Land Use in City Simcoe

The Development of
City Simcoe

_____

_____

_____

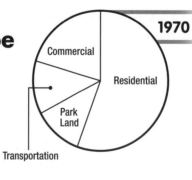 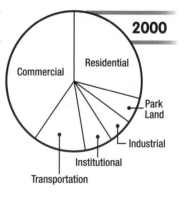

_____

_____

_____

_____

_____

C.   Find the population density of each city. Then answer the questions.

1.   **City A**

Land area: 362 534 km²

No. of people: 4 534 016

Population Density:

City B

Land area: 730 253 km²

No. of people: 9 540 755

Population Density:

City C

Land area: 642 619 km²

No. of people: 7 165 342

Population Density:

2a. Which city has the highest population density?   _____

 b. Give two possible site factors and two possible situation factors to explain why people would prefer to live in that city.

Site Factor

_____

_____

Situation Factor

_____

_____

D.   Identify the type of industry shown in each picture. Write "Primary Industry", "Secondary Industry", or "Tertiary Industry" on the line.

1. _____

2. _____

3. _____

E. Identify the characteristics of different economic systems. Write the letters under the correct economic system.

(A) The government decides how goods and services are disturbuted to the people.

(B) Producers will produce in whatever way they can to be competitive and profitable.

(C) The government controls all factors of production.

(D) What consumers want dictates what will be produced.

(E) Goods are produced in the same way they were produced in the past.

(F) Whatever was produced in the past will continue to be produced.

Traditional Economy   Command Economy   Market Economy

_____   _____   _____

F. Explain the terms "push factor" and "pull factor" for human migration. Then identify each of the following as a push factor or pull factor for migration.

1. Push Factor: _____

    Pull Factor: _____

2. Factors for Migration

    a. employment opportunities   _____

    b. human conflicts   _____

    c. poverty   _____

    d. political violence   _____

    e. safety   _____

G. **Circle the correct answers.**

1. Find the factors that make migration difficult.

   a.

   > My family wants to move to that country, but they have laws that prevent us from doing so. Perhaps if I was an aerospace engineer instead of a fisherman, we would be allowed to immigrate.

   legal   political   physical barriers

   b.

   > People from my country are rarely allowed to immigrate to that country.

   emotional adjustments   financial   political

2. In which province would it be likely to find a logging business?

   Yukon   British Columbia   Newfoundland

3. Which natural resource can be found in Saskatchewan?

   gold   potash   gravel

4. Which province or territory is abundant in zinc?

   Prince Edward Island   New Brunswick   Manitoba

5. Which of these was an early Canadian industry?

   agriculture   service   construction

6. What is the term used to describe people who are forced to move from one place to another?

   producer   immigrants   refugees

SCIENCE

Cell Theory

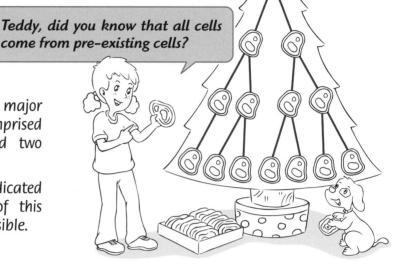

Teddy, did you know that all cells come from pre-existing cells?

- The cell theory is one of the major foundations of biology, and is comprised of three main postulates and two exceptions.

- Without technology and dedicated individuals, the formulation of this theory would not have been possible.

A. Fill in the blanks to complete the postulates of the cell theory and its exceptions. Then give each picture a caption with the postulate or the exception that it illustrates.

Postulates of Cell Theory

1. All living things are made up of _____ .

2. All cells are a _____ to carry out functions to sustain life. _____ flow occurs within cells.

3. All cells come from _____ cells.

first

pre-existing

viruses

structure

energy

cells

Exceptions

1. The _____ cell did not come from an already existing cell.

2. _____ do not contain a cell structure, so they are not living.

Picture 1
Animals: Plants:

Picture 2

Yeah, I understand that, but where did the first cell come from?

_____

_____

B. **To complete the timeline, fill in the blanks with the names of people and events that led to the Cell Theory.**

Thedor   Robert   Anton   Zacharias   cell   microscope   membrane
Rudolph   Charles-Francois   Matthias   arise   products   live

Events that Led to the Cell Theory:

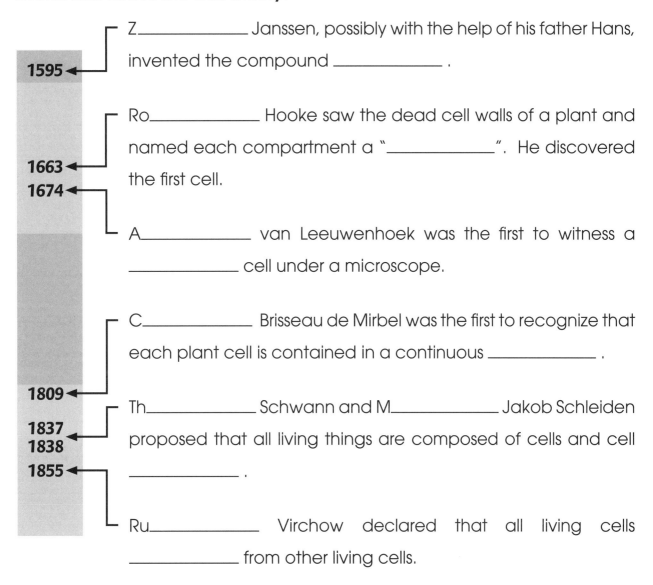

1595 — Z_____ Janssen, possibly with the help of his father Hans, invented the compound _____ .

1663 — Ro_____ Hooke saw the dead cell walls of a plant and named each compartment a "_____". He discovered the first cell.

1674 — A_____ van Leeuwenhoek was the first to witness a _____ cell under a microscope.

1809 — C_____ Brisseau de Mirbel was the first to recognize that each plant cell is contained in a continuous _____ .

1837
1838 — Th_____ Schwann and M_____ Jakob Schleiden proposed that all living things are composed of cells and cell _____ .

1855 — Ru_____ Virchow declared that all living cells _____ from other living cells.

Science Fact

Long ago, it was believed that life could arise out of non-life. Spontaneous generation, as it was known, was a way for people to explain how maggots could appear on rotting meat, or how frogs could rise up from the muddy banks of the Nile River.

2

Animal and Plant Cells

- Both animal and plant cells contain some of the same types of structures, but not all.

- Photosynthesis and respiration are important functions of plant and animal cells, respectively.

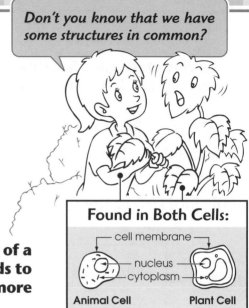

Don't you know that we have some structures in common?

Found in Both Cells:

- cell membrane
- nucleus
- cytoplasm

Animal Cell   Plant Cell

A. **Unscramble the words to label the diagram of a typical animal cell. Then use the same words to complete the passage. Words can be used more than once.**

1. **A Typical Animal Cell**

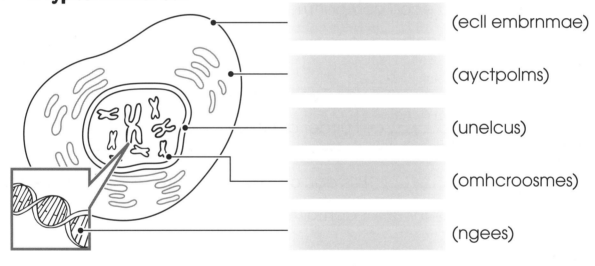

(ecll embrnmae)

(ayctpolms)

(unelcus)

(omhcroosmes)

(ngees)

2. The a._____ is the control centre of the cell. It contains

the b._____ , which are thread-like structures that contain

genetic information. This information, stored in c._____ , is

the information needed to define characteristics of the individual. The

material that suspends the d._____ and other structures in

the cell is called the e._____ . The whole cell is enclosed in a

f._____ , which is not a complete barrier, but rather one that

allows some materials to pass in and out of the cell.

B. Fill in the blanks with the words in the diagram.

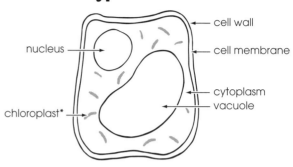

A Typical Plant Cell

cell wall

nucleus

cell membrane

cytoplasm
vacuole

chloroplast*

*Chloroplasts are members of a class of organelles known as plastids.

1. A _____ is a protective and supportive structure external to the cell membrane that is found in plants, fungi, bacteria, and algae.

2. This _____ contains chlorophyll, which is a green pigment used in photosynthesis.

3. A large part of the cytoplasm is occupied by a _____ , which is a fluid-filled cavity that may contain water, minerals, sugars, and proteins.

4. A _____ is an organelle found in both plants and algae. It is involved in food production and storage.

C. Read what Amy says. Complete the flow diagrams with the words in bold.

*Green plant cells perform a chemical reaction called photosynthesis, where they use the **energy** from the sun to change **carbon dioxide** and water into food and **oxygen**.*

*Animal cells undergo **respiration**, where they change sugar (food) and oxygen into **carbon dioxide**, **water**, and energy.*

Photosynthesis

_____ + water + _____ ⟶ sugar + _____

Respiration

sugar + _____ ⟶ _____ + _____ + energy

Science Fact

One of the main functions of the plant cell wall is to prevent the cell from bursting when it absorbs water.

3

Structures and Organelles in Cells

I can see it clearly under an electron microscope.

- Advances in microscope technology have made it possible to identify the various structures and organelles inside cells.

- These organelles have particular jobs to do inside the cell.

A. **Read what Simon says. Identify whether the microscope is a "light" or "electron" microscope. Then sort the structures into the correct groups.**

> *Using a light microscope, we can observe many different structures inside a cell. These include the nucleus, cell membrane, and the cell wall (in plant cells only). Other specialized structures in the cytoplasm, known as organelles, can only be seen under an electron microscope.*

_____ microscope

- _____
- _____
- _____
- _____

_____ microscope

- _____
- _____
- _____
- _____
- _____

endoplasmic reticulum

cytoplasm

cell membrane

Golgi apparatus

lysosomes

cell wall

mitochondria

nucleus

ribosomes

B. The organelles of the cell have specific forms and functions. Use the diagram and the given words to complete the information chart.

canals   cell respiration   recycle   toxic
proteins   oval-shaped   cytoplasm   sac-like

A Typical Cell

Ribosomes
Lysosome
Golgi apparatus
Endoplasmic reticulum
Mitochondrion

The Organelles of the Cell

1. R_____ (Form: free or attached)

   Function: assemble _____

2. M_____ (Form: _____)

   Function: make energy through photosynthesis or _____

3. Endoplasmic reticulum (Form: _____)

   Function: carry materials through the _____

4. G_____ a_____ (Form: stacked like pancakes)

   Function: packages proteins and _____ materials

5. Lysosome (Form: _____)

   Function: contain proteins that break down and _____ larger molecules

Science Fact

The number of mitochondria a cell contains seems to be related to the type of cell in which they are found. Cells that need a lot of energy to perform their job typically have a high number of mitochondria.

Diffusion and Osmosis

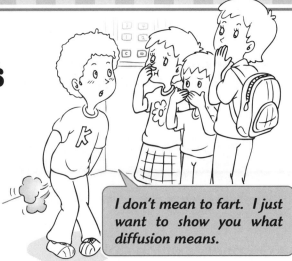

- Diffusion is the movement of molecules from an area of high concentration to an area of low concentration.

- Osmosis is the movement of water molecules from an area of high concentration to an area of low concentration.

> *I don't mean to fart. I just want to show you what diffusion means.*

A. Fill in the blanks by unscrambling the letters to complete what Sally says. Then write 1 to 5 to number the sentences that describe the movement of molecules during diffusion.

1.

> *Diffusion occurs on a molecular level when molecules move from an area of _____ (ihgh) concentration to an area of _____ (wlo) concentration.*

food colouring (solute)

water (solvent)

> *Liquid food colouring comes in concentrated form, and when a drop is put into a glass of water, it diffuses.*

2. **Movement of Molecules During Diffusion:**
   (Add a drop of food colouring into a glass of water.)

   ( ) The molecules of the food colouring "glob" collide with other molecules that they are close to, and are sent off in all directions, only to collide with more.

   ( ) There is no longer a "glob", as the food colouring molecules have spread themselves out evenly throughout the water.

   ( ) Before meeting with water, the highly concentrated food colouring molecules are close together, forming a "glob" as it begins to fall through the water.

   ( ) Due to the randomness of the collisions, the food colouring molecules spread out and "intermingle" with the water molecules.

   (1) According to the Kinetic Theory of Matter, the molecules in both the concentrated food colouring and water are in constant motion.

B. **Fill in the blanks with the given words. Then put ">", "<", or "=" in the circles.**

Osmosis
equal membrane osmosis water out

When salt is used on roadways to combat icy conditions, roadside plants can be destroyed. This happens as a result of 1._____ . Under normal conditions, the concentration of water inside the cells of the plant is 2._____ to the concentration of water outside. Water flows equally in and out of the cells through a selectively permeable 3._____*. When salt is added to roads, it forms a salt solution with the melting ice. The concentration of water inside the plant cells is no longer equal to the concentration outside. More water flows 4._____ of the cells than into the cells through the cell membrane, damaging the cell, and leaving it without the 5._____ it needs to make food.

* a membrane that only allows some materials to pass through it

Plant Cell when Exposed to Salt Water

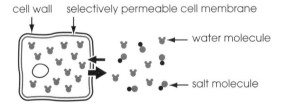

concentration of water
inside the cell ◯ outside the cell

Plant Cell with Continued Exposure to Salt Water

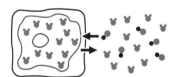

concentration of water
inside the cell ◯ outside the cell

The size of the arrows indicates the amount of water moving from one place to another.

Science Fact

Turgor pressure is the pressure of the cell's contents against the cell wall. This pressure is a direct result of osmosis and it gives the plant rigidity and strength.

The Organization of Cells

Some life forms on Earth are single-celled; some are multi-celled. Sea sponges are animals that display the move from being single-celled to multi-celled.

- Cellular differentiation is displayed in multi-cellular organisms.
- Cells in multi-cellular organisms are specialized and organized into three levels: tissues, organs, and systems.

A.   Complete the passage about the five differentiated types of cells in a sponge with the help of the diagram. Then fill in the missing information.

The body of a sponge is made up of different types of cells in a jelly-like mass substance called a mesoglea. 1. C_____ are "colour cells" that function as the sponge's digestive system in that they have flagellum to beat and create the sponge's water current. They also filter the water to trap and engulf food. 2. P_____ are

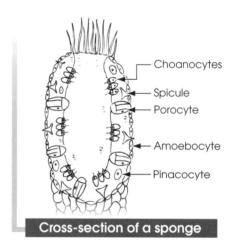

Choanocytes
Spicule
Porocyte
Amoebocyte
Pinacocyte

Cross-section of a sponge

cells that make up the pores in the body, making openings that allow water to flow through the body. 3. A_____ move around in the sponge's body, storing and carrying food to other cells that they get from choanocytes. 4. S_____ are made from calcium carbonate. They provide protection and structure. 5. P_____ form the outer covering of the sponge.

6.

Cell and Its Function

- _____ : Make up the pores in the body.
- Choanocytes   : _____
- Amoebocytes : _____
- Pinacocytes   : _____
- _____ : Protect and support the body.

B.   Read what Simon says. Then fill in the blanks.

> Organisms on Earth come in many different forms, but all of them are composed of cells. The organization of different types of cells is highly complex. The cells must work together.

organs
cells
tissues

1.   Groups of _____ that specialize in performing the same function are called tissues.

2.   Organs are groups of _____ working together.

3.   Several _____ that work together to perform a function are called an organ system.

C.   Answer the children's questions.

1.   _Which organ system does the kidney belong to?_

_____

digestive system
excretory system
respiratory system
circulatory system
nervous system

2.   Amy asks, "Which system is responsible for the ingestion and breakdown of food into tiny pieces so that it can pass into cells?"

_____

3.   Kevin asks, "Which system is comprised of these organs: heart, arteries, veins, and capillaries?"

_____

Science Fact

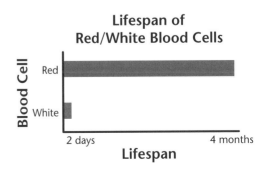

White blood cells have a lifespan of about two days, while red blood cells can live for four months.

6

About Systems

- Systems are groups of parts that work together to do something. They can be found in nature or constructed by humans.

- Systems can be made up of smaller systems, or subsystems, that work together to make up the whole.

This is my audio system.

A.   Circle the letter for the correct ending to each sentence that describes systems.

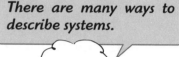

There are many ways to describe systems.

1.   Systems are designed to

    A.   get things done.

    B.   run without stopping.

    C.   break down eventually.

2.   Systems can

    A.   be human-made only.

    B.   be human-made, or occur in nature.

    C.   only occur in nature.

3.   Systems are characterized by

    A.   parts that work together to accomplish a task.

    B.   mechanical parts.

    C.   electrical parts.

4.   The goal of a system is to

    A.   produce resources.

    B.   retain as many resources as possible.

    C.   use resources more efficiently.

B. Look at the pictures. Identify the various types of systems.

mechanical system   body system   optical system
electrical system   hydroelectric power system

1. _____

2. _____

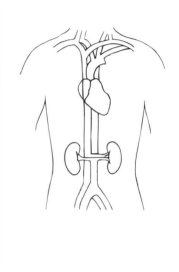

3. _____

4. _____

5. _____

C. Identify three different subsystems that work inside the larger system of a bicycle.

_____

_____

_____

_____

_____

_____

Many systems contain smaller systems, or subsystems, working together to make the larger system work.

Science Fact

Some systems are very old. The cuneiform writing system of the Sumerians, for example, was invented about 5000 years ago. This Sumerian system was one of the first writing systems in the world.

Cuneiform Writing

Examples:

bird   ➤✦Ⳇ   water ⳇⳇ

Systems: Input and Output

Input: electricity

Output: light

- All systems have a purpose – something they are meant to create.
- Systems include an input and an output.

> Look at my vaned lighting system at home. The purpose of this system is to give me light. This system allows me to work at night.

A. Identify the purpose, input, and output of the different systems. Fill in the missing information.

1. **System:** home heating

   Purpose: heat home

   Input: fuel

   Output: _____

2. **System:** bicycle

   Purpose: move from one place to another

   Input: _____

   Output: _____

3. **System:** digestive system

   Purpose: digest food

   Input: _____

   Output: _____

4. **System:** farm

   Purpose: _____

   Input: _____

   Output: _____

5. **System:** grandfather clock

   Purpose: _____

   Input: _____

   Output: _____

B. Identify the input and output of each system. Write "input" or "output" in the boxes.

1.

2.

3.

4.

Science Fact

Sometimes the output of one system can be the input of another. For example, the output of the logging industry's timber could be the input for a home heating system as logs for a fireplace.

input

output

The Work Systems Do

- The terms energy, force, work, and efficiency have scientific meanings that differ from their meanings in our everyday use of the words.

- Work, in the scientific sense of the word, is only being done if the force is causing movement of an object in the same direction as the force being applied.

Dad, look at the windmill. Is work being done?

Yes. The wind is doing the work.

A. For each picture, write the term that is being used. Then write whether it is an everyday use or a scientific use of the term.

Term: energy   force   work   efficiency

1.
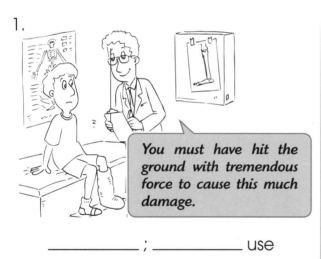

You must have hit the ground with tremendous force to cause this much damage.

_____ ; _____ use

2.

They have lots of energy.

_____ ; _____ use

3.

Our new machine works with a higher efficiency than the old one. We get a lot more output for the same amount of input.

_____ ; _____ use

4.

I'm going to be late for work.

_____ ; _____ use

B. **Fill in the blanks with the given words to define the scientific meanings of the terms.**

> useful   work   pull   effort

scientific meanings

Energy: the capacity to do 1._____

Force: a push, 2._____ , or other factor that makes an object change speed, shape, or direction

Work: the amount of 3._____ expended in moving an object

Efficiency: how much of the energy used is 4._____

C. **Read each situation. Decide whether or not work is being done. If so, explain how it is being done; otherwise, suggest ways to make work happen.**

1. A conveyor belt is moving heavy auto parts through a factory.

   Is work being done?   _____

   Explain: _____

2. The circulatory system moves oxygen to cells throughout the body.

   Is work being done?   _____

   Explain: _____

3. A man pushes a piano, but no matter how hard he pushes, it does not move.

   Is work being done?   _____

   Explain: _____

Science Fact

The Industrial Revolution certainly made work easier and more efficient for humans, but it also brought about major changes to society, including pollution and job displacement.

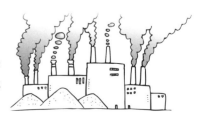

Work, Mechanical Advantage, and Efficiency

- Work, mechanical advantage, and efficiency are all elements of simple machines, complex machines, and mechanical systems.

Jason, do you know that the output force increases if we use a longer screwdriver to open the can? It is because we gain a mechanical advantage from it.

A. Fill in the blanks to complete the paragraph. Then use the formula to calculate the amount of work being done in each situation.

Force is a push or pull that is exerted on an object. It is

measured in 1._____ (N). 2._____

is done when a continuous force is applied to an

object and the object moves a certain distance in

3._____ (m) in the direction of the force.

It is measured in 4._____ (J) and can be

calculated using the formula:

Work = Force x Distance

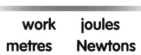

| work | joules |
| metres | Newtons |

See how much work I have done!

distance travelled

5. A car was pushed across a parking lot. Two students applied a force of 800 N for a distance of 40 m. How much work was done?

6. 4 kJ of work was done when a box was pushed along the floor for 10 m. What amount of force was applied?   `1 kJ = 1000 J`

_____

_____

B. Use the formula to determine the mechanical advantage (MA) of each simple machine. Then answer the question.

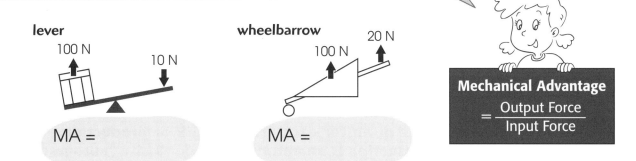

Many machines and mechanical systems are designed to multiply an input force. This multiplied force makes work easier for us. To calculate the mechanical advantage of a machine, simply divide the output force by the input force.

lever

100 N

10 N

MA =

wheelbarrow

100 N

20 N

MA =

Mechanical Advantage

$$= \frac{\text{Output Force}}{\text{Input Force}}$$

Which has greater mechanical advantage? _____

C. Use the formula to determine the efficiency of each simple machine. Then fill in the blank.

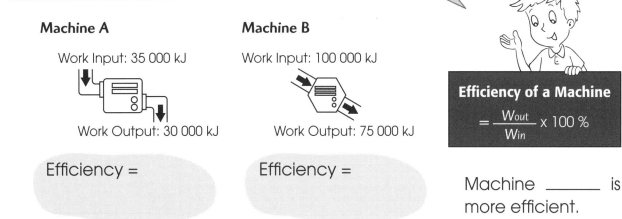

We know how efficient a machine is by comparing its output work to its input work. To calculate efficiency, simply divide the output work (W_{out}) by the input work (W_{in}) and then multiply by 100%. The higher the percent, the higher the efficiency.

Machine A

Work Input: 35 000 kJ

Work Output: 30 000 kJ

Efficiency =

Machine B

Work Input: 100 000 kJ

Work Output: 75 000 kJ

Efficiency =

Efficiency of a Machine

$$= \frac{W_{out}}{W_{in}} \times 100\%$$

Machine _____ is more efficient.

Science Fact

In 1763, James Watt had an idea for improving the incredibly inefficient steam engine of the time. His design made the new steam engine four times as powerful, making it much more efficient.

10

Evolving Systems

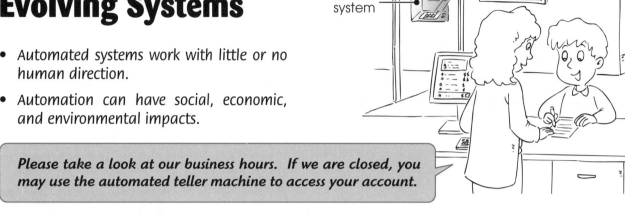

an automated system

- Automated systems work with little or no human direction.
- Automation can have social, economic, and environmental impacts.

Please take a look at our business hours. If we are closed, you may use the automated teller machine to access your account.

A. **Two different tasks are given for each area of work or production. Decide whether or not each situation is an automated task. Write "automated" or "not automated" on the line.**

1. a.   mail delivery   _____

    b.   mail sorting   _____

2. a.   long-distance phone calls   _____

    b.   operator-assisted phone calls   _____

3. a.   garden hose and spray nozzle   _____

    b.   automatic sprinklers   _____

4. a.   automatic weaving machine   _____

    b.   knitting needles   _____

5. a.   b.

_____   _____

B. **Complete the sentences to find out some of the positive and negative impacts of automation on society.**

environment   economic   social

1. One of the _____ impacts of automation is the deterioration of workmanship in goods that are now mass-produced.

2. Positive _____ impacts of automation are increased productivity and reduced costs.

3. A negative _____ and _____ impact of automation is job losses.

4. Automated devices can be sophisticated and powerful, but in industries such as shipping and nuclear power, errors may have a catastrophic impact on the _____ .

C. **Think about an automated system that you use. Write a paragraph to describe the social, economic, or environmental impact it has had since its automation.**

_____

_____

_____

_____

_____

Here are some suggestions.

Movie-theatre-ticket booth
Home heating/air conditioning
Automatic ice-maker

🧪 **Science Fact**

Not long ago, the job of a pinsetter was to set up bowling pins that had been knocked down and to roll the balls back to the bowler. This gruelling job became obsolete with the introduction of the automatic pinsetter in 1946.

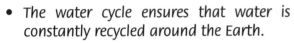

Where on Earth Is Water?

- The water cycle ensures that water is constantly recycled around the Earth.

- Water is present in different states all over the Earth.

- All living things need water, and very little is available to humans.

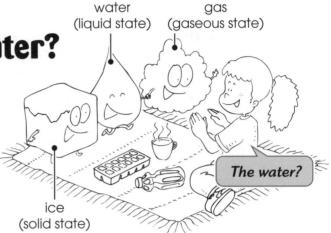

water (liquid state)   gas (gaseous state)

The water?

ice (solid state)

A. **Complete and label diagram with the help of the passage and the given words. Use arrows to show the directions of the movement of water. Then answer the questions.**

Fueled by the sun, water from oceans, lakes, puddles, and even dewdrops on leaves enter the atmosphere through evaporation. There, water exists as a gas. It may condense again on the outside of a cold glass, or around dust particles in the air, forming clouds. From clouds, water may precipitate in the form of snow, hail, or rain, saturating a field and flowing to wherever gravity takes it. No new water is ever formed. All the water that ever was is the same water that exists now, and it is all that we will ever have. This is the water cycle.

1. **Water Cycle**

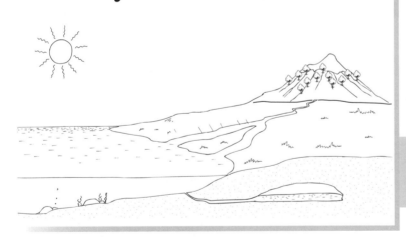

precipitation	condensation
evaporation	groundwater
runoff	transpiration

2. Which three processes describe how the atmosphere transports water from one place to another?

   _____

3. How do plants release evaporated water into the atmosphere?

   _____

B. **Circle the ten hidden words that show where water is distributed on Earth. Label the circle graph with the help from the information points. Then answer the question.**

1.

a	n	p	o	n	d	s		y	w
g	l	o	m	e	c	k	p	g	a
r	c	l	o	u	d	s	T	l	t
o	n	a	c	s	n	t	j	a	e
u	e	r	i	v	e	r	s	c	r
n	a		i	n	t	e	t	i	
d	b	i	x	i	v	w	r	e	v
w	r	c	j	s	o	c	e	r	a
a	c	e	n	t	e	r	a	s	p
t	i		r	h	u		m	a	o
e	o	c	e	a	n	s	s	e	u
r	k	a	b	e	s	i	p	u	r
m	n	p	i	c	w	d	e	w	w
o	c	s		m	h	o	l	e	t

- more than 97% of the water on Earth is salt water
- almost 3% is freshwater (with more than 2% in the polar ice caps or glaciers)

Distribution of Water on Earth

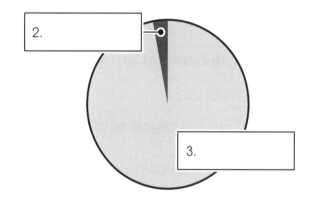

2.

3.

4.

Humans can only use unfrozen, fresh water for drinking. Approximately what percentage of all the water on Earth is available for human use?

_____

C. **Write an example of water on Earth given in part B for each state of matter.**

Solid	Liquid	Gas
_____	_____	_____

Science Fact

Some facts about the distribution of the world's freshwater can be surprising! For instance, there is more water in the atmosphere – in the air – than there is in all of Earth's rivers.

12

What Is a Watershed?

- A watershed is an area of land in which all the water drains into the same body of water.

- Water in a watershed is replenished through precipitation or melted ice from higher ground.

> Look at our watershed model. Don't you think it's great?

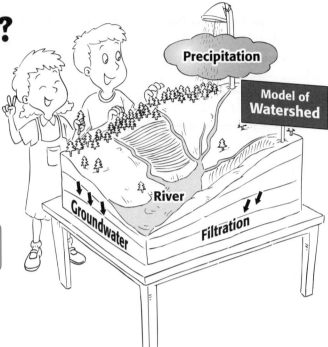

A.   Check the correct answers.

1.   A watershed is

   Ⓐ   a safe place to store water.

   Ⓑ   a geographical area where all the water runs to the same place.

2.   New water in a watershed comes from

   Ⓐ   precipitation or ice/snowmelt.

   Ⓑ   the mountains.

3.   Water in a watershed travels

   Ⓐ   from low land to high land.   Ⓑ   from high land to low land.

4.   The downward travel of water in a watershed is caused by

   Ⓐ   gravity.   Ⓑ   heat.   Ⓒ   water pressure.

5.   Watersheds are separated by

   Ⓐ   areas of lower elevation.

   Ⓑ   areas of higher elevation.

   Ⓒ   bodies of water.

B.   Match each physical component of a watershed with its description.

river   lake   glacier   wetland   precipitation   groundwater aquifer

1. _____
   a large mass of ice formed by the compaction and recrystallization of snow under freezing conditions; it moves slowly down slopes or moves outward due to its own weight

2. _____
   solid or liquid water that falls from clouds to the ground

3. _____
   an underground layer of water-bearing permeable rock; groundwater can usually be extracted using a well

4. _____
   any inland body of standing water, usually freshwater, larger than a pool or a pond

5. _____
   an extensive network across land; a natural drainage channel for surface water

6. _____
   an area with soft and wet land intermingled with surface water; a marsh

   (valuable because it provides a habitat for many plants and animals and for its ability to clean polluted water)

C.   Colour the map to show the major watersheds in Canada that drain into the oceans below.

- **Green:**   Pacific Ocean
- **Blue:**   Atlantic Ocean
- **Yellow:** Arctic Ocean
- **Red:**   Gulf of Mexico
- **Brown:**   Hudson Bay

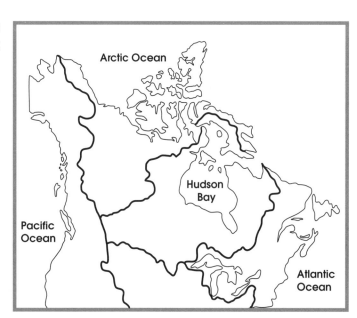

Topography (physical features), soil type, and land use are some of the factors that determine how quickly water reaches its final drainage point – and whether an area is prone to flooding.

13

The Water Table

- Underground water is below the water table when all the spaces among particles of soil and rock are filled with water – in other words, where the earth is saturated.

- The level of the water table increases and decreases due to natural and human-caused events.

Jason, let me show you what "water table" means.

No, it doesn't mean a table with water. A water table is the upper surface of groundwater that is available under the soil.

A. Complete the diagram with the given words. Then follow Wayne's direction.

ground level   water table   saturated zone
bedrock   surface water   unsaturated zone

1.

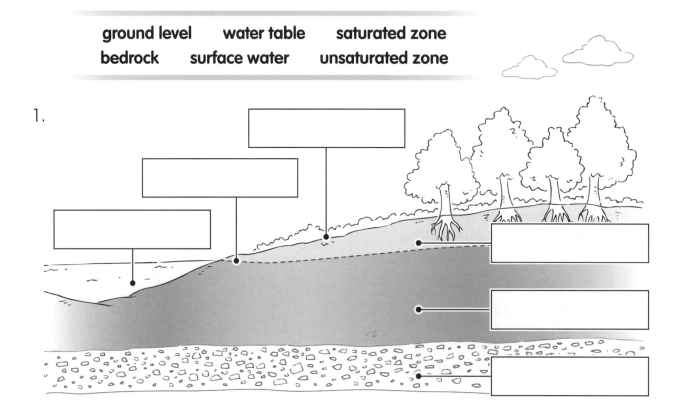

2.

A successful well taps into the groundwater below the water table. Draw a well in the diagram.

B. **Write "true" or "false" for each sentence.**

1. Heavy rainfall or water from melted snow and glaciers can cause the water table to rise. _____

2. A water table can change due to natural causes such as drought. _____

3. Groundwater can enter impermeable rock. _____

4. Once lowered, the water table cannot return to its previous level. _____

5. A rising water table will never reach ground level and cause flooding. _____

6. Underground water is replenished by precipitation and water from melted glaciers and snow packs. _____

7. The soil below the water table has air spaces, as it does above the water table. _____

8. Lawn-watering, inefficient showers and toilets, and the bottled water industry are all human causes of lowered water tables. _____

C. **Write the meaning of each word that is related to groundwater.**

1. saturated: _____

2. impermeable: _____

3. groundwater: _____

4. water table: _____

Science Fact

The Russian city of Saint Petersburg is situated on a river delta with a high water table. This makes for shallow wells, but the underground transportation system had to be built extra deep; it is over 100 m below the Earth's surface.

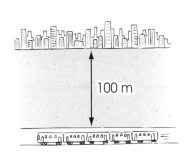

100 m

343

14

Glaciers and Polar Ice Caps

- Precipitation and temperature affect the size of polar ice caps and glaciers.
- All glaciers and ice caps are dynamic, with patterns of movement.
- Melting ice caps and glaciers affect both local and global water systems.

A. Fill in the blanks with the given words to complete the paragraph.

Glaciers and 1._____ do not stay the same size year after year, or even within a year. These enormous stretches of ice respond to fluctuating 2._____ of the seasons, to 3._____ , and to global 4._____ change. Sometimes, when all factors equal out, they may stay 5._____ for a time. But usually they are dynamic, 6._____ and retreating at distances often only noticeable over years.

ice caps
temperatures
advancing
precipitation
stationary
climate

B. Label the two glaciers below as a valley glacier or a continental glacier.

1.

_____

2.

_____

Experiment

Melting glaciers and ice caps affect water systems around the world. Try this experiment to find out how melting ice caps affect sea levels.

Materials:

- a tray of ice cubes
- tape
- two partially filled bowls of water
- a plastic lid small enough to float in bowl

Steps:

1. Put half the ice cubes in the first bowl of water.

2. Put the remaining ice cubes on the plastic "land" that is floating in the second bowl.

3. Mark the top of the water line on each bowl with a piece of tape.

4. Allow the ice cubes to melt.

While you wait, write down what you predict will happen to the water level in each bowl.

Bowl 1 (ice cubes in water): _____

Bowl 2 (ice cubes on "land"): _____

5. Check the water level of each bowl when all ice cubes have completely melted. Write your observation.

Bowl 1 (ice cubes in water): _____

Bowl 2 (ice cubes on "land"): _____

Antarctica is completely covered in an ice sheet that is kilometres thick. The Arctic ice cap, however, is floating on the ocean. Based on your findings in this experiment, which ice cap would have a bigger effect on sea levels when it melts?

_____

Approximately 75% of the Earth's freshwater is in the form of glaciers, with almost all of that in the Antarctic ice cap.

Glacier
Antarctic Ice Cap

15

Water Conservation

- Three of the main uses we have for water are domestic, agricultural, and industrial.

- The water we use comes from a watershed and is returned to a watershed.

- Human activity within a watershed affects our water supply.

Domestic Water Use

drink — wash hands — wash dishes

When washing dishes, never let water run while rinsing. Instead, fill one sink with soapy water and the other with rinsing water. It helps conserve water that way.

A. Read the descriptions of the different ways we use water. Then answer the questions.

Domestic Water Use

We use water for personal hygiene and cleanliness. We drink and cook with it. Water is flushed down our toilets, pressure-sprayed on our driveways, and used to clean our cars. The water we use is groundwater from a well or lake treated and filtered at a water treatment plant. After we use it, water that disappears into the sewage system is treated, while water that flows into storm drains is not treated, before returning to the water system. Water that soaks into the Earth goes through a natural water filtration through soil and rock before reaching the water table.

Agricultural Water Use

The agricultural industry uses the most freshwater because many crops require enormous amounts of water. In dry climates, underground aquifers can be depleted. Conservation efforts are important, and growers are switching to less wasteful irrigation methods. Agriculture can also pollute water systems by leaching pesticides and fertilizers into the water supply.

Industrial Water Use

Industrial demands for freshwater increase with industrialization. Water is used as a solvent, a coolant, and a transport agent. It is also a source of energy in the production of wood and paper products, steel, plastics, and many other items. Toxic waste is an inevitable byproduct of industry. It is difficult to filter out because water is a good solvent. In addition, water used to cool industrial machinery is returned to a water body at a higher temperature, causing thermal pollution.

1. Name two possible ways that we get our water at home. _____

2. Where does water from a bathtub drain go? _____

3. Where does water sprayed on a paved driveway go? _____

4. Name one agricultural use of water. _____

5. Which agricultural pollutants can leach into the water supply? _____

6. List two ways industry uses water. _____

7. Why would it be better to wash a car on grass than on pavement?

    _____

    _____

8. What is one way to conserve water in agriculture?

    _____

9. What kind of pollution results from the disposal of warm water into a cold water body?

    _____

B. List three different ways you use water in a day. Then describe how you conserve water in at least one of your water uses.

    _____

    _____

 Science Fact

Desalinated Water

Desalination, or the removal of salt from salt water to make it freshwater, is one of the ways drier countries deal with water shortages.

16

Fluids and Density

- The particle theory of matter explains how the different states of matter vary in density.

- Liquids and gases are fluids because they flow.

- Mass, volume, and density relate as a property of matter.

Our boxes are the same size, but the cubes in my box are closely packed. The density of my box is higher than that of yours.

A. Unscramble the letters to fill in the blanks. Then label the diagrams with "solid", "liquid", or "gas".

Solids have _____ (rmoe) density than liquids, which have more density than _____ (esgas). The particle theory of matter explains this by showing the particles closely packed, as in a solid, or loosely together, as in a gas.

Solid water is one of the few exceptions to this rule; although ice is a solid, it is less dense than liquid water.

General Density of the Three States of Matter

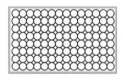   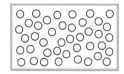   

_____   _____   _____

B. Circle the fluids in the list of matter.

We recognize fluids by the fact that they flow under force and take the shape of the container they fill.

orange juice	calculator	chair	honey
helium	shoe	maple syrup	clock
water vapour	oxygen	marble	air

C. Fill in the blanks to complete the paragraph about density.

mass   decreases   temperature   volume   density   fluid

Density is the amount of matter in a given 1._____ of fluid. Every fluid has a characteristic density that does not change with a change in 2._____ or a change in volume. Indeed, one litre of milk has the same 3._____ as one tablespoon of milk. However, density can vary with 4._____ . With most fluids, density increases when a fluid's temperature 5._____ . In other words, the colder a 6._____ is, the denser it will be.

D. Use the equation to find the density of water at room temperature.

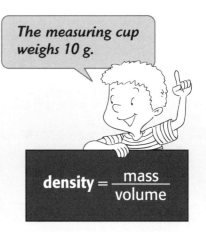

The measuring cup weighs 10 g.

density = mass / volume

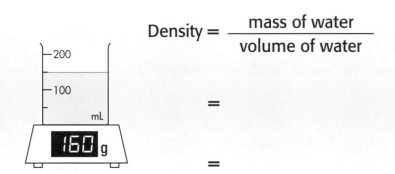

$$\text{Density} = \frac{\text{mass of water}}{\text{volume of water}}$$

=

=

The density of water at room temperature is _____ g/mL.

Science Fact

A hydrometer is an instrument that measures the density of liquids. It specifically measures a liquid's density relative to the density of water. These instruments have a wide range of use, from breweries and dairies to the petroleum industry.

hydrometer

17

Viscosity

- Viscosity is not just a measure of the thickness or thinness of a fluid; it measures a fluid's flow, as well as how other substances move through it.

- Generally, heat reduces a fluid's viscosity while cold increases it.

"Oil" reaches the finish line first. So, "ketchup" has a higher viscosity.

A. Fill in the blanks with the given words and circle the correct words to complete the sentences.

> cohesion   adhesion   fluids   viscosity   temperature   viscous

1. _____ are solids / matter that flow when a force pushes or pulls them.

2. _____ is a measure of a fluid's resistance / reaction to flowing.

3. Generally, the more density / mass a fluid has, the more _____ it is.

4. The viscosity of a fluid usually increases / decreases when its _____ increases.

5. The particles of a fluid have a force of repulsion / attraction called _____ that causes them to move towards each other.

6. _____ is the force between a fluid's particles and the particles of another substance / fluid , such as the fluid's container.

B. Which of the following determine the viscosity of a fluid? Check the correct letters.

Determine the Viscosity of a Fluid

(A) the colour of a fluid   (B) how much space a fluid takes up

(C) the rate of a fluid's flow   (D) the temperature of a fluid

(E) how long it takes for a peanut to sink to the bottom of a fluid

---

Experiment – How the viscosity of a fluid changes with different temperatures

Choose two or more of the following fluids to use in the experiment. You will need two sets of each in small amounts: one to be refrigerated and one to be at room temperature.

Steps:

1. Pour a little more than a teaspoon of liquid into each container. There should be two containers of each liquid.

2. Refrigerate one set of your chosen liquids. Let the other set sit at room temperature.

3. One at a time, pour the room-temperature liquids onto a teaspoon.

4. Record how each liquid flows, numbering them in order of viscosity, from least to greatest.

5. Do the same with the refrigerated liquids.

Materials:

• Fluids: water   maple syrup
          honey   chocolate sauce
          vinegar ketchup

• small containers, (4 for 2 different liquids, 6 for 3 different liquids)

• teaspoons

Record

Fluids	Observation
room temp.	
refrigerated	
room temp.	
refrigerated	

How did each room-temperature liquid compare with the same refrigerated liquid? Write down if there was a change and what the change was.

Science Fact

Viscosity is very important in the production of motor oil. Viscosity modifiers are added to oil so it can flow freely through a vehicle's engine in the cold winter and in the hot summer.

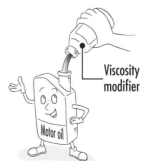

Viscosity modifier

Motor oil

18

Buoyancy

I can float because the gas inside me has a lower density than the air.

- Buoyancy is *a property of fluids.*
- *The force of buoyancy exerted on an object depends on a fluid's density.*

A. Fill in the blanks with the given words to complete the descriptions.

buoyancy	gravity	densities

Helium balloons, toy sailboats, and cruise liners all float. Matter floats as a result of another property of fluids: 1._____ . When the force of 2._____ pushes an object down on a fluid, the fluid pushes back with the force of 3._____ . If the force of buoyancy is greater than gravity's force, the object will float. Objects float differently in different types of fluid because of their different 4._____ . The more density a fluid has, the more buoyancy it can exert on an object. So, buoyancy is created by the difference in density between the fluid and the object that floats on it.

5. *Force of* _____ $>$ *Force of* _____ → **Float**

B. Draw arrows to show the directions of the forces. Then write what the forces are.

1.

2.

C. **Read what Dr. Simmons says. Figure out which glass and pitcher contain "salt water" and "fresh water". Label each container with "salt water" or "fresh water". Then answer the questions.**

An uncooked egg will sink in a glass of fresh water as a result of the low density of the fresh water. If salt is added to fresh water, the result will be different. This is because salt water has a higher density than fresh water. It exerts a stronger force of buoyancy on the egg to keep it afloat.

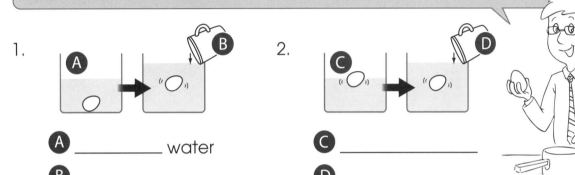

1.

A _____ water

B _____

2.

C _____

D _____

3. For question 1, which liquid has a greater density? How do you know?

_____

_____

4. For question 2, which liquid has a greater density? How do you know?

_____

_____

5. Why does matter float differently in different liquids?

_____

6. Is it possible to have buoyancy without gravity? _____

Science Fact

Any swimmer will notice a difference in buoyancy between a pool of fresh water and an ocean. The Dead Sea has such a high salt concentration and high level of buoyancy force that a swimmer could stop, lay back, and read a book.

Compressed Fluids –
Hydraulics and Pneumatics

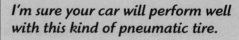

I'm sure your car will perform well with this kind of pneumatic tire.

- Gases and liquids are both fluids, but they are not equally compressible.

- Confined liquids under pressure are the basis of hydraulic systems. Confined air under pressure is the basis of pneumatic systems.

A. **Look at the microscopic view of gas and liquid particles. Draw the particles of gases and liquids when they are confined and put under pressure. Circle the correct words and answer the question.**

1.

Gas Particles

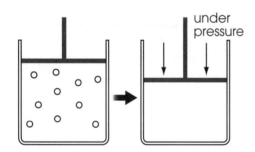

under pressure

Liquid Particles

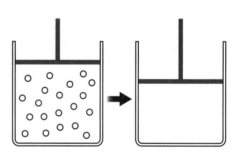

2. Gas particles have   lots of / little   space between them.

3. Liquid particles can move around but have   more / less   space to do it.

4.

How does the particle theory of matter explain why a gas has more compressibility than a liquid?

_____

_____

_____

_____

B. Match each system with its descriptions.

hydraulic system   pneumatic system

When force is applied at one point of a _____ , an even stronger force is transmitted at another point further along in the system. Liquids are used as a source of power, and their force can be multiplied many times.

A _____ , usually using air, operates in a similar manner but with different applications. The compressibility of air makes a pneumatic system less suitable for things that require the force a hydraulic system is capable of.

C. Look at the diagrams of the simple hydraulic systems. Then answer the questions.

Hydraulic Systems

Which hydraulic system would be good for

a. shooting water a long distance?   _____

b. lifting a heavy object?   _____

D. Find an example of one hydraulic system and one pneumatic system in your home, school, or neighbourhood. Describe the work each system does.

Hydraulic System: _____

_____

Pneumatic System: _____

_____

Science Fact

Hydraulic and pneumatic systems were discovered, but not invented, by humans. The movement of blood through our hearts, arteries, and veins is a hydraulic system. Our respiratory system is a very important pneumatic system.

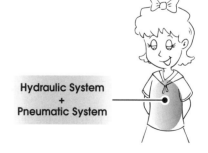
Hydraulic System
+
Pneumatic System

20

Using Fluids

We make use of one of the properties of fluids – force; it helps us to do work. This jackhammer has a pneumatic system which is powered by compressed air.

Work in Progress

- Properties of fluids affect how they are used.
- Human use of fluid mirrors the way fluid is used in nature.
- Fluid technology has social, economic, and environmental impacts.

A. Which property of fluid is important to consider when using each of the following? Fill in the blanks using the words in bold.

1. submarine _____

2. airplane cabin _____

3. streamlined race car

   _____

4. airplane wings in flight

   _____

5. pump for an air mattress

   _____

Properties of Fluids

1. **flow**

2. **pressure**
   - increases with depth
   - is exerted in all directions

3. fluids transmit **force** when confined, causing movement in another part of a system
   - liquids are less compressible than gases, and respond more quickly as a result
   - hydraulic systems use liquids to multiply a force
   - pneumatic systems use gases to multiply a force

B. Match the human-made uses of fluid with the corresponding natural uses of fluid.

(A) Fish can inflate and deflate their bladders to give themselves the amount of buoyancy they need at any time.

(B) Valves in our circulatory system direct the movement of fluid, opening for blood flowing in one direction, and closing in response to pressure from reverse flow.

(C) Scuba divers wear a buoyancy compensator vest, which can take in and release gases, to lower themselves and rise to different depths in the water.

(D) Gases produced from the burning of fuel in the internal combustion engine only move in one direction due to valves that prevent two-way movement.

Human-made use
vs
Natural use

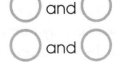

◯ and ◯

◯ and ◯

C. **Read about the impacts of fluid technology on our world. Then answer the questions.**

Technology that is based on the properties of fluid impact our world socially, economically, and environmentally; there are advantages and disadvantages of fluid technology.

Medical hydraulic systems can save many lives, but the costs of tests and treatments mean they are not available to everyone. It is a difficult social dilemma to solve.

Fluid technology is used to make amusement rides run and to allow pilots to train in realistic flight simulators. It increases productivity in backhoes and other heavy machinery. Things are made with less human labour, but this is a disadvantage to the employee who is no longer needed.

Fluid technology has an environmental cost as well. Hydraulic devices can pollute the air. Spills during transport can be harmful to animal and plant habitats as well as our fresh water supply.

While we enjoy the benefits of fluid technology, we must also find better ways to distribute the technology, and use it in a responsible manner.

1. What is one of the social dilemmas regarding fluid technology?

    _____

    _____

2. Give an example of an economic advantage of fluid technology.

    _____

3. Describe how fluid spills harm the environment.

    _____

 **Science Fact**

The fantastic special effects used in the production of your favourite movies likely owe their success to pneumatic or hydraulic systems.

A Trail of Terra!

Review

A. Name the diagrams. Then complete the descriptions.

A Typical Animal Cell

nucleus   genes   chromosomes
cytoplasm   cell membrane

A Typical Plant Cell

nucleus   cell wall   cell membrane
vacuole   cytoplasm   chloroplasts*

*Chloroplasts are members of a class of organelles known as plastids.

1.

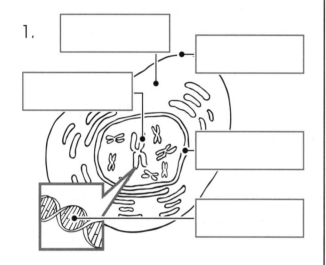

2.

3.

Animal Cell

_____ : the control centre of the cell

_____ : thread-like structures that contain genetic information

_____ : stores information that defines characteristics of the individual

_____ : encloses the cell, but allows some materials to pass in and out

4.

Plant Cell

_____ : contains chlorophyll, which is a green pigment used in photosynthesis

_____ : an organelle found in both plants and algae, which is involved in food production and storage

_____ : a fluid-filled cavity that may contain water, minerals, sugars, and proteins

B. **Complete the flow diagrams to show the process of photosynthesis and respiration.**

| carbon dioxide | oxygen | water | sugar | energy |

Photosynthesis

_____ + water + _____ ➝ _____ + _____

Respiration

_____ + sugar ➝ _____ + _____ + _____

C. **Write the meanings of diffusion and osmosis. Then explain each term with the help of the diagrams.**

1. **Diffusion:** _____

    Explanation:

    _____

    _____

    _____

    _____

    _____

    _____

Movement of Molecules During Diffusion

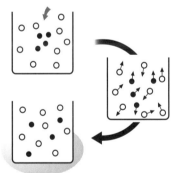

2. **Osmosis:** _____

    Explanation:

    _____

    _____

    _____

    _____

Plant Cell when Exposed to Salt Water

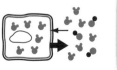 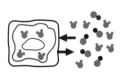

❤ water molecule   🐟 salt molecule

359

D. **Look at the pictures. Identify the various types of systems. Then write the purpose, input, and output of the different systems.**

Types of Systems

mechanical system   water system   optical system
body system   electrical system

1. Wagon: _____ system

   Purpose: _____

   Input: _____

   Output: _____

2. Circulatory system: _____

   Purpose: _____

   Input: _____

   Output: _____

E. **Solve the problems.**

1. A worker pushes a wheelbarrow over a distance of 10 m with a force of 450 N. What is the work done by the worker?

   _____

2. Mr. Karr applies a force of 600 N to pull a box along a road. If 2100 J of work is done, how far is the box moved?

   _____

3. The efficiency of a machine is 75%. If the input work of machine A is 24 kJ, what is the output work?

   _____

F.   Answer the questions with the help of the diagram.

1.   What are the meanings of the words labelled in the diagram?

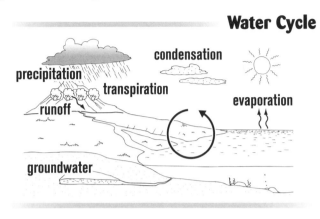

Water Cycle

_____

_____

_____

_____

_____

_____

2.   What is the water cycle?

_____

_____

G.   Complete the diagram by drawing a line to show the water table and by labelling it with the given words. Then answer the questions.

saturated zone
unsaturated zone
water table
bedrock
ground level
surface water

2.   What things can cause the water table to rise? Give two examples.

_____

3.   Where can underground water be found?

_____

H. **Label each glacier as a valley glacier or a continental glacier. Then answer the question.**

1.

A : _____

B : _____

2. What causes the change in size of glaciers and ice caps?

_____

_____

I. **Answer the questions.**

1. What is density?

_____

2. Use diagrams to show the general density of the three states of matter. Then complete the sentences.

a. General Density of the Three States of Matter

Solid   Liquid   Gas

b. _____ have more density than liquids.

c. _____ have less density than liquids.

3. In general, the denser a fluid is, the   more / less   viscous it is.

J.   Check the correct sentences.

1. **Watershed**

    (A) A watershed is a geographical area where all the water runs into the same place.

    (B) Water in a watershed travels from low land to high land.

    (C) Watersheds are separated by areas of high elevation.

    (D) A wetland is a physical component of a watershed.

    (E) New water in a watershed comes from rivers.

2. **Viscosity**

    (A) Viscosity is a measure of a fluid's ability to move.

    (B) The viscosity of a fluid usually decreases when its temperature increases.

    (C) The colour of a fluid determines its viscosity.

    (D) The time that it takes a peanut to sink to the bottom of a fluid can be used to determine the viscosity of a fluid.

    (E) The particles of a fluid have a force of attraction called cohesion, which causes the particles to move towards one another.

3. **Fluids**

    (A) Hydraulic systems use confined liquid under pressure to multiply a force.

    (B) A bicycle pump is an example of a pneumatic system.

    (C) An uncooked egg will float in a glass of fresh water as a result of the low density of the fresh water.

    (D) The more density a fluid has, the more buoyancy it can exert on an object.

    (E) If the force of buoyancy is smaller than gravity's force, the object will float.

ANSWERS

1 Exponents

1. 3 ; 2
2. 4 ; 2
3. 2.5^2 x 8^2
4. 1.7^4 x 5^2
5. 5^2 x 9^3
6. 4.6^2 x 7^3
7. 2^2 x 7.8^4 x 10^3
8. 5^3 x 6.3^3 x 13 x 14^2
9. 3^4 x 4^5 x 5.5^2
10. 27 ; 3 ; 9 ; 3 ; 3 ; 3 ; 3^4
11. 5^3
12. 6^4
13. 3^5
14. 10^4
15. 4^5
16. 2^7
17. 2 ; 16
18. 7 x 7 x 7 ; 343
19. 1.5 x 1.5 x 1.5 ; 3.375
20. $\frac{1}{3}$ x $\frac{1}{3}$ x $\frac{1}{3}$ x $\frac{1}{3}$; $\frac{1}{81}$
21. 8 ; 24
22. 216 ; 9 ; 207
23. 10 + 7.2 = 17.2
24. 3^4 ÷ 1 + 8 = 89
25. 3
26. 2
27. 343
28. 76
29. 0
30. 101
31. 11
32. 980
33. 4 ; 64 ; 8 ; 512
34. 91.125 cm^3
35. 3375 m^3
36. 0.216 m^3
37. 1 ; 8 ; 27 ; 64 ; 125 ;
    0.125 ; 1.728 ; 15.625 ; 39.304 ; 74.088
38. 2 ; 2
39. 2.5 ; 2.5
40. 4 ; 4
41. 1.2 ; 1.2
42. base
43. 5^2
44. 2^3 x 5
45. 2 x 3 x 7
46. 2 x 3^2
47. 2^3 x 3^2
48. 2^3 x 7
49. 2^5 x 3
50. 2^2 x 5^2
51. 2^2 x 3 x 5^2
52. 3 x 5 ; 3^2 x 5 ; 3, 5, 15
53. 2^3 x 3 x 5 ; 2^2 x 3 x 5 x 7 ; 2, 3, 4, 5, 6, 10, 12, 15, 20, 60

2 Square Roots

1. 9
2. 11
3. 19
4. 25
5. 30
6. 1.3
7. 0.5
8. 4 ; 16
9. $10^2 = 100$
10. $(1.5)^2 = 2.25$
11. a
12. itself
13. 9 ; 3
14. $\sqrt{121} = 11$
15. $\sqrt{10\,000} = 100$
16. b
17. itself
18. $\sqrt{16}$; $\sqrt{25}$; $\sqrt{36}$; $\sqrt{81}$; $\sqrt{121}$; $\sqrt{144}$
19-22. (Individual guess-and-check)
19. 3 ; 4 ; 3.6
20. $\sqrt{25}$; $\sqrt{36}$; $\sqrt{25}$ = 5 and $\sqrt{36}$ = 6 ; $\sqrt{28}$ ≈ 5.3
21. $\sqrt{144}$; $\sqrt{169}$; $\sqrt{144}$ = 12 and $\sqrt{169}$ = 13 ; $\sqrt{150}$ ≈ 12.2
22. $\sqrt{81}$; $\sqrt{100}$; $\sqrt{81}$ = 9 and $\sqrt{100}$ = 10 ; $\sqrt{85}$ ≈ 9.2
23. <
24. <
25. >
26. <
27. =
28. >
29. $\sqrt{100}$, 11, 4^2
30. $\sqrt{13^2}$, 14, $\sqrt{255}$, 7^2
31. 5^2, $(\sqrt{26})^2$, $\sqrt{33^2}$

32. $(\sqrt{10})^2$, $\sqrt{11^2}$, 12, $\sqrt{169}$
33. 9 cm^2
    6 cm x 6 cm = 36 cm^2
    3 cm x 9 cm = 27 cm^2
    9 cm x 9 cm = 81 cm^2
34. 32 cm^2
    4 cm x 4 cm ÷ 2 = 8 cm^2
    4 cm x 4 cm = 16 cm^2
    8 cm x 8 cm = 64 cm^2

35.

Square	Side Length	Perimeter
A	4 cm	16 cm
B	8 cm	32 cm
C	16 cm	64 cm

ribbon left: 150 – (16 + 32 + 64) = 38 (cm)
Yes, she will have enough ribbon and 38 cm of ribbon left.

36a.

Field	Side Length	Perimeter
Corn	2.2 km	8.8 km
Carrot	3.2 km	12.8 km

Total fencing: 8.8 + 12.8
         = 21.6 (km)
About 21.6 km of fencing is needed.

b. Side length of wheat field: 21.6 ÷ 4 = 5.4 (km)
The side length is 5.4 km.

c. Side length of Tom's Field:
5.4 x 2 = 10.8 (km)
Area of Tom's field:
10.8 x 10.8 = 116.64 (km^2)
Area of Jack's field:
5.4 x 5.4 = 29.16 (km^2)
No. The area of Tom's field is not two times as that of Jack's.

3 Pythagorean Theorem

1. legs ; hypotenuse ; longest
2.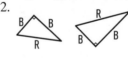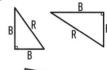
3.
4.

2.8 cm, 5 cm ; 5.7 cm   4.5 cm, 1.6 cm, 4.8 cm

5. B
6. A
7. A
8. 2^2 ; 3^2
9. $h^2 = 4^2 + 5^2$
   $h^2 = 4 + 9$ $h^2 = 16 + 25$
   $h^2 = 13$ $h^2 = 41$
   h = 3.6   h = 6.4
10. $h^2 = 6^2 + 20^2$
    $h^2 = 36 + 400$
    $h^2 = 436$
    h = 20.9
11. $h^2 = 5^2 + 8^2$
    $h^2 = 25 + 64$
    $h^2 = 89$
    h = 9.4

12. $h^2 = 9^2 + 9^2$
$h^2 = 81 + 81$
$h^2 = 162$
$h = 12.7$

13. 8 cm   14. 4.47 cm   15. 4.9 cm
16. 6.63 cm ; 8.31 cm   17. 2.65 cm ; 1.87cm
18.
$5^2 + 12^2$	13^2
$25 + 144$	169
169	169 ✔

It is a right triangle.

19.
$8^2 + 10^2$	13^2
$64 + 100$	169
164	169 ✘

It is not a right triangle.

20.
$5^2 + 7^2$	11^2
$25 + 49$	121
74	121 ✘

It is not a right triangle.

21.
$6^2 + 8^2$	10^2
$36 + 64$	100
100	100 ✔

It is a right triangle.

22. Side length of square: $\sqrt{8^2 - 5^2} = 6.24$ (m)
Area of square: $6.24^2 = 39$ (m²)

23. Length of rectangle: $\sqrt{10^2 - 6^2} = 8$ (m)
Width of rectangle: $\sqrt{5^2 - 3^2} = 4$ (m)
Area of rectangle: 8 x 4 = 32 (m²)

24. Base of triangle: $5 + \sqrt{5.8^2 - 5^2} = 7.94$ (m)
Area of triangle: 7.94 x 5 ÷ 2 = 19.85 (m²)

25. $\sqrt{2.5^2 + 1.2^2} = 2.77$ (m)
The length of the ramp is 2.77 m.

26. Walk along the border: 30 + 20 = 50 (m)
Walk diagonally: $\sqrt{30^2 + 20^2} = 36.06$ (m)
Janet will walk less: 50 – 36.06 = 13.94 (m)
Janet will walk 13.94 m less.

27.
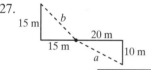
Length of a: $\sqrt{20^2 + 10^2} = 22.36$ (m)
Length of b: $\sqrt{15^2 + 15^2} = 21.21$ (m)
The second slice of cake is closer.

4   Integers

1. 2
2. 3 ;
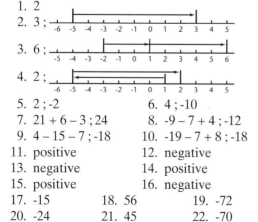
3. 6 ;
4. 2 ;
5. 2 ; -2   6. 4 ; -10
7. 21 + 6 – 3 ; 24   8. -9 – 7 + 4 ; -12
9. 4 – 15 – 7 ; -18   10. -19 – 7 + 8 ; -18
11. positive   12. negative
13. negative   14. positive
15. positive   16. negative
17. -15   18. 56   19. -72
20. -24   21. 45   22. -70

23. 48   24. -64   25. 27
26. -108   27. (-5)   28. (-5)
29. 6   30. (-2)   31. (-4)
32. (-2)
33. positive ; + ; +
negative ; - ; -
34. -4   35. -5   36. 13
37. -27   38. -14   39. 38
40. 2   41. 5   42. 4
43. -4
44. (-32) ; -44
45. (13 x (-5)) ; (-65) ÷ 2 ; -32.5
46. ((-20) ÷ (-4)) ; 5 + (-18) ; -13
47. (-4 + 2) ; (-11) x (-2) ; 22
48. (3^2 – 21) ; (-12) ÷ (-2) ; 6
49. ((-30) ÷ 6) ; (-5) + (-5) ; -10
50. -32 ; 64 ; -128 ; Start with 1. Multiply by -2 each time.
51. -75 ; 149 ; -299 ; Start with 2. Multiply by -2 and subtract 1 each time.
52. -4 ; 2 ; -1 ; Start with 128, divide by -2 each time.
53. -16 ; 5 ; -2 ; Start with -1276. Add 1 and divide by -3 each time.
54. -768, -3072 ; -12 288 ; Start with -3. Multiply by 4 each time.
55a. -42   b. -7
56a. -18°C   b. -18.5°C

5   Order of Operations

1. 8 ; 64 ; 16 ; 64 ; 8 ; 72
2. 5^2 x 8 – 5^2 = 25 x 8 – 25 = 175
3. 52   4. 11   5. 7
6. 0   7. 14   8. 154
9. 9   10. 128
11. 2^2 – 1 = 3   12. $22 – 4^2 = 6$
13. 1.8^3 – 0.2 = 5.632   14. 1.5^2 x 10^2 = 225
15. 1.5^2 x 2^2 = 9   16. 1.331 + 3.3 = 4.631
17. 202   18. 162
19. 2   20. $(-4)^2 = -4$ x -4 = 16
                             $-4^2 = -4$ x 4 = -16
21. $(-2)^3 = -2$ x -2 x -2 = -8
    $-2^3 = -2$ x 2 x 2 = -8
22. 81 ; -81   23. 25 ; -25
24. -1024 ; -1024
25. +   26. -   27. C
28. A   29. B   30. B
31. -125 – 49 x (-216) = -125 + 10 584 = 10 459
32. (-11) x 9 = -99   33. 44 ÷ 4 = 11
34. 36 ÷ 9 = 4   35. 8
36. 2   37. -215
38. 192   39. A ; 39.06 cm²
40. C ; 87   41. B ; 227 cm³

6 Expanded Form and Scientific Notation

1. 20 ; 4 ; 2 x 10 ; 4 x 1 ; 2 ; 4
2. 200 + 50 + 3
   = 2 x 100 + 5 x 10 + 3 x 1
   = 2 x 10^2 + 5 x 10^1 + 3 x 10^0
3. 800 + 90 + 6
   = 8 x 100 + 9 x 10 + 6 x 1
   = 8 x 10^2 + 9 x 10^1 + 6 x 10^0
4. 1000 + 600 + 20 + 5
   = 1 x 1000 + 6 x 100 + 2 x 10 + 5 x 1
   = 1 x 10^3 + 6 x 10^2 + 2 x 10^1 + 5 x 10^0
5. 40 000 + 7000
   = 4 x 10 000 + 7 x 1000
   = 4 x 10^4 + 7 x 10^3
6. 1.75 x 10^8 7. 1.06 x 10^5 8. 4 x 10^4
9. 9.7 x 10^6 10. 1.52 x 10^4 11. 7.06 x 10^4
12. 10 000 ; 4
13. 9.21 x 1000 = 9.21 x 10^3
14. 7.08 x 10 000 = 7.08 x 10^4
15. 3.145 x 10 000 = 3.145 x 10^4
16. 2.5   17. 3 270 000 000
18. 3.145 x 10^7 19. 1 008 000
20. 8.012 x 10^6 21. 63 240 000
22. 1.927   23. 10^{13}
24. 10^9 25. 10^7
26. 10 ; 240
27. 5 x 1000 + 2 x 100 + 8 x 10 = 5280
28. 80 232   29. 302 021
30. 212 070   31. 3.7 x 10^6 ; 3.7 x 10^4
32. 4.107 x 10^6
33. 6.54 x 10^2, 5.46 x 10^3, 4.56 x 10^4
34. 1.09 x 10^7, 9.01 x 10^7, 1.09 x 10^8
35. 2.43 x 10^a, 3.42 x 10^a, 2.34 x 10^{a+2}
36. 4.56 x 10^b, 4.65 x 10^b, 6.54 x 10^b
37. Jupiter, Mars, Earth, Venus, Mercury
38. 5.97 x 10^{25} kg

7 Ratio and Proportion

1. $\frac{1}{2}$; 2:1 ; $\frac{2}{1}$; 1:5 ; $\frac{1}{5}$
2. 1:1 ; $\frac{1}{1}$; 2:3 ; $\frac{2}{3}$; 3:8 ; $\frac{3}{8}$
3. (The pattern will have 4 ▨, 10 ⬚, 7 ▨ and 6 ⊞)
4. $\overset{\times 6}{\frac{2}{p}} = \frac{12}{6}$
   $p = 1$
5. $\frac{8}{3}$ x 9 = $\frac{s}{9}$ x 9
   $s = 24$
6. $\frac{3}{7}$ x 14 = $\frac{q}{14}$ x 14
   $q = 6$
7. $\frac{n}{10}$ x 10 = $\frac{8}{20}$ x 10
   $n = 4$

8. $\overset{\times 6}{\frac{3}{4}} = \underset{\times 6}{\frac{b}{24}}$
   $b = 18$
9a. $\frac{2}{3} = \frac{10}{n}$ b. $\frac{3}{5} = \frac{15}{m}$
   $n = 15$ $m = 25$
10. $\frac{11}{2} = \frac{p}{10}$; $p = 55$; There are 55 balls in the bag.
11. $\frac{3}{1.5} = \frac{x}{3}$ 12. $\frac{8}{16} = \frac{2}{a}$
   $x = 6$ $a = 4$
13. $\frac{9}{16} = \frac{4.5}{r}$ 14. $\frac{3}{5} = \frac{5}{t}$
   $r = 8$ $t = 8\frac{1}{3}$
15. 100 000
16. a. $\frac{1}{100\,000} = \frac{2}{p}$; $p = 200\,000$ (cm) ; 2000 m
    b. $\frac{1}{100\,000} = \frac{6}{q}$; $q = 600\,000$ (cm) ; 6000 m
    c. $\frac{1}{100\,000} = \frac{3.5}{r}$; $r = 350\,000$ (cm) ; 3500 m
17. a. 1:2 400 000   b. 108 km ; 84 km
    c.
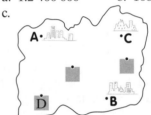
18. No. of heart stickers: $\frac{4}{5} = \frac{320}{n}$; $n = 400$
    No. of stickers in difference: 400 – 320 = 80
    There are 80 more heart stickers.
19. No. of heart stickers: $\frac{2}{7} = \frac{n}{14}$; $n = 4$
    No. of star stickers: $\frac{3}{6} = \frac{m}{4}$; $m = 2$
    There are 2 star stickers on the hat.

8 Rate

1. 68   2. 55   3. 17
4. 1.4   5. 2.25   6. 15
7. A ; 1.84 ; 2/L ; 2.10/L
8. A ; 1.60 ; 2.40/kg ; 2/kg
9. $1.28 x 3 = $3.84 ;
   cost of 3 L = $1.30 x 3 = $3.90 ;
   cost of 3 L = $1.42 x 3 = $4.26 ;
   apple
10. cost of 200 g = $0.02 x 200 = $4 ;
    cost of 200 g = $0.021 x 200 = $4.20 ;
    cost of 200 g = $0.018 x 200 = $3.60 ;
    corned beef

11.

USD ($)	CAD ($)	HKD ($)
1	1.23	7.75
3	3.69	23.25
5	6.15	38.75
7	8.61	54.25
9	11.07	69.75
10	12.30	77.50
20	24.60	155
30	36.90	232.50

12a. 1.23   b. 6.30   c. 0.13

13. $37.03

14. 180 g ; $\frac{3}{4}$ cup ; $4\frac{1}{2}$ bananas ; $\frac{3}{4}$ teaspoon ; $4\frac{1}{2}$ teaspoons

15. $1.97   16. 1 teaspoon

17. 40 servings

18a. $\frac{3}{2} = \frac{n}{6}$

$n = 9$

9 bananas are needed.

b. $\frac{3}{120} = \frac{n}{240}$

$n = 6$

6 bananas are needed.

19a. 2.22 kg   b. $14.40

20a $2.88   b. $2.40

21a. Michelle makes: 57 (cookies)
Jane makes: 60 (cookies)
Total no. of cookies made: 117 (cookies)
They made 117 cookies in 1.5 hours.

b. Michelle makes: 114 (cookies)
Jane makes: 120 (cookies)
The ratio is 114:120 or 19:20.

9   Application of Percent

1. 9 ; $\frac{9}{78}$; $\frac{9}{78}$; 11.54% ; 12%

2. 5 ; $\frac{5}{51}$; $\frac{5}{51}$ x 100% ; 9.8%

3. 18 ; $\frac{18}{160}$; $\frac{18}{160}$ x 100% ; 11.25%

4. **Way 1:**
Discount: $110.50 x 30% = $33.15
Sale Price: $110.50 – $33.15 = $77.35
Way 2:
Discount in Percent: 1 – 30% = 70%
Sale Price: $110.50 x 70% = $77.35

5. **Way 1:**
Discount: $59.24 x 30% = $17.77
Sale Price: $59.24 – $17.77 = $41.47
Way 2:
Discount in Percent: 1 – 30% = 70%
Sale Price: $59.24 x 70% = $41.47

6. **Way 1:**
Discount: $82.88 x 30% = $24.86
Sale Price: $82.88 – $24.86 = $58.02
Way 2:
Discount in Percent: 1 – 30% = 70%
Sale Price: $82.88 x 70% = $58.02

7. Discount in Percent: 1 – 10% = 90%
Sale Price: ($77.35 + $41.47 + $58.02) x 90% = $159.16 ; $159.16

8. Robot:
PST: $59.50 ; $4.76
GST: $59.50 ; $2.98
Total Cost: $59.50 + $4.76 + $2.98 = $67.24
Remote Car:
PST: $98.70 x 8% = $7.90
GST: $98.70 x 5% = $4.94
Total Cost: $98.70 + $7.90 + $4.94 = $111.54
Riding horse:
PST: $110.54 x 8% = $8.84
GST: $110.54 x 5% = $5.53
Total Cost: $110.54 + $8.84 + $5.53 = $124.91

9. Stove Top: $1139 ; $91.12 ; $56.95 ; $1287.07
Oven: $1513 ; $121.04 ; $75.65 ; $1709.69
Bike: $142.03 ; $11.36 ; $7.10 ; $160.49

10. The total cost of the oven is $1718.73. So, this is not a better buy.

11. $2500 ; 9% ; 5 ; $1125

12. $39 000 x 5% x 3 ; $5850

13. $19.80   14. $7\frac{1}{2}$ 15. 2%

16. $522 = $5800 x r x $2\frac{1}{2}$; $r = 3.6\%$

The interest rate is 3.6%.

17. $19 385 x 5.5% x $\frac{9}{12}$ = $799.63

He will pay back an interest of $799.63 after 9 months.

10   Fractions

1. $\frac{21}{56}$; $\frac{16}{56}$; $\frac{5}{56}$ 2. $\frac{7}{12} + \frac{2}{12}$; $\frac{3}{4}$

3. $2\frac{9}{21} + \frac{16}{21}$; $3\frac{4}{21}$ 4. $1\frac{4}{12} - \frac{1}{12}$; $1\frac{1}{4}$

5. $3\frac{8}{30} + 1\frac{7}{30}$; $4\frac{1}{2}$ 6. $1\frac{3}{4} + 1\frac{2}{4}$; $3\frac{1}{4}$

7. $8\frac{1}{6}$; $3\frac{1}{6}$ 8. $13\frac{7}{9}$; $6\frac{2}{9}$

9. $4\frac{5}{6}$; $2\frac{17}{30}$ 10. $2\frac{5}{8}$; $\frac{1}{8}$

11. $\frac{2}{21}$ 12. $\frac{5}{22}$ x $\frac{11}{4}$ = $\frac{5}{8}$

13. $\frac{19}{12}$ x $\frac{2}{5}$ = $\frac{19}{30}$ 14. $2\frac{1}{2}$

15. $3\frac{3}{16}$ 16. $2\frac{6}{13}$ 17. $17\frac{3}{5}$

18. $1\frac{3}{4} \times \frac{1}{3} = \frac{7}{4} \times \frac{1}{3} = \frac{7}{12}$

He has travelled $\frac{7}{12}$ km.

19. $3\frac{3}{4} \times \frac{1}{3} = \frac{15}{4} \times \frac{1}{3} = 1\frac{1}{4}$

$1\frac{1}{4}$ kg of flour is needed to make the cake.

20. $\frac{19}{14}$ 21. $\frac{5}{6}$ 22. $\frac{7}{9}$

23. $\frac{11}{50}$ 24. 3 25. $\frac{1}{5}$

26. 16 27. $\frac{8}{13}$ 28. $\frac{1}{33}$

29. 1 30. $5\frac{1}{2}$ 31. $\frac{5}{28}$

32. $8\frac{3}{4} \div 1\frac{1}{4} = \frac{35}{4} \times \frac{4}{5} = 7$

He needs 7 bags.

33. $1\frac{1}{4} \div 5 = \frac{5}{4} \times \frac{1}{5} = \frac{1}{4}$

Each apple weighs $\frac{1}{4}$ kg on average.

34. $(\frac{4}{14} + \frac{5}{14}) \times \frac{8}{15}$ 35. $\frac{10}{3} \times \frac{3}{8} - \frac{6}{7}$

$= \frac{9}{14} \times \frac{8}{15}$ $= \frac{5}{4} - \frac{6}{7}$

$= \frac{12}{35}$ $= \frac{11}{28}$

36. $\frac{11}{8} - \frac{2}{5}$ 37. $\frac{5}{6}$

$= \frac{55}{40} - \frac{16}{40}$

$= \frac{39}{40}$

38. $1\frac{1}{5}$ 39. $\frac{5}{13}$ 40. $\frac{11}{14}$

41. $(3 - \frac{1}{2}) \div \frac{1}{6} = \frac{5}{2} \times 6 = 15$

There are 15 guests.

42. $3\frac{2}{3} \times 4\frac{1}{2} = \frac{11}{3} \times \frac{9}{2} = 16\frac{1}{2}$

She has $16\frac{1}{2}$ L of juice.

43. $16\frac{1}{2} \div \frac{3}{8} = \frac{33}{2} \times \frac{8}{3} = 44$

The jars can fill 44 cups.

11 Decimals, Fractions, and Percents

1. $0.\overline{9}9999... = 0.\overline{9}$
2. $1.\overline{13}1313 1... = 1.\overline{13}$
3. $1.\overline{024}02402... = 1.\overline{024}$
4. $5.0\overline{81}81818... = 5.0\overline{81}$
5. $3.1\overline{234}2342... = 3.1\overline{234}$
6. $2.78\overline{132}1321... = 2.78\overline{132}$
7. $1.17\overline{184}18418... = 1.17\overline{184}$
8. $4.0\overline{53}3053053... = 4.0\overline{53}$
9. 0.6 ; T   10. $0.\overline{2}$; R   11. $0.0\overline{675}$; R
12. 2.875 ; T   13. $0.58\overline{3}$; R   14. 1.48 ; T

15. $3.\overline{72}$; R   16. $4.8\overline{3}$; R   17. $\frac{1}{6}$; $0.1\overline{6}$
18. $\frac{5}{9}$; 55.56% 19. $0.\overline{6}$; 66.67%
20. $\frac{2}{15}$; $0.1\overline{3}$; 13.33% 21. $\frac{6}{11}$; $0.\overline{54}$; 54.55%
22. $\frac{7}{11}$; $0.\overline{63}$; 63.64%

23. $=$ 24. $<$ 25. $<$
26. $>$ 27. $<$ 28. $>$
29. $>$ 30. $=$ 31. $<$
32. $2.00\overline{6}, 2.00\overline{6}, 206\%, 2.0\overline{6}$
33. $1.0\overline{6}, 1.16, 1\frac{1}{6}, 1\frac{6}{9}$
34. $\frac{33}{90}, 63.3\%, 0.6\overline{3}, \frac{7}{11}$
35. $1.20\overline{7}, 1.\overline{207}, 1.20\overline{7}$
36. 2.81 37. 8070 38. 50.6
39. 1130 40. 140 41. 4
42. 40 43. 4 44. 0.3
45. 90 46. 0.01 47. 2.023
48. 1.08 49. 0.05 50. 0.4
51. 7.2 52. 0.5 53. 0.5
54. 1.2 55. 0.15

56.

0.25	0.025
45	4.5
3.4	0.34

57.

1.4	140
0.279	27.9
0.26	26

58.

0.7	7
1.86	18.6
0.029	0.29

59.

0.18	0.9
0.8	4
1.56	7.8

60.

0.15	3
0.5	10
1.2	24

61.

0.9	300
0.18	60
1.8	600

62. $1.78 \times (1 - 35\%) = 1.78 \times 0.65 = 1.16$
There are 1.16 kg of ground beef.

63a. $0.65 + \frac{7}{12} \times 0.98 = 0.65 + 0.57 = 1.22$
He will get 1.22 L of soup base.

b. $(0.98 - 0.57) \times (1 - 45\%) = 0.41 \times 0.55 = 0.23$
0.23 L of beef stock is left.

12 Nets

1. top ; side ; front   2. front ; side ; top
3. side ; top ; front   4. C ; B ; E
5. cross out the front view ;
6. cross out the side view ;
7. cross out the front view ;
8. cross out the top view ;
9.   10.   11.

12.

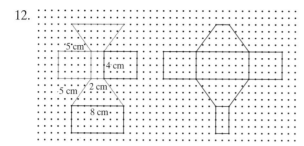

The net is formed by 2 identical trapezoids, 2 identical rectangles, 1 large rectangle, and 1 small rectangle.

13.

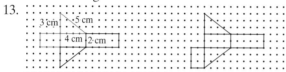

The net is formed by 2 identical right triangles, and 3 rectangles in different sizes.

14. B ;   15. A ;

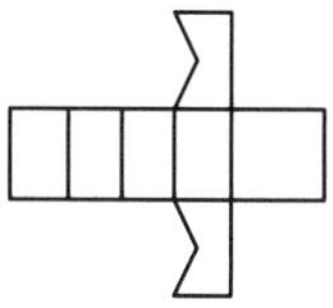

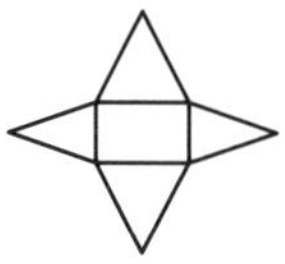

16a.

Solid	Rectangular Prism	Triangular Pyramid	Pentagonal Pyramid
No. of Vertices (V)	8	4	6
No. of Faces (F)	6	4	6
No. of Edges (E)	12	6	10
V + F − E	2	2	2

b. 2

17. The solid has 12 edges. It is a hexagonal pyramid.

13 Circumference and Area

1. radius   2. diameter
3. circumference   4. diameter
5.

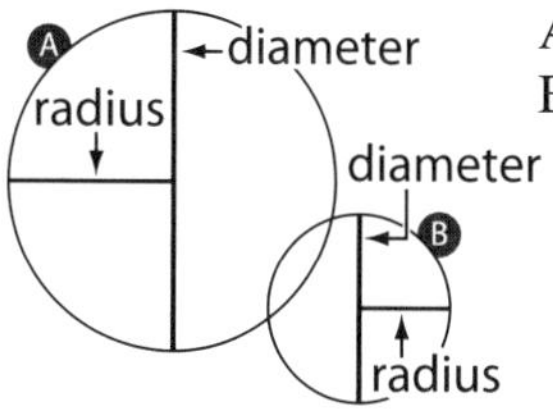

[diagram showing circle A with diameter and radius labels, and circle B with diameter and radius labels]

A: 2.7 cm ; 5.4 cm
B: 2 cm ; 4 cm

6. The length of diameter is two times the length of radius.

7. π ; 3 ; 9.42 (cm)   8. 2 x π x 10 ; 62.83 (m)
9. 2 x π x 0.5 ; 3.14 (cm)
10. π x 0.68 ; 2.14 (m)
11. π x 7 ; 22 (cm)   12. 2 x π x 1 ; 6.28 (m)
13. 7.32 cm   14. 4 cm

15. 16.12 cm   16. 5 cm
17. π x 1^2 = 3.14 (cm^2)
18. π x 3.9^2 = 47.78 (cm^2)
19. π x 20^2 = 1256.64 (cm^2)
20. A: 153.94 cm^2 ; B: 63.62 cm^2 ; C: 50.27 cm^2
21. area: 153.94 + 63.62 + 50.27 = 267.83 (cm^2)
    radius: $\sqrt{267.82 \div \pi}$ = 9.23 (cm)
    The radius of the big circle is 9.23 cm.
22. $\sqrt{267.83 \div 3 \div \pi}$ = 5.33 (cm)
    The radius of each circle is 5.33 cm.
23.

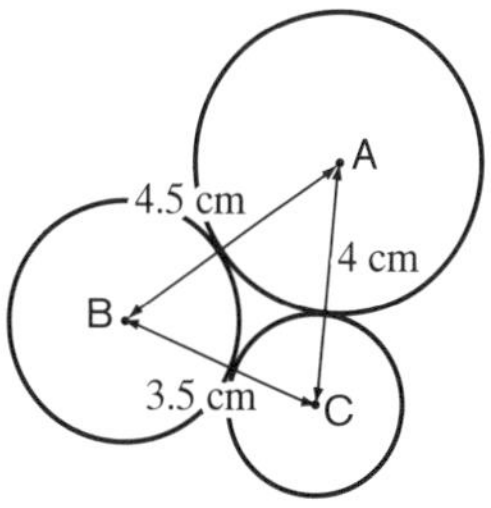

[diagram showing three circles A, B, C with measurements 4.5 cm, 4 cm, 3.5 cm connecting them]

24. The length of $\overline{AB}$ is the sum of the radius of circles A and B which is 4.5 cm. Use the same way to find the lengths of $\overline{BC}$ and $\overline{AC}$. The lengths of $\overline{BC}$ and $\overline{AC}$ are 3.5 cm and 4 cm respectively.
25. area: π x $(\frac{20}{2})^2$ = 314.16 (cm^2)
    The area of the spinner is 314.16 cm^2.
26. circumference: 20π = 62.83 (cm)
    62.83 cm of ribbon will be needed.

14 Surface Area and Volume

1. πr^2 ; h   2. $\pi 5^2$ x 4 = 314.16
3. $\pi 3.5^2$ x 6 = 230.91   4. $\pi 9.2^2$ x 5.5 = 1462.47
5. A: V = 1017.88 cm^3 B: V = 1628.6 cm^3
   C: V = 603.19 cm^3 D: V = 14.53 cm^3
6. A: 4.02 L   B: 2.62 L   C: 1.36 L
7. 1.85 L   8. 0.68 L   9. 12 cups
10. 8.19 cm   11. 17.41 cm
12.

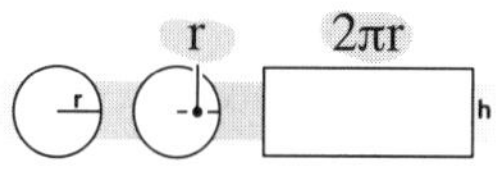

[diagram showing a circle with r, and 2πr rectangle with h, labels ; r ; 2πr]

13. $2\pi 8^2$ + 2π8 x 25 = 1658.76 (cm^2)
14. surface area: $2\pi 7^2$ + 14π x 9 = 703.72 (cm^2)
15. surface area: $2\pi 7.5^2$ + 15π x 24 = 1484.4 (cm^2)
16. surface area: $2\pi 4^2$ + 8π x 4.5 = 213.63 (cm^2)
17. h = 9 cm   18. h = 11 cm
19. h = 34.98 cm   20. r = 9 cm ; h = 12.5 cm
21. The volume of the cylinder is 0.24 m^3.
22. The surface area of the cylinder is 2.28 m^2. So, he needs 9 cans of paint.
23. The surface area of each small cylinder will be 1.02 m^2.

Review 1

1. 2 x 2 x 3 ; 2 x 3 x 3 x 5 ; 2, 3, 6
2. 40 = 2 x 2 x 2 x 5 ; 60 = 2 x 2 x 3 x 5 ; 2, 4, 5, 10, 20
3. 30 = 2 x 3 x 5 ; 84 = 2 x 2 x 3 x 7 ;
   126 = 2 x 3 x 3 x 7 ; 2, 3, 6
4. 75 = 3 x 5 x 5 ; 245 = 5 x 7 x 7 ;
   315 = 3 x 3 x 5 x 7 ; 5
5. 3 ; 4 ; 3.7
6. between $\sqrt{64}$ and $\sqrt{81}$; $\sqrt{64}$ = 8 ; $\sqrt{81}$ = 9
   So, $\sqrt{79} \approx 8.9$.
7. between $\sqrt{36}$ and $\sqrt{49}$; $\sqrt{36}$ = 6 ; $\sqrt{49}$ = 7
   So, $\sqrt{38} \approx 6.2$.
8. between $\sqrt{100}$ and $\sqrt{121}$; $\sqrt{100}$ = 10 ; $\sqrt{121}$ = 11
   So, $\sqrt{105} \approx 10.2$.
9. 9.6 cm
10. 43.8 cm
11. 9.85
12. 16.58
13. 7.62
14. 7.62
15. 14.14
16. 13.42
17. 33 – 21 = 12
18. 14 x 10 – 81 = 59
19. -27 + 49 + 16 = 38
20. (-13) x (-5) = 65
21. 9
22. 9
23. 1
24. 0.1
25. 17
26. 16
27a. 2 ; 1
   b. $4 \times 10^4 + 6 \times 10^2 + 8 \times 10 + 5$
   c. $3 \times 10^5 + 8 \times 10^3 + 2 \times 10^2 + 5 \times 10$
28a. 7.1×10^4 b. 3.5681×10^4
   c. 4.7×10^5 d. 3×10^4
   e. 4.0206×10^5 f. 3.70309×10^5
29a. $\frac{3}{8} = \frac{j}{240}$; j = 90 ; Jennifer got 90 candies.
   b. $\frac{5}{8} = \frac{e}{240}$; e = 150 ; Elsa got 150 candies.
   c. $\frac{2}{3} = \frac{r}{90}$; r = 60 ; Elsa got 60 red candies.
30. Steak:
   A: 4.50   B: $4.85/kg
   C: $4.20/kg ; C
   Chicken Wings:
   A: $0.92/wing   B: $0.96/wing
   C: $1.03/wing ; A
31. (16.42 – 6.30) ÷ 0.92 = 11
   Mrs. Collins bought 11 chicken wings in total.
32. Toaster: 60.18 ; $60.18
   Blenders: 38.10 ; $76.20
   Sub-Total: $136.38
   PST: $10.91
   GST: $6.82
   Total: $154.11
33. $49.56 x (1 – 25%) x (1 – 30%) x 1.13 = $29.40
   James pays $29.40 for an iron.
34. $2\frac{13}{18}$
35. $4\frac{1}{20}$
36. $\frac{2}{3}$
37. $\frac{2}{9}$
38. 2
39. $4\frac{2}{7}$

40. $\frac{1}{24}$
41. $2\frac{1}{4}$
42. $\frac{4}{5}$
43. $1\frac{1}{6}$
44. $\frac{7}{24}$
45. 4
46. A: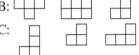
   B:
   C:
47. hexagonal prism   48. triangular prism
49. triangular pyramid
50.

circle A: 50.27 cm^2 ; 25.13 cm
circle B: 28.27 cm^2 ; 18.85 cm
circle C: 12.57 cm^2 ; 12.57 cm
51. 1696.46 cm^3 ; 791.68 cm^2
52. 3 cm ; 263.89 cm^2
53. 7 cm ; 22 cm^3
54. The volume of the largest cylinder is 311.02 cm^3
   and she will have 150.98 cm^3 of clay left.

15 Volume and Surface Area of Solids (1)

1. volume = 360 cm^3 ; surface area = 336 cm^2
2. volume = 35 cm^3 ; surface area = 76.2 cm^2
3. volume = 156 cm^3 ; surface area = 180.8 cm^2
4. volume = 600 cm^3 ; surface area = 486 cm^2
5. volume = 505 cm^3 ; surface area = 452 cm^2
6. volume = 453 m^3 ; surface area = 436.5 m^2
7. volume = 189 cm^3 ; surface area = 270 cm^2
8.

	A	B	C
V.	176 cm^3	176 cm^3	176 cm^3
S.A.	256 cm^2	240 cm^2	256 cm^2

9. the same   10. different
11. 512 cm^3 12. 152 cm^2
13. 8 blocks
14a. The total surface area to be painted is 2008 cm^2.
   b. The volume will be 5568 cm^3.
15. The total surface area is 250 cm^2.
16a. The volume of each piece of cake is 450 cm^3.
   b. The total surface area of each piece is 447.56 cm^2.
   So, she needs 5 bags of icing.

16 Volume and Surface Area of Solids (2)

1. volume = 1306.9 cm^3 ; surface area = 735.79 cm^2
2. volume = 1428 cm^3 ; surface area = 749.7 cm^2
3. volume = 1979.2 cm^3 ; surface area = 1602.2 cm^2
4. volume of cylinder: 785.4 cm^3
   surface area of cylinder: 471.24 cm^2
   volume of cube: 1000 cm^3
   surface area of cube: 600 cm^2
   The cube has a greater volume and surface area.
5. The greatest volume of cylinder is 2199.11 cm^3.
   So, 1720.89 cm^3 of clay is left.
6a. $(6 \times 6 \times \pi \times 20) \div (12 \times 12) = 15.71$
   The height is 15.71 cm.
  b. The total surface area to be painted is 2022.26 cm^2.
7. cylinder A: $\pi(3^2)(5) = 141.37$ (cm^3)
   cylinder B:

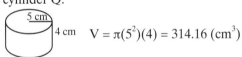

   $V = \pi(6^2)(5) = 565.49$ (cm^3)

   cylinder C:

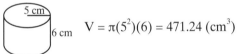

   $V = \pi(9^2)(5) = 1272.35$ (cm^3)
8. 4   9. 9
10. 1800 cm^3 ; 4050 cm^3
11. cylinder P:
    $\pi(5^2)(2) = 157.08$ (cm^3)
    cylinder Q:

    $V = \pi(5^2)(4) = 314.16$ (cm^3)

    cylinder R:

    $V = \pi(5^2)(6) = 471.24$ (cm^3)
12. 2   13. 3
14. The volume of the container is 2700 cm^3.

17 Angle Properties of Intersecting Lines

1. 180° ; supplementary
2. the same ; opposite
3. 90° ; complementary
4. 180° ; supplementary
5a. complementary   b. supplementary
  c. opposite   d. supplemenary
6a. supplementary   b. complementary
  c. opposite   d. opposite

7. Complementary Angles:
   ∠b ; ∠k ; ∠m
   Supplementary Angles:
   ∠d ; ∠j ; ∠g
   Opposite Angles:
   ∠e ; ∠l ;
   ∠i ; ∠j
8. complementary ; 90° ; 90° ; 55°
9. opposite ; 62°
10. supplementary ; 180° ; 180° ; 134°
11. ∠FOH = ∠AOB (opposite angles)
    ∠FOH = 35°
12. ∠HOI + ∠BOI= 180° (supplementary angles)
    ∠HOI = 180° – 62° – 35°
    ∠HOI = 83°
13. ∠DOF = ∠AOI (opposite angles)
    ∠DOF = 62°
14. ∠COD + ∠DOF = 90° (complementary angles)
    ∠COD = 90° – 62°
    ∠COD = 28°
15.   16.
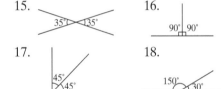
17.   18.
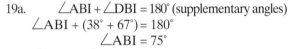
19a.   ∠ABI + ∠DBI = 180° (supplementary angles)
    ∠ABI + (38° + 67°) = 180°
                    ∠ABI = 75°
  b. ∠BCD = ∠ICF (opposite angles)
    ∠BCD = ∠ICF = 39° + 37° = 76°
  c.   ∠GEF + ∠DEG = 90° (complementary angles)
    ∠GEF + (90° – 38°)= 90°
              ∠GEF = 38°

18 Angle Properties in Parallel Lines

1. Corresponding
2. Interior
3. Alternate

4. corresponding ; alternate ; interior
5. corresponding ; alternate ; interior
6. alternate angles: ∠e ; ∠h ; ∠f and ∠g
   corresponding angles: ∠c ; ∠d ; ∠e and ∠g
   interior angles: ∠e ; ∠c ; ∠d and ∠h

7. alternate angles: $\angle$s ; $\angle$y ; $\angle$p and $\angle$y
   corresponding angles: $\angle$w ; $\angle$x ; $\angle$s and $\angle$y
   interior angles: $\angle$r ; $\angle$x ; $\angle$p and $\angle$t
8. $\angle$a = 70° ; $\angle$b = 110° ; $\angle$c = 110° ; $\angle$d = 70°
9. $\angle$e = 76° ; $\angle$f = 104° ; $\angle$g = 104° ; $\angle$h = 104°
10. $\angle$i = 100° ; $\angle$j = 80°
11. $\angle$m = 130° ; $\angle$n = 50°
12. corresponding ;
    alternate ; $\angle$a = 132° ;
    180° ; supplementary ; $\angle$c = 48° ;
    alternate ; corresponding ;
    180° ; supplementary ; $\angle$f = 40°
13. $\angle$a = 86° (corresponding angles)
    $\angle$b = 86 °(alternate angles)
    $\angle$e = 180° – 128° = 52° (interior angles)
    $\angle$f = 128° (corresponding angles)
    $\angle$d = 180° – 128° (supplementary angles)
    $\angle$d = 52°
    $\angle$c + $\angle$b + $\angle$e = 180° (sum of angles in a $\triangle$)
        $\angle$c = 42°
14. $\angle$a + 35° = 90° (complementary angles)
        $\angle$a = 55°
    $\angle$c = 180° – 55° = 125° (interior angles)
    $\angle$d = 125° (corresponding angles)
    $\angle$b = 125° (corresponding angles)
    $\angle$e = 125° (alternate angles)
15. B ; corresponding
16. A ; supplementary
17. B ; interior
18. A ; interior
19.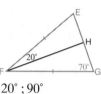
    Let x be the measure of the small angle.
    $x + x + 10°= 180°$
        $x = 85°$
    So, the measure of the angles are 85° and 95°
    (85° + 10°).

19 Angle Properties in a Triangle

1. $\angle$a = 48° ; $\angle$b = 72° ; $\angle$c = 60° ;
   $\angle$d = 27° ; $\angle$e = 32° ; $\angle$f = 42°
2. A   3. B
4. B   5. A
6. $\angle$a + 62° + 45° = 180° (sum of angles in a $\triangle$)
        $\angle$a = 73°
   $\angle$b + 45° = 180° (supplementary angles)
        $\angle$b = 135°
7. $\angle$x + 68° + 68°= 180° (sum of angles in a $\triangle$)
        $\angle$x = 44°
   $\angle$y + 44° = 180° (supplementary angles)
        $\angle$y = 136°

8. $\angle$m + 120° = 180° (supplementary angles)
        $\angle$m = 60°
   $\angle$n + 60° + 90°= 180° (sum of angles in a $\triangle$)
        $\angle$n = 30°
9. $\angle$p = 32°   10. $\angle$q = 70°   11. $\angle$r = 69°
12. 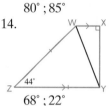 13.
    80° ; 85°   20° ; 90°
14.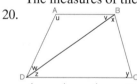
    68° ; 22°
15.   16.

    109°   40°
17. vertex angle: 360° ÷ 5 = 72°
    base angle: (180° – 72°) ÷ 2 = 54°
    The measures of the angles are 72°, 54°, and 54°.
18. x + 3x + 6x = 180
            x = 18
    Since 1:3:6 = 18:54:108, so the measures of the
    angles are 18°, 54°, 108°.
19. y + 4y + 4y = 180°
            y = 20°
    The measures of the angles are 20°, 80°, 80°.
20.
    $\angle$u + $\angle$v + $\angle$w = 180° (sum of angles in a $\triangle$)
    $\angle$x + $\angle$y + $\angle$z = 180° (sum of angles in a $\triangle$)
    Therefore, the sum of the angles in the trapezoid
    is 360° (180° + 180°).

20 Constructing Bisectors

1. midpoint ; right
a.   b.
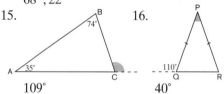

2. vertex ; two

3.

4.

5. 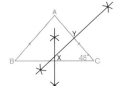 6.

48°   90°

7.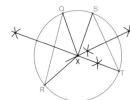

8a. 2 cm   b. 2 cm
 c. 2 cm   d. 2 cm
9. X is the centre of the circle because the distance between X and any one of the points on the circle is the same.

10a.   b. perpendicular
                c. 90°

11. 135° is the sum of 90° and 45°.
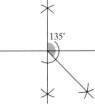

12-13.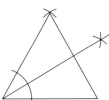

14. equilateral   15. 60°
16. Draw a 90° angle by constructing a perpendicular bisector. Then construct an equilateral triangle on the perpendicular bisector.
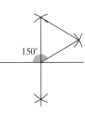

17.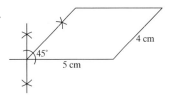

21 Transformations (1)

1. A, E, M ;
   D, F ;
   C, I, J, P ;
   B, G, K, L
2. H, N
3. A and G ; F and J ; D and I ; K and L ; H and P
4. D and M ; B and C ; P and N ; I, J, and L
5. H   6. N   7. E, P
8. A(4,2) ; B(2,-2) ; C(-3,-2) ; D(-5,4) ; E(1,1) ;
   F(-2,3) ; G(4,-5) ; H(-4,0) ; I(-5,-6) ; J(-2,-6) ;
   K(6,-3) ; L(6,-6) ; M(3,4) ; N(0,-4) ; P(-4,-4)

9-10.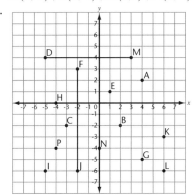

9a. horizontal
 b. (Suggested answers)
    (-5,4), (-4,4), and (-3,4)
 c. They have the same y-coordinates.
10a. vertical
  b. (Suggested answers)
     (-2,3), (-2,2), and (-2,1)
  c. They have the same x-coordinates.
11. a horizontal line
12.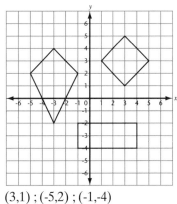

(3,1) ; (-5,2) ; (-1,-4)

375

13.

	Area (square units)	Perimeter (units)
Square	8	11.31
Kite	12	14.6
Rectangle	10	14

14. triangle: E
    trapezoid: P, T
    L-shape: U, W
15. A   16. B
17. -2,5 ; -2,3 ; -5,3
18. 4,-3 ; 3,-5 ; 2,-3

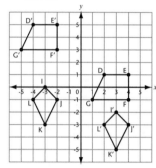

19. Translate 6 units left and 4 units up.
20. Translate 6 units right and 2 units down.

22 Transformations (2)

1.

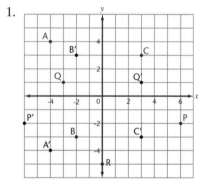

A′(-4,-4) ; B (-2,-3) ; B′(-2,3) ; C(3,3) ; C′(3,-3)
P(6,-2) ; P′(-6,-2) ; Q(-3,1) ; Q′(3,1) ; R(0,-5) ;
R′(0,-5)

2a. stays the same   b. changes in sign
3a. changes in sign   b. stays the same
4-5.

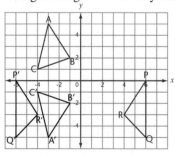

4. A(-3,5), B(-1,2), C(-4,1)
   A′(-3,-5), B′(-1,-2), C′(-4,-1)

5. P(6,0), Q(6,-5), R(4,-3)
   P′(-6,0), Q′(-6,-5), R′(-4,-3)
6. (-15,3), (-18,3), (-18,-1), (-13,-1)
7.

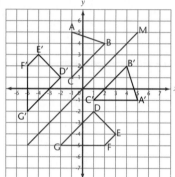

a. A(-1,5) ; A′(5,-1)   B(2,4) ; B′(4,2)
   C(-1,1) ; C′(1,-1)
b. D(1,-2) ; D′(-2,1)   E(3,-4) ; E′(-4,3)
   F(2,-5) ; F′(-5,2)   G(-2,-5) ; G′(-5,-2)
8. The coordinates of each point are interchanged.
9a-d.

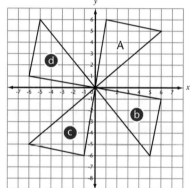

b. (6,-1), (5,-6), (0,0)   c. (-1,-6), (-6,-5), (0,0)
d. (-6,1), (-5,6), (0,0)
10. 90° ; 180° ; 270° clockwise
11a. (2,3), (6,0), (8,7)   b. (-2,-3), (-6,0), (-8,-7)
   c. (-3,2), (0,6), (-7,8)
12-14.

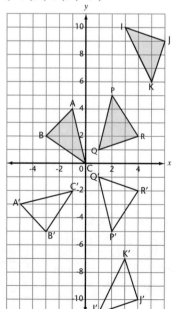

12. I′(1,-11), J′(4,-10), K′(3,-7)
13. P′(2,-5), Q′(1,-1), R′(4,-2)
14. A′(-5,-3), B′(-3,-5), C′(-1,-2)
15a. (-1,4), (2,1), (6,1)
 b. (1,4), (-2,1), (-6,1)
16a. (4,-5), (7,-5), (5,0), (2,0)
 b. (-5,4), (-5,7), (0,5), (0,2)

23 Number Patterns

1. 3 ; 3
 3 x 3 = 9
 3 x 4 = 12
 3 ; 1
2a. 31   b. 43
 c. 79   d. 106
3a. $4n - 1$ b. 39 ; 63
                 99 ; 119
4a. $3n - 2$ b. 25 ; 49
                 58 ; 97
5a. 4 ; 10 ; 16 ; 22 ; 28
 b. $6n - 2$
 c. 46 ; 88 ; 118
 d. figure 9 ; figure 12 ; figure 18
6a. 3 ; 6 ; 9 ; 12 ; 15 ; $3k$; 90
 b.

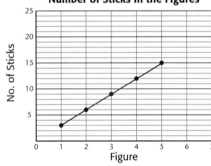

Number of Sticks in the Figures

7a.

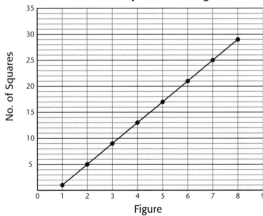

Number of Squares in the Figures

 b. $4n - 3$; 129   c. figure 25

8. $1^2 ; 2^2 ; 3^2 ; 16\,(4^2) ; 25\,(5^2) ; k^2$
9a. 64   b. 121   c. 225
10a. 20   b. 16   c. 19
11a.

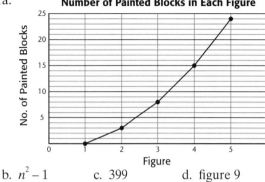

Number of Painted Blocks in Each Figure

 b. $n^2 - 1$ c. 399   d. figure 9

24 Algebraic Expressions

1.

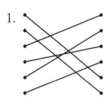

2. $x + y$ 3. xy
4. $4x - y$ 5. $5x + y$
6. $2x + \dfrac{1}{3}y$
7a. $\$2m$ b. $\$0.25n$
 c. $\$(2i + 5j)$ d. $\$(x + 0.01y)$
8. $(\dfrac{c}{2} + 4d)$ coins
9a. $\$8m$ b. $\$3p$
 c. $\$(5m + 3n)$ d. $\$(9m + 3k)$
10. $\dfrac{\$(3m + 3r)}{4}$
11. $(\dfrac{32}{m} + \dfrac{d}{3})$ cones and cups
12. $\$(9m + 3p + 12)$
13a. 34   b. 6
14a. 13   b. 33
15a. 0   b. 3
16. 94   17. 10   18. 10
19. 38   20. 56   21. -2
22. 3   23. 0   24. 2
25. 11   26. 12
27.

x	y	$2(x + y)$	$2x + y$	$2x + 2y$
-2	0	-4	-4	-4
-1	1	0	-1	0
0	2	4	2	4
1	3	8	5	8
2	4	12	8	12

28. $2(x + y), 2x + 2y$
29. A ; 53   30. A ; 28   31. B ; 8

25 Equations

1. $35 ; 9 ; 70 ; 18 ; 88$
2. $= 3 \times 9 + 3 \times 7$
   $= 27 + 21$
   $= 48$
3. $= 4 \times 20 + 4 \times 6 + 4 \times 5$
   $= 80 + 24 + 20$
   $= 124$
4. $= 6 \times 5 + 6 \times 5 + 6 \times 5$
   $= 30 + 30 + 30$
   $= 90$
5. $3x ; 2y ; 12x ; 8y$
6. $= 4(5) + 4(4p)$
   $= 20 + 16p$
7. $= 9(2m) + 9(3n)$
   $= 18m + 27n$
8. $6p + 10q$
9. $10a + 15b$
10. $3b$
11. 7
12. $4m$
13. $7p$
14. $2x ; 18z$
15. $3j ; 2k ; 7i$
16. $3(5 + 7a) = 15 + 21a$
17. $2(4x + y) = 8x + 2y$
18a. $2(3x + 8) = 6x + 16$
   b. $4(p + q) = 4p + 4q$
   c. $5(3 + m) = 15 + 5m$
19a. $6(x + 3y) = 6x + 18y$
   b. $4(m + n) = 4m + 4n$
   c. $9a(b + 15) = 9ab + 135a$
20. $x = 22$
21. $y = 15$
22. $a = 84$
23. 3
24. 6
25. 105
26. 1
27. 32
28. 18
29. $x ; x ; 4 ; 4 ; 4$
   Left side: $5(4) = 20$
   Right side: $16 + 4 = 20$
30. $2y - 4 - y = y + 8 - y$
   $y - 4 + 4 = 8 + 4$
   $y = 12$
   Left side: $2(12) - 4 = 20$
   Right side: $12 + 8 = 20$
31. $4n - 5 - n = n + 13 - n$
   $3n - 5 + 5 = 13 + 5$
   $\dfrac{3n}{3} = \dfrac{18}{3}$
   $n = 6$
   Left side: $4(6) - 5 = 19$
   Right side: $6 + 13 = 19$
32. $d ; 74$
   $d = 4$
   Left side: $27(4) + 74 = 182$
   Right side: 182
   4
33. Let n be the number of marbles that Annie has.
   $n + 2n = 4n - 8$
   $n = 8$
   Left side: $8 + 2(8) = 24$
   Right side: $4(8) - 8 = 24$
   Annie has 8 marbles.

34. Let r be the growth rate of the plant.
   $21 + 3r = 21 \times 2$
   $r = 7$
   Left side: $21 + 3(7) = 42$
   Right side: $21 \times 2 = 42$
   The growth rate is 7 cm/year.
35. Let m be the number of marbles that Jack has.
   $m + 3m = 2(m + 13)$
   $m = 13$
   Left side: $13 + 3(13) = 52$
   Right side: $2(13 + 13) = 52$
   Jack has 13 marbles.

26 Data Management (1)

1a. sample   b. census   c. sample
   (Check b)
2a. census   b. sample   c. sample
   (Check a)
3a. sample   b. sample   c. census
   (Check b)
4. No. Because there are more people (29) who voted for other types of movies than those who voted for "fantasy" (12).
5. (Individual answer)
6. B and C
7. (Individual answer)
8. The number of male and female teachers in Collingview Public School from 1997 to 2009.
9. There will be about 35 teachers in 2012.
10. (Individual answer)
11.

Years of Experience vs Income

12. The more the experience, the higher the annual income.
13. It will be about $50k.

14.

Superhero	No. of Children	Sector Angle	Percent
Batman	17	$\frac{17}{65}$ x 360° ≈ 94°	$\frac{17}{65}$ x 100% = 26%
Spiderman	15	$\frac{15}{65}$ x 360° ≈ 83°	$\frac{15}{65}$ x 100% = 23%
Superman	13	$\frac{13}{65}$ x 360° ≈ 72°	$\frac{13}{65}$ x 100% = 20%
X-men	9	$\frac{9}{65}$ x 360° ≈ 50°	$\frac{9}{65}$ x 100% = 14%
Ironman	11	$\frac{11}{65}$ x 360° ≈ 61°	$\frac{11}{65}$ x 100% = 17%
Total	**65**	**360°**	**100%**

15.

Our Favourite Superhero

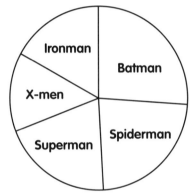

16. About 875 children have Batman as their superhero.
17. (Individual answer)

27 Data Management (2)

1.

Height of the Plants

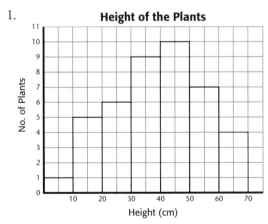

2. (Individual answer)
3a. scatter plot
  b. double line graph
  c. circle graph
  d. double bar graph
  e. histogram
  f. scatter plot

4.

No. of Participants at Each Age

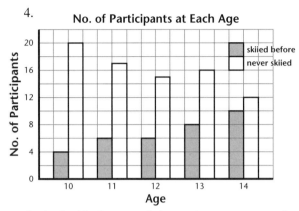

skiied before
never skiied

5. A double bar graph is used to represent the data because it can show two sets of discrete data.
6. (Individual answer)
7. She should use a circle graph because it can display a part to whole relationship.
8. 2   9. 5 ; 97
10. 3 ; 7   11. No outliers
12. 5 ; 102 ; 180
13. 6 ; 96 ; 96
14. with the outliers: 47.5 ; 40.5 ; 41
   without the outliers: 39.6 ; 40 ; 41
15a. No. Because the mean is affected by every data. So, it is not a good idea to use mean to represent the data if there are some outliers.
  b. Yes. Because every data is used to calculate the mean. So, the mean is the best average.

28 Probability

1. $\frac{favourable}{possible} = \frac{2}{3}$
2. equal ; 1 ; $\frac{5}{5}$; 1
3. numerator ; 0 ; $\frac{0}{5}$; 0

4.

Blouse	Skirt	Combination
plain	black	plain, black
	grey	plain, grey
with ruffles	black	with ruffles, black
	grey	with ruffles, grey
with lace	black	with lace, black
	grey	with lace, grey

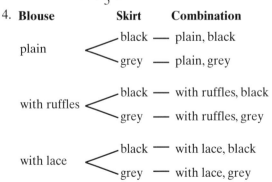

5a. $\dfrac{1}{6}$ b. $\dfrac{1}{3}$

c. $\dfrac{2}{3}$ d. $\dfrac{1}{2}$

6. B

7. 31%   8. 0%

9. 69%   10. 81%

11. 100%

12a. $\dfrac{1}{5}$ b. $\dfrac{2}{5}$

c. $\dfrac{4}{5}$ d. $\dfrac{4}{5}$

13a. $\dfrac{1}{6}$ b. $\dfrac{5}{6}$

c. $\dfrac{1}{2}$ d. $\dfrac{1}{2}$

14. P(not getting a vowel) = $\dfrac{3}{5}$

P(not getting a composite number) = $\dfrac{2}{3}$

No, the probability of not getting a composite number is higher.

15a. 1 to 14 ; 14 to 1   b. 6 to 9 ; 9 to 6

c. 4 to 11 ; 11 to 4   d. 6 to 9 ; 9 to 6

e. 9 to 6 ; 6 to 9

16. 45% ; 55% ; 9 to 11

17. 19 to 6

Review 2

1. 8.5 m^3 ; 30 m^2

2. 201.06 cm^3 ; 214.8 cm^2

3. 120 m^3 ; 160.83 m^2

4. 357.08 cm^3 ; 330.81 cm^2

5. 219.4 cm^3 ; 243.96 cm^2

6. 90° ; complementary ; 20°
   70° (opposite angles)

7. 180° – 60° (interior angles)
   = 120°
   60° (alternate angles)

8. $\angle$ABC + $\angle$ACB + 50° = 180°
   $\angle$ABC + $\angle$ACB = 130°
   $\angle$ACB = 65°
   $\angle m$ = 180° – 65° = 115° (supplementary angles)
   $\angle n$ = 180° – 115° – 31° = 34° (sum of angles in a $\triangle$)

9. $\angle s$ + 90° + 45° = 180° (sum of angles in a $\triangle$)
   $\angle s$ = 45°
   $\angle$ABD + 25° + 45° + 45°= 180° (sum of angles in a $\triangle$)
   $\angle$ABD = 65°
   $\angle t$ = 65° (alternate angles)

10-13. (Individual drawings)

14.

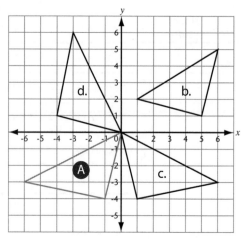

a. (0,0), (-1,-4), (-6,-3)

b. (6,5), (5,1), (1,2)

c. (0,0), (1,-4), (6,-3)

d. (0,0), (-4,1), (-3,6)

15a. x-axis

b. translated 2 units left and 1 unit down

c. rotated 180° at (0,0)

16a. A′(-2,3), B′(-2,-1), C′(-9,-1)

b. A′(1,-2), B′(1,2), C′(-6,2)

c. A′(-1,-2), B′(-1,2), C′(6,2)

17a. X′(4,-1), Y′(1,-4), Z′(10,-5)

b. X′(-2,1), Y′(1,-2), Z′(-8,-3)

c. X′(-1,2), Y′(2,-1), Z′(3,8)

18.

Term No.	Term Value
1	0
2	4
3	8
4	12
5	16

a. $4n - 4$ b. 32 ; 56   c. 11

19.

Term No.	Term Value
1	4
2	10
3	16
4	22
5	28

a. $6n - 2$ b. 58 ; 118   c. 15

20. 7 ; -2 ; 14 – 8 ; 6

21. = 3(7 + 3)   22. = 3^2(-2 + 1)
    = 30   = -9

23. $= -2(5 - 1)$
    $= -8$
24. $3e \div d = 3(5) \div 3 = 5$
    There are 5 candies in each jar.
25. $4a = 16$
    $a = 4$
26. $10 + b = 21$
    $b = 11$
27. $2n + n = 3$
    $3n = 3$
    $n = 1$
28. $36 - 6 = 4k - k$
    $3k = 30$
    $k = 10$
29. $m + 2 = 3$
    $m = 1$
30. $n - 4 = 33$
    $n = 37$
31. 6
32. 5
33. 7
34. 3
35.

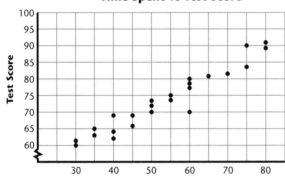

Time Spent vs Test Score

36. The more time spent on studying, the higher the test score.
37. double bar graph
38. scatter plot
39. histogram
40. circle graph
41a. 1 to 1 ; 1 to 7
  b. 7 to 1 ; 15 to 1
  42. (Suggested answer)
      The probability of drawing a number is 50%. So, a coin can be used to simulate the chance of drawing a number.

1   Polar Bears – Did You Know?

A.   1. C
     2. B
     3. B ; C
     4. A
B.   1. BI
     2. PRP
     3. G
     4. F
     5. TI
     6. PP
     7. BI
C.   (Individual writing)

2   Cambodia's Angkor Wat: Endangered by Tourism

A.   Paragraph 1: B
     Paragraph 2: D
     Paragraph 3: E
     Paragraph 4: C
     Paragraph 5: A
B.   1. It was built in the early 12th century as a Hindu place of worship, but evolved into a revered Buddhist temple as the religion and inhabitants changed.
     2. For this reason, while other countries in the region, such as Thailand and Malaysia, began to prosper and invite foreign tourists on a large scale, Cambodia, with little infrastructure, was still a place that outsiders knew little about.
     3. A few years ago (2004) over a million foreigners came to Cambodia, and more than half said they had come to visit Angkor Wat.
C.   (Individual additional non-progressive verbs)
     Sense: feel ; hear ; see ; taste
     Mental State: believe ; know ; remember ; want
     Emotional State: fear ; hate ; like ; mind
     Existence: appear ; be ; contain ; seem
     Possession: belong ; have ; own ; possess
D.   (Individual writing)

3   Canadian Nobel Prize Laureates

A.   1. prestigious
     2. established
     3. bequest
     4. inventor
     5. economics
     6. personal
     7. prestige
     8. attention
     9. impressive
     10. scientists
     11. founded
     12. shared
     13. Peace
     14. efforts
B.   1. came about
     2. broke in
     3. carried on ; took down
     4. died down
     5. get over
     6. has gone through
     7. keep to
C.   (Individual definitions and sentences)

4   The Naming of a Public Holiday

A.   1. B
     2. C
     3. B
B.   (Individual answer)
C.   1. on
     2. for
     3. from
     4. in
     5. from
     6. in
     7. about
     8. of
     9. to
     10. for
     11. with
     12. for
D.   1. at
     2. of
     3. with

4. to ; for
5. with
6. for
E. 1. for
2. about
3. about
4. about
5. of
6. with
7. of
8. of
9. of
10. in
11. of
12. about
F. (Individual writing)

5 The History of Christmas Giving

A. 1. He was actually a man named Nicholas who gave his inherited wealth to the poor and became a monk. He helped the needy and became known as the protector of children and sailors, and was later made a saint.
2. He gave fruits, nuts, and candies to good children and lumps of coal to naughty ones.
3. Nicholas tried to help a poor girl who needed a wedding dowry, and he threw a sack of gold coins through her window, which landed in her stocking that had been hanging up to dry.
4. It attracted shoppers with Christmas-themed window displays and kept its doors open until midnight on Christmas Eve.
5. (Individual answer)
B. 1. gorgeous, tall, green Christmas
2. most popular European
3. precious, heavy gold
4. special, old German
5. beautiful, long, silver wire
6. interesting, miniature, colourful paper
7. expensive, big, new doll
8. famous, big, old, American department
C. (Individual writing)

6 The Remarkable Journey of Al Gore

A. 1. Al Gore received about 500 000 more votes than George W. Bush in the 2000 presidential race.
2. (true)
3. The documentary *An Inconvenient Truth* was turned into a best-selling book with the same title.
4. Al Gore shared the 2007 Nobel Peace Prize with the scientists of the Intergovernmental Panel on Climate Change for their efforts in addressing the problem of global warming and climate change.
B. (Individual answer)
C. (Suggested answers)
1. When did Al Gore run for the presidency against the Republican candidate George W. Bush?
2. How many more votes did Al Gore receive than George W. Bush?
3. How did Al Gore present his message about global warming?
4. Where was the film *An Inconvenient Truth* shown?
5. Why do many people hope that Al Gore will run for the presidency again?
D. (Suggested answers)
1. Schools and town halls were the places where Al Gore went to impart his message about global warming. /
Al Gore went to schools and town halls where he imparted his message about global warming.
2. 1965 was the year when Gore enrolled in Harvard University.
3. The media wanted to know why Gore enlisted in the U.S. military.
4. There was a time when Gore struggled to make a decision about joining the U.S. military.
5. This is the cathedral where Gore married Tipper.
6. Gore gave a speech about why he supported the use of green energy.

7　The Wisdom of a Baseball Player: Yogi Berra's Quotes

A. 1. "Those" refers to stand-up comedians and writers of humour.
2. He is revered as a humorist because he often came up with quotes containing misused words with comic effects.
3. It implies "open to all".
4. (Individual answer)
5. (Individual answer)

B. 1. Stand-up comedy shows started to be popular long ago.
2. ✔
3. I never find it easy to be a person of humour.
4. It is certainly amusing to read Yogi Berra's one-liners.
5. Being humorous is completely different from being silly.

C. 1. My brother never finds it hard to make me laugh.
2. The comedian is so famous that he drew an extremely large audience to his show.
3. His performance is humorous enough to bring laughter to everyone throughout the two-hour show.
4. Lester commented quite casually on the controversial issue.
5. Yogi Berra is widely known for his sense of humour.
6. His is always quick at coming up with new one-liners.
7. You can usually discover great philosophy in what he says.

8　Too Much of a Good Thing: the "Law of Unintended Consequences"

A. 1. Purpose: to control the greyback cane beetle that was devastating sugar cane crops
Consequence: The toad population has now grown to more than 200 million, severly damaging the native Australian ecosystem.
2. Purpose: to stabilize soil erosion
Consequence: It grew like a weed, threatened the natural flora, and got in the way of forest rejuvenation.

3. Purpose: to prevent and reduce forest fires
Consequence: Old trees that are susceptible to pests and disease were not burned down, allowing accumulated matter on the forest floor to remain, so new seedlings could not sprout and new trees could not grow. Now the forests are seriously threatened by pests such as the pine beetle.
4. (Individual answer)

B. 1. Surprisingly, the government did not do any research before introducing the species to the country.
2. Theoretically, the cane toad can control the damage done by greyback cane beetles to the sugar cane.
3. Ideally, the whole population of cane beetles could be wiped out from Australia.
4. Honestly / Frankly, I don't think this policy will work without causing other problems.
5. Clearly / Obviously, the Australian government is facing another serious pest problem – the cane toad.

C. (Individual writing)

9　How to Talk Like a Fashion Trendsetter

A. 1. Hipster cool
2. Punk rock
3. Preppy chic
4. Bollywood
5. Goth glam
6. Boho chic

B. (Individual answer)

C. 1. when ; S
2. and ; or ; and ; C
3. whether...or ; CR
4. If ; S
5. and ; C
6. Both...and ; CR
7. or ; C
8. Although ; S

D. (Suggested answers)
1. You can buy either the belt or the necklace.
2. Try both jackets on before you decide which one to buy.

3. My friend, Sean, likes the punk rock style, but I prefer the classic style.
4. Both Sharon and Angela have decided to wear something purple to the prom.
5. Kenneth is saving up his allowance because he wants to buy a pair of leather gloves for his mom's birthday.
6. Jeans are a favourite for many young people and they have been popular since the 1950s.

10 Watch out for Those Language Bloopers!

A. (Individual answers)
B. 1. We need an energy bill that encourages conservation.
   2. Rarely is the question asked: are our children learning?
C. 1. SC
   2. A
   3. OC
   4. SC
   5. OP
   6. OV
   7. S
   8. OP
D. (Individual writing)

11 Don't Be a Dope: Drugs in Sports

A. 1. During the two world wars, soldiers were given cigarettes because cigarettes were considered to be able to provide extra protection against colds and boost concentration.
   2. ✔
   3. The use of performance-enhancing drugs in competitive sports during the early days was considered acceptable as they helped athletes perform better.
   4. Gene doping refers to the activity of altering cells, genes, and other genetic material for the purpose of improving athletic performance.
B. 1. Some new drug-testing policies have been introduced by the World Anti-Doping Agency.

2. The WADA Athlete Guide can be obtained from their website.
3. The hard evidence that some performance-enhancing drugs have resulted in long-term harmful consequences for those who took them cannot be disputed.
4. "Gene doping" is considered to be as sinister as drug doping (by many people).
C. (Suggested answers)
   1. The organizing committee had all athletes tested for performance-enhancing drugs before the commencement of the competitions.
   2. They want to get the samples examined as soon as possible.
   3. Methods of detecting various performance-enhancing drugs need improving.
   4. People need educating about the harmful effects of doping.

12 One of the World's Most Published Editorials

A. (Suggested answers)
   1. They think that if they do not understand certain things, then these things simply do not exist.
   2. Life would lack lustre without childhood dreams and imaginations.
   3. If you have faith, fancy, poetry, love, and romance, you will be able to open up yourself to the beauty and glory of the things you cannot see.
B. 1. It explained to Virginia that there really is a Santa Claus, just like there is love, generosity, and devotion.
   2. (Individual answer)
C. 1. IND
   2. SUB
   3. SUB
   4. IMP
   5. IND
   6. IMP
   7. SUB
   8. IND

D. (Suggested answers)
1. Cindy wishes she had not asked the silly question.
2. If I were Keith, I would not have turned down the offer.
3. If Jan saw fairies, she could take pictures of them.
4. If Timothy were Molly, he wouldn't have believed in that story.

E. (Individual writing)

13 Steven Fletcher, an Exceptional Public Servant

A. 1. A
2. B
3. B
4. C

B. (Suggested answers)
1. He was twice elected president of the University of Manitoba Students' Union.
2. He was recently inducted into the Terry Fox Hall of Fame.
3. Soon the family moved back to Canada, and Fletcher grew up in Manitoba.
4. He soon found work in his chosen profession in the environment he loved, and life was good.
5. A year later, while Fletcher was driving to a job site in northern Manitoba, his vehicle hit a moose.
6. When his busy schedule allows, he likes visiting the Fort Whyte Centre.
7. Doctors told him he would be spending the rest of his life in an institution, but Fletcher decided things would be otherwise, and after a long and painful period of rehabilitation, during which time Fletcher regained the ability to speak, he returned to university to obtain a Master of Business Administration Degree.

C. 1. Fletcher has been inducted into the Terry Fox Hall of Fame and he has received the King Clancy Award.
2. Fletcher had won the Manitoba kayak competition two times before the accident happened.

3. If you like the outdoors, you can visit the Fort Whyte Centre and you can hike along the pond and listen to the sounds of water foul there.

D. (Individual writing)

14 The Seven Sacred Teachings

A. (Suggested answers)
Wisdom is the ability to think before we act and understand clearly what is good and bad, or right and wrong.
Love means giving kindness without asking for or expecting anything in return.
Respect is the ability to honour others' sincere and healthy beliefs although they may be different from ours.
Courage is being brave enough to stand alone to do what we believe in, and to do things differently because we know the outcome would be better that way.
Honesty means saying, thinking, and doing only the things we really mean.
Humility is the ability to admit that we don't know everything, to admit mistakes, to be successful without being arrogant, to let others take the credit, and to set aside what we want for the needs of others.
Truth is the ability to tell the truth and the desire to be truthful.

B. (Suggested answers)
1. Below is a list of what we consider the "Seven Sacred Teachings".
2. How can we become better people?
3. What a wonderful world it would be if everyone followed the Seven Sacred Teachings!
4. Try to say, think, and do only the things you really mean.

C. (Suggested answers)
1. How can I improve myself?
2. The "Seven Sacred Teachings" include wisdom, love, respect, courage, honesty, humility, and truth.
3. Hand in your project ideas on First Nations culture next Friday.
4. What is the play about, Christine?
5. Come to see my performance, Matthew.
6. Where is the school hall?
7. What a great show!

Review 1

A. 1. think ; invented
   2. fishing ; sailing
   3. endangered ; trodden
   4. appreciating ; engaging
   5. to offer ; to explore
   6. swim

B. 1. in
   2. across
   3. up ; with
   4. into
   5. to
   6. on

C. 1. No one dared to open the mysterious, big, old wooden chest in the attic.
   2. The famous, Canadian rock band will hold a concert this Saturday.
   3. Jessica put the lovely, small pink shell carefully in the gift box.
   4. Oh, I've completely forgotten my half-eaten pizza in the fridge. /
      Oh, I've forgotten my half-eaten pizza in the fridge completely.
   5. The steps to making an origami crane are simple enough for everyone to follow.

D. 1. How
   2. where
   3. why
   4. Why
   5. when
   6. Where / When

E. 1. and
   2. but
   3. not only / both
   4. but also / and
   5. and
   6. because / since
   7. Even if
   8. Although / Though
   9. so
   10. If

F. 1. B
   2. F
   3. D
   4. E
   5. I
   6. H
   7. A
   8. J
   9. G
   10. C

G. 1. Canada's culture has been influenced by British and French cultures.
   2. Each of the children was given a sketchbook and some crayons by the teacher. /
      A sketchbook and some crayons were given to each of the children by the teacher.
   3. A pair of mittens was left under the chair after the seminar.
   4. Their excellent performance will not be forgotten.

H. (Individual writing)

I. 1. SUB
   2. IMP
   3. SUB
   4. IND
   5. IMP

J. (Suggested answers)
   1. The Williams checked into the hotel. After that, they met their friends in the lobby. The tour guide then took them to different attractions in the city.
   2. I can say that was the best clam chowder I've ever had and the price was reasonable.
   3. Although the film has won many Oscars, including Best Picture and Best Director, Derek has no intention of seeing it.
   4. We were watching television in the living room when all the lights went out and we were in complete darkness.
   5. Wilfred has been elected the Best Student of the Year.
   6. What is the fastest way to the airport?
   7. What an amazing show!
   8. Please tell me what is going on.

15 Twenty Thousand "Oskar Schindlers": the Holocaust Rescuers

A. 1. It stands for one who risked one's life to save Jews during Hitler's era of Nazi atrocities in Europe.

387

2. Most of these diplomats did so secretly, or even against the express orders of their own governments!

3. Although he failed to convince the Canadian government to take in Jewish refugees when he was Canada's top diplomat in France as World War II began, Vanier's continued efforts helped change Canada's immigration policy and enabled more than 186 000 European refugees to settle in Canada between 1947 and 1953.

4. (Suggested answer)
Canada could benefit from accepting Jewish refugees because the capital and expertise they brought to Canada could boost the economy.

B. 1. so that they could travel out of the danger zone ; ADV
2. whom Schindler rescued ; ADJ
3. while he served as the Japanese Consul General in Lithuania ; ADV
4. when he returned to Japan ; ADV
5. which Georges Vanier's son, Jean, founded ; ADJ
6. Exactly how many "Schindlers" there were ; N
7. why someone risked his or her life to save others ; N

C. (Individual writing)

16 An Ancient Story about the Sun and the Moon

A. "The Sun and the Moon" described three physical phenomena. First, it explained how the solar system came about and how it evolved around the sun. It also explained why there are tidal changes in oceans and seas. The eclipse of the moon was accounted for in "The Sun and the Moon", too.

B. (Individual writing)

C. 1. Linda told Julie that the Star and the Crab were children of the Sun and the Moon.
2. Timothy says that there are a lot of similarities among the folktales of different countries around the world.
3. Ginny told Kingsley that her mom had bought her a set of books on Greek mythology.

4. Mom said that she would tell me an interesting folktale before I went to bed.

D. 1. Jerry asked Shirley who had told her that there had been ten suns in the past.
2. The teacher asked the children if / whether they wanted to learn more about their country's legends.
3. Cedric asked where he could find the illustrations of ancient heroes.
4. The librarian reminded us not to write or draw in the books.
5. Mr. Willis told me to create another story about the sun and the moon.

17 Do Aliens Exist?

A. 1. C
2. A
3. C
4. C

B. 1. then
2. that day
3. that night
4. the next day / the following day
5. the year before / the previous year
6. the next Monday / the following Monday
7. eight years before
8. five days from then
9. the next month / the following month
10. three weeks before
11. the weekend before / the previous weekend
12. the next Christmas / the following Christmas
13. that afternoon

C. 1. Jenny said that she had borrowed that book from the library the week before / the previous week.
2. Sandra asked Dave if / whether he believed there really were aliens then.
3. Mr. and Mrs. Hayes said that they had seen a UFO hover over their house six years before.
4. Anna said that they / we could go to the Ontario Science Centre the next weekend / the following weekend.
5. Emily told Sam that a seminar about the existence of life on other planets would be held there the next Friday / the following Friday.

D. (Suggested answers)
    1. Nelson asked me, "Will you watch the program about aliens on the Discovery Channel tomorrow?"
    2. "Research into the atmospheric conditions of different planetary bodies started some years ago," the astronomer explained to us.
    3. "My uncle bought me these cute alien dolls last summer when he came to visit," Tammy said.
    4. Ricky's sister told him, "I have to hand in a book report on a science fiction book in two weeks."

18 Saving Lake Winnipeg

A. Paragraph 1: B
    Paragraph 2: B
    Paragraph 3: B
    Paragraph 4: A
    Paragraph 5: B
    Paragraph 6: A
B. (Individual writing)
C. 1. If I owned a cottage in Manitoba, I would spend every summer there.
    2. ✔
    3. If Macy had been to Winnipeg before, she would have known more about the city.
    4. If the pollution problem of Lake Winnipeg continues, all wildlife will be adversely affected.
    5. Lake Winnipeg would recover if everyone started using phosphate-free detergents today.
    6. ✔
    7. I would teach everyone how to make phosphate-free detergent if I had the formula.
    8. If I were a citizen of Manitoba, I would do everything I could to help save Lake Winnipeg.

19 Depression in Teenagers: a Very Treatable Condition

A. 1. Depression is a common ailment affecting about one out of every 25 teens each year.
    2. ✔
    3. Depression can be caused by a chemical imbalance in the brain.
    4. Medication is one of the many ways to treat depression.
    5. ✔
    6. People suffering from depression may have sudden outbursts of anger or tears over relatively small matters.
B. (Individual writing)
C. (Individual writing)

20 The Start of the Sagas

A. 1. Dagur
    2. Borr
    3. Laxdœla
    4. Valkyries
    5. Heimskringla
    6. Odin
    7. Loki
    8. Niflheim
    9. Bestla
    10. Búri
    11. Delling
    12. Múspell
B. (Individual writing)
C. (Individual writing)

21 Green Iceland: a Letter from Uncle Josh

A. Reykjavik: capital city of Iceland; filled with parks and gardens
    The Blue Lagoon: an outdoor geothermal pool with water full of minerals
    Gulfoss: a great waterfall in Iceland

Geysir: a place with a lot of colourful bubbling mud pots, steam vents, and a few geysers
Thingvellir National Park: the site of the world's oldest parliament

B. 1. As there are a lot of volcanoes in Iceland, they trap the heat energy and use it to generate electricity and provide hot water.
   2. He thinks that Icelanders are trying to live in an environmentally friendly way and they reduce as far as possible the emission of carbon dioxide, which is one of the major causes of global warming.

C. 1. Iceland was ranked as the most developed country in the world in 2007 by the United Nations' Human Development Index.
   2. Ocean-fresh seafood is served by many restaurants in Iceland.
   3. The ancient language of the Vikings is still spoken by Icelanders.

D. 1. Many Icelanders do believe in the existence of elves.
   2. The hotel does provide free shuttle services to many attractions around the city.
   3. It's not usual to see polar bears in Iceland but I did see one on my trip there.

E. 1. Never did we expect to see the Northern Lights in Iceland.
   2. Little does Keith know about Iceland.
   3. Seldom do Icelanders add salt to their food.
   4. Hardly had the tourists arrived at the geyser when it erupted.

F. 1. What we all must try is the Icelandic skyr.
   2. What some tourists to Iceland want to see is the Northern Lights.
   3. What many people do not know is that it is not that cold in Iceland.

22 Countries that Are Younger than You

A. USSR: Armenia, Azerbaijan, Belarus, Estonia, Georgia, Kazakhstan, Kyrgyzstan, Latvia, Lithuania, Moldova, Russia, Tajikistan, Turkmenistan, Ukraine, Uzbekistan
Yugoslavia: Slovenia, Croatia, Macedonia, Bosnia, Herzegovina, Serbia, Montenegro
Czechoslovakia: Czech Republic, Slovakia

B. (Individual writing)
C. (Individual writing)

23 High Flight – a Poem by John Gillespie Magee, Jr.

A. (Suggested answers for 1 – 3)
   1. Noonan has the ability to make references to other great works, and reinterpret them to achieve the effect she desires.
   2. It could be interpreted as "broke away from the centre of gravity and soared high into heaven".
   3. Magee expressed in his poem the thrill of being up in the air where few could reach, not even larks or eagles.
   4. B
   5. (Individual answer)
B. (Individual writing)
C. (Individual writing)

24 Hannah Taylor and the Ladybug Foundation

A. 1. It refers to Hannah seeing a man eating out of a garbage can.
   2. It refers to her effort in helping the homeless.
   3. (Suggested answer)
      She wanted to draw more attention to the event.
   4. (Individual answer)
B. (Suggested answers)
   1. too ; also ; furthermore
   2. in the same way ; by the same token ; in like fashion
   3. instead ; nevertheless ; on the other hand
   4. such as ; namely ; to illustrate
   5. indeed ; of course ; above all
   6. then ; later on ; subsequently
   7. usually ; ordinarily ; generally speaking
   8. as ; because ; due to
   9. so ; therefore ; consequently

10. except ; other than ; exclusive of
11. in brief ; to sum up ; all in all
C. (Individual writing)

25 Shania Twain – More than a "Rags to Riches" Story

A. 1. She is admired by fans of country music, but legions of pop and rock-and-roll devotees also love her music.
    2. Shania's new family after her mother's second marriage did not have much money, and Shania had to sing in bars around town at the age of eight to make money.
    3. She changed her name from "Eilleen" to "Shania", an Ojibway word meaning "on my way".
    4. In 1991, a music executive from Nashville offered to produce a demo for Shania, and her first album was released in 1993.
    5. It means "staying away from the glamour and limelight associated with a world-famous figure".
B. (Individual writing)

26 Yoga: a Most Healthful Form of Exercise

A. Viniyoga: synchronizing breathing techniques with postures
    Ashtanga yoga: performing postures in a fast-paced, flowing sequence
    Kundalini yoga: unlocking a powerful energy that exists at the base of the spine
    Jivamukti yoga: intense, physical postures performed with chanting and meditation
    Power yoga: more rigorous form of Ashtanga yoga postures to build up a sweat
    Forrest yoga: yoga sequences with other core strengtheners
    Happy Face yoga: a series of 30 facial exercises, along with deep breathing and relaxation in between

B. (Individual writing)
C. (Individual writing)

27 Tips for Effective Public Speaking

A. 1. e
    2. c
    3. b
    4. d
    5. f
    6. a
B. (Individual writing)
C. (Individual writing)

28 A Volunteer and a Tourist?

A. Paragraph 2: B
    Paragraph 3: A
    Paragraph 4: A
    Paragraph 5: B
B. (Individual answer)
C. 1. Even brief periods of voluntouring give everyone involved insight into the lives of people in other countries.
    2. According to the Travel Industry Association of America, over 55 million Americans have participated in a voluntouring project.
    3. One-quarter of people planning for a vacation are considering a service-oriented one.
    4. Some of the work voluntourists do on their trips includes: teaching English, planting trees, building bridges, and repairing trails.
    5. Jamie found two organizations that provide voluntouring projects on the Internet, but neither of them was a non-profit organization.
D. (Individual writing)

Review 2

A. 1. How the plane went missing in such good weather conditions ; N
    2. unless you follow all the steps of installation ; ADV
    3. whom Mrs. Mitchell requested to see ; ADJ
    4. who can tell me why the meeting has been cancelled ; ADJ
    5. Although there have not been many reported sightings of the Ogopogo ; ADV
    6. where we used to stay every summer ; ADJ
    7. that Olivia was the actual writer of the book ; N
    8. Whoever comes onto the political scene ; N
    9. before you sign up for the outing ; ADV
    10. because it is the best surviving example of a planned British colonial settlement in North America ; ADV

B. 1. Jane told her friend to meet her there at noon the next day / the following day.
    2. Mr. Ward asked Heather if / whether she thought she could draw up a new plan a week from then.
    3. Mom says that she has always had a great liking for country music.
    4. Mrs. Cooper told her daughter that they would probably stay in Old Quebec City for two days.
    5. The teacher told her students that Paris is the capital city of France.

C. (Suggested answers)
    1. "I have seen this stranger outside my house a number of times this week," Mark said.
    2. Kelly asked her mother, "Why can't I get a video game for my birthday?"
    3. Ned told Raymond, "I do walk my dog after school every day."
    4. "We took a course in interior design together last year," the twin sisters said.

D. 1. If I were a government leader, I would try every way to help children in poor countries.
    2. Ryan would not have made this kind of mistake if he had had enough sleep the night before.
    3. ✔
    4. If Jimmy had not put on his seat belt, he could have been more seriously injured.

5. You must answer at least three questions correctly if you want to join the club.
6. ✔
7. If Helen were Leona, she would not have agreed to wear that weird costume.
8. Mom will let me sleep over at your place if I can get all my work done this afternoon.

E. (Individual writing)

F. 1. The first hot air balloon capable of carrying passengers was built by the Montgolfier brothers.
    2. The soybean has been used as food by people in many Asian countries for thousands of years.
    3. A large sum of money has been donated to World Wildlife Fund Canada. /
       World Wildlife Fund Canada has been donated a large sum of money.
    4. The famous Christmas song "Rudolph the Red-Nosed Reindeer" was written by Robert Lewis May.

G. (Suggested answers)
    1. Little can we do to solve the problem at this stage.
    2. Never have we seen anything as strange and unimaginable as this.
    3. I did meet the famous author J. K. Rowling on my trip to England.
    4. We do have a member to take care of the registration of new members.
    5. What Rita bought for her grandmother was a beautiful crystal brooch.

H. 1. likewise ; similarity
    2. for instance ; example
    3. As a result ; consequence
    4. In fact ; emphasis

I. (Individual writing)

1 British North America: Before Confederation

A. 1. Canada East
    2. Newfoundland
    3. Prince Edward Island
    4. Nova Scotia
    5. New Brunswick
    6. Canada West
    7. British Columbia
    8. Vancouver Island

B. 1. British North American colonies traded less with Britain and more with the United States.
    2. (Suggested answer)
       The minority could lose their culture and language if they united with the majority.

2 Confederation

A. 1. Manifest Destiny ; British North American
    2. Reciprocity Treaty ; 1866
    3. Fenian Raids ; united

B. 1. September
    2. Nova Scotia
    3. Canada
    4. union
    5. 1864
    6. resolutions
    7. Quebec
    8. 1866
    9. Dominion
    10. Ontario
    11. July
    12. confederation

3 Growth of Canada

A. 1. Quebec
    2. Nova Scotia
    3. Northwest Territories
    4. Ontario
    5. province
    6. British Columbia
    7. gold rush
    8. Dominion
    9. Prince Edward Island
    10. Britain
    11. Yukon
    12. American
    13. Saskatchewan
    14. growth
    15. Newfoundland
    16. referendum
    17. Nunavut
    18. Northwest Territories

B. 1. 1867
    2. any year from 1999 to 2009

4 People to Know

A. 1. Sir John Alexander Macdonald ; prime minister
    2. responsible government ;
       Fathers of Confederation
    3. George-Etienne Cartier ; confederation ; Canadiens
    4. conferences ; Royal Proclamation

B. 1. children ; vote
    2. women ; leadership
    3. Black community ; discrimination
    4. First Nations ; Europeans
    5. Chinese ; less

5 Into the West

A. 1. Vancouver Island ; coal mining
    2. Red River ; rebellion
    3. Prairies ; prairie
    4. Winnipeg, Calgary ; factories
    5. Dawson City ; North
    6. Vancouver ; CPR
    7. Alberta ; buffalo ; smallpox

B. (Individual design)

6 Canadian Pacific Railway

A. 1. Immigrants ; C
    2. Chinese workers ; B
    3. Farmers ; D
    4. Tourists ; A

B. 1. connect
    2. Shield

3. immigrants
4. workers
5. British
6. leadership
7. Rebellion
8. spike

3. C
4. B
5. B
6. B
7. C
8. A
9. A

7 The Riel and Northwest Rebellions

A. Event 1: 3 ; 1 ; 2
   Event 2: 3 ; 2 ; 1
   Event 3: 2 ; 1 ; 3
B. 1. Métis
   2. Parliament
   3. provisional government
   4. Gabriel Dumont
   5. Poundmaker
   6. Canadian Pacific Railway
   7. treason

8 Two Kinds of Gold

A. 1. settlement
   2. immigration
   3. industries
   4. Yukon
B. did not require ;
   new, improved ;
   high
C. 1. prospector
   2. Marquis
   3. outfitters
   4. Dawson City
   5. agricultural economy

9 The Origins of the Royal Canadian Mounted Police

A. 1873: NWMP
   1904: RNWMP
   1920: RCMP
B. Check A, D, and E.
C. 1. B
   2. A

10 Changes in Canada: 1885-1914

A. 1. Canada's Changing Role within the British Empire
   2. Rapid Industrialization
   3. Canadian / American Relations
   4. Challenges of Increased Migration and Settlement
   5. Rapid Advances in Technology
B. 1. The Boer War
   2-3. Alaska boundary dispute resolved ;
        Chinese head tax raised ;
   4-5. PEI banned automobiles ;
        Canada's first gas station
C. 1. moving pictures
   2. automobiles
   3. wireless transmission
   4. radio broadcasts
   5. airplanes

11 People Who Made a Difference: 1885-1914

A. 1. Mohawk ; Native Canadians
   2. Prime Minister ; compromise
   3. landscape ; novels
   4. activist ; vote
   5. native villages
   6. immigration
B. 1. Nellie McClung
   2. Clifford Sifton
   3. Emily Carr
   4. Sir Wilfred Laurier
   5. Pauline Johnson
   6. Lucy Maude Montgomery

12 Living and Working in Canada

A. 1. death ; compensation
    2. children ; mines
    3. Factory ; Women
B. 1. labour unions
    2. Labour laws
C. (Individual   answers   for   today's   living
    conditions)
    1. different
    2. different
    3. different
    4. different

8. American
9. settlement
G. C ; B ; A ; D

Review

A. Canada East ;
    Reciprocity Treaty ;
    Manifest Destiny ;
    conferences ;
    Dominion
B. 1867: ON, QC, NS, NB
    1873: PEI
    1905: AB, SK
    1949: NL
    1999: NU
C. John A. Macdonald: C, D
    Joseph Howe: A, E
    George-Etienne Cartier: B, F
D. 1. Métis
    2. cities
    3. gold rush
    4. Chinese
    5. Vancouver
    6. logging
    7. Smallpox
    8. First Nations
E. 1. A
    2. C
    3. B
    4. C
    5. C
F. 1. immigrants
    2. outfitters
    3. prospectors
    4. guides
    5. NWMP
    6. terrain
    7. Yukon

1 Human Settlement Patterns

A. Lakeside Paradise:
canoeing, water-skiing, swimming, archery, camping, hiking
Mount Utopia:
downhill skiing, cross-country skiing, snowshoeing, tobogganing

B. 1.

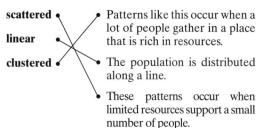

2a. scattered
b. linear
c. clustered
d. clustered
e. scattered

2 Factors That Affect Settlement

A. 1. site
2. harbour
3. natural resources
4. crossroads
5. strategic
6. Situation
7. climate
8. employment
9. transportation

B. 1. situation
2. site
3. situation
4. site

C. (Individual observation)

3 Populations – High/Low Density

A. 1. NB: 10.23
BC: = 4.44
ON: = 13.4
YK: = 0.06
PEI: = 23.9

2. Fredericton: = 386.71
Victoria: = 3966.31
Toronto: = 3939.44
Whitehorse: = 49.13
Charlottetown: = 725.78

3. Prince Edward Island
4. Whitehorse

B. 1. valid
2. invalid
3. valid
4. invalid
5. invalid

C. 1. (Individual answer)
2. (Suggeseted answer)
hospitals, schools, libraries, fire department, police

4 How We Use Land

A. 1. Residential
2. Transportation
3. Institutional
4. Industrial
5. Commercial
6. Park land / Open space

B. 1.

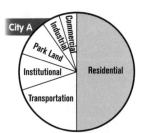

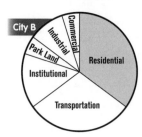

2. City B

C. (Individual answers)

5 What Is an Economic System?

A. 1. Goods: cell phones, shoes, clothes, musical instruments, hair products, automobiles
     Services: communication, travel tour, bus driver, music lesson, haircut, transportation
   2-3. (Individual answers)

B. 1. A
    2. C
    3. B

C. 1. producers
    2. industry
    3. market
    4. goods
    5. services
    6. distribution
    7. consumers
    8. competition

6 Types of Economic Systems

A. 1. Command
    2. Traditional
    3. Market

B. Command Economy
    1. government
    2. production
    3. distributed
    Traditional Economy
    1. continue
    2. the same
    3. past
    Market Economy
    1. consumers
    2. competitive
    3. money

C. Traditional Economy: B, F
    Command Economy: C, D
    Market Economy: A, E

7 Industry

A. 1. Primary Industry ; C, F, I
    2. Tertiary Industry ; B, D, E, H
    3. Secondary Industry ; A, G

B. (Suggested answers)
    1. pulp and paper mill ; stationery store
    2. sugar refinery ; grocery store
    3. stone manufacturing plant ; furniture store
    4. oil refinery ; gas station
    5. fishery ; restaurant
    6. (Individual example)

8 Canadian Industry

A. 1. gold, zinc, lead, coal, salmon, timber, copper, oil, natural gas, potash, wheat, nickel, salt, fruit, fish, tin, sand, gravel, potatoes, hydro electric power, maple syrup, asbestos
    2. British Columbia
    3. Alberta
    4. British Columbia and New Brunswick

B.

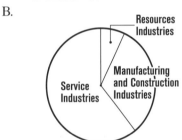

C. 1. fur trade
    2. agriculture
    3. timber
    4. mining

D. (Individual answer)

9 Human Migration

A. 1. transportation
    2. barriers
    3. immigration
    4. accessibility
    5. mobility
    6. migration
    7. emigration
    8. push factors
    9. refugees
   10. pull factors

B. 1. push
    2. push
    3. push
    4. push
    5. push
    6. pull
    7. push
    8. push
    9. pull
    10. push
    11. push
    12. pull
C. 1. banishment
    2. (Individual example)

10 What Makes Migration Difficult?

A. 1. B
    2. B
    3. D
    4. E
    5. B
    6. A
    7. C
    8. E
    9. D
B. 1. The man is more mobile than the woman because he has the ability to connect with people through technology.
    2. The farmer is less mobile than the doctor because the doctor is more financially stable and has a secure occupation.
    3. The people in the country on the right are more mobile because the community has language support and other services provided for the newcomers.
    4. The woman is more mobile because her financial standing is better than the man's.

11 Migration and Culture

A. 1. (Suggested answers)
    Food: Dim Sum ; Sushi ; Poutine
    Music: Symphony ; Hip hop ; Salsa
    Clothing: Hawaiian shirt ; Traditional Indian dress ; Cowboy hat and boots

Art and Dance: Irish dance ; West coast native art ; Chinese dragon dance
Celebrations: Yom Kippur ; Robbie Burns Day ; Jewish New Year
    2. (Individual answer)
B. 1. Japanese
    2. Italian
    3. Danish
    4. German
    5. Italian
    6. French
    7. Mexican
    8. Chinese
C. Welkom ; Velkommen ; Bienvenue ; Willkommen ; Aloha ; Swaagetam ; Yokoso ; Witamy ; Yindii ton rap

12 Migration and Canada

A. 1. French settlers
    2. persecution
    3. Irish Potato Famine
    4. opening of the West
    5. Russian Mennonites
    6. Europeans and Americans
    7. head tax
    8. Chinese Exclusion Act
B. 1. a cause
    2. a push factor
    3. Irish Potato Famine
C.

Review

A. 1. scattered: pattern occurs when the limited resources support a small number of people
    linear: the population is distributed along a line
    clustered: pattern occurs when a lot of people gather in a place rich in resources

2. clustered ; linear ; scattered

B. The land in the city was mostly for residential use in 1970. 30 years later, more land was used for commercial purposes. Industrial and institutional buildings were also developed. The land used for residential purposes and parks was reduced. More employment opportunities were provided in the city.

C. 1. City A: = 12.51 people/km^2
   City B: = 13.06 people/km^2
   City C: = 11.15 people/km^2
   2a. City B
   b. (Individual answers)

D. 1. Tertiary Industry
   2. Secondary Industry
   3. Primary Industry

E. Traditional Economy: E, F
   Command Economy: A, C
   Market Economy: B, D

F. 1. Push Factor:
   The reasons people have for leaving a particular area
   Pull Factor:
   The basis for people choosing a new place of residence
   2a. pull
   b. push
   c. push
   d. push
   e. pull

G. 1a. legal
   b. political
   2. British Columbia
   3. potash
   4. Manitoba
   5. agriculture
   6. refugees

1   Cell Theory

A.   Postulates of Cell Theory:
1. cells
2. structure ; Energy
3. pre-existing
Exceptions:
1. first
2. Viruses
Picture 1: All living things are made up of cells.
Picture 2: The first cell did not come from an already existing cell.

B.   1595: Zacharias ; microscope
1663: Robert ; cell
1674: Anton ; live
1809: Charles-Francois ; membrane
1837-1838: Thedor ; Matthias ; products
1855: Rudolph ; arise

2   Animal and Plant Cells

A.   1. cell membrane
cytoplasm
nucleus
chromosomes
genes
2a. nucleus
b. chromosomes
c. genes
d. nucleus
e. cytoplasm
f. cell membrane

B.   1. cell wall
2. chloroplast
3. vacuole
4. plastid

C.   Photosynthesis:
carbon dioxide ; energy ; oxygen
Respiration:
oxygen ; carbon dioxide ; water

3   Structures and Organelles in Cells

A.   light microscope ;
• nucleus
• cytoplasm

• cell membrane
• cell wall
electron microscope ;
• ribosomes
• Golgi apparatus
• endoplasmic reticulum
• lysosomes
• mitochondria

B.   1. Ribosomes ; proteins
2. Mitochondrion ; oval-shaped ; cell respiration
3. canals ; cytoplasm
4. Golgi apparatus ; toxic
5. sac-like ; recycle

4   Diffusion and Osmosis

A.   1. high ; low
2. 3 ; 5 ; 2 ; 4

B.   1. osmosis
2. equal
3. membrane
4. out
5. water
Plant Cell when Exposed to Salt Water: >
Plant Cell with Continued Exposure to Salt Water: =

5   The Organization of Cells

A.   1. Choanocytes
2. Porocytes
3. Amoebocytes
4. Spicules
5. Pinacocytes
6. Porocytes ;
Beat and create the sponge's water current. ;
Store and carry food to other cells. ;
Form the outer covering of the sponge. ;
Spicules

B.   1. cells
2. tissues
3. organs

C.   1. excretory system
2. digestive system
3. circulatory system

6 About Systems

A. 1. A
   2. B
   3. A
   4. C
B. 1. optical system
   2. mechanical system
   3. hydroelectric power system
   4. electrical system
   5. body system
C. (Suggested answer)
   3 subsystems are: gears and drivers ; wheel and axles ; frames and materials

7 Systems: Input and Output

A. 1. heat
   2. push ; movement
   3. food ; energy
   4. grow food or plants ;
      water, sunshine, and nutrients ;
      food and other plants
   5. tell time ;
      electricity ;
      movements of the clock hands
B.

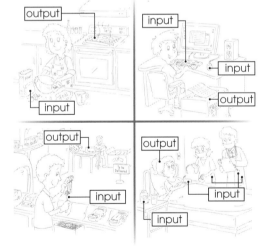

8 The Work Systems Do

A. 1. force ; scientific
   2. energy ; everyday
   3. efficiency ; scientific
   4. work ; everyday
B. 1. work
   2. pull
   3. effort
   4. useful
C. 1. Yes ; The machine is providing the force that moves the objects in the same direction as the force.
   2. Yes ; Red blood cells carry the oxygen molecules from one place to another.
   3. No ; The piano would have to move for work to happen.

9 Work, Mechanical Advantage, and Efficiency

A. 1. Newtons
   2. Work
   3. metres
   4. joules
   5. 800 N x 40 m = 32 000 J ;
      32 000 J of work was done.
   6. 4000 J ÷ 10 m = 400 N ;
      400 N of force was applied.
B. lever: $\frac{100}{10} = 10$
   wheelbarrow: $\frac{100}{20} = 5$
   lever
C. Machine A: $\frac{30\,000}{35\,000}$ x 100% = 85.7%
   Machine B: $\frac{75\,000}{100\,000}$ x 100% = 75%
   A

10 Evolving Systems

A. 1a. not automated
   b. automated
   2a. automated
   b. not automated
   3a. not automated
   b. automated

4a. automated
   b. not automated
5a. automated
   b. not automated
B. 1. social
   2. economic
   3. economic ; social
   4. environment
C. (Individual answer)

11 Where on Earth Is Water?

A. 1.

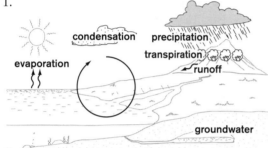

   2. evaporation, precipitation, and condensation
   3. Plants release evaporated water into the atmosphere through transpiration.
B. 1.

a	n	p	o	n	d	s			y	w
g	l	o	m	e	c	k	p	g	a
r	c	l	o	u	d	s	T	l	t
o	n	a	c	s	n	t	j	a	e
u	e	r	i	v	e	r	s	c	r
n	a		i	n	t	e	t	i	
d	b	i	x	i	v	w	r	e	v
w	r	c	j	s	o	c	e	r	a
a	c	e	n	t	e	r	a	s	p
t	i		r	h	u		m	a	o
e	o	c	e	a	n	s	s	e	u
r	k	a	b	e	s	i	p	u	r
m	n	p	i	c	w	d	e	w	w
o	c	s		m	h	o	l	e	t

   2. freshwater
   3. salt water
   4. 1%
C. Solid: glacier
   Liquid: ponds
   Gas: water vapour

12 What Is a Watershed?

A. 1. B
   2. A
   3. B
   4. A
   5. B
B. 1. glacier
   2. precipitation
   3. groundwater aquifer
   4. lake
   5. river
   6. wetland
C.

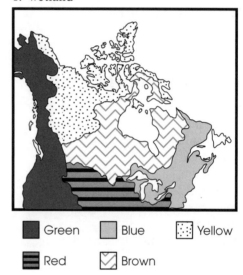

■	Green	▨	Blue	⋰	Yellow
▤	Red	▨	Brown		

13 The Water Table

A. 1-2.

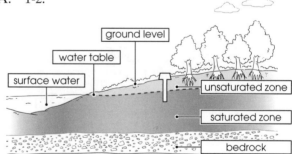

B. 1. true
   2. true
   3. false
   4. false
   5. false
   6. true

7. false
8. true
C. 1. where all spaces are filled with water
   2. where water is unable to enter or pass through
   3. water within the soil/rock underground
   4. the top level of the saturated zone underground

14 Glaciers and Polar Ice Caps

A. 1. ice caps
   2. temperatures
   3. precipitation
   4. climate
   5. stationary
   6. advancing
B. 1. valley glacier
   2. continental glacier
   Experiment:
   (Individual record)
   Antarctica would have a bigger effect on sea levels when it melts because the ice is on a land mass and would raise the ocean level if it was to melt.

15 Water Conservation

A. 1. wells, water treatment plants
   2. sewage system
   3. storm drain
   4. irrigation
   5. pesticides ; fertilizers
   6. solvent ; coolant
   7. Soap and dirty water would be filtered through the ground rather than return to a stream or a lake through a storm drain.
   8. Use less wasteful irrigation methods.
   9. thermal pollution
B. (Individual answer)

16 Fluids and Density

A. more ; gases
   solid ; liquid ; gas
B. orange juice
   honey
   helium

maple syrup
water vapour
oxygen
air
C. 1. volume
   2. mass
   3. density
   4. temperature
   5. decreases
   6. fluid
D. Density $= \dfrac{(160-10)}{150}$

$ = \dfrac{150}{150}$

$ = 1 \ (g/mL)$

17 Viscosity

A. 1. Fluids ; matter
   2. Viscosity ; resistance
   3. density ; viscous
   4. decreases ; temperature
   5. attraction ; cohesion
   6. Adhesion ; substance
B. C ; D ; E

18 Buoyancy

A. 1. buoyancy
   2. gravity
   3. buoyancy
   4. densities
   5. Buoyancy ; Gravity
B. 1.

force of buoyancy

force of gravity

   2.

force of buoyancy

force of gravity

C. 1. A: fresh water
      B: salt water
   2. C: salt water
      D: fresh water

3. Liquid B has a greater density. After pouring B into A, the solution has a stronger force of buoyancy to exert on the egg to keep it afloat.
4. Liquid C has a greater density. After pouring D into C, the density of C is reduced, which provides a smaller force of buoyancy to keep the egg afloat.
5. Different fluids have different densities, and therefore exert different amounts of buoyancy.
6. No

19 Compressed Fluids – Hydraulics and Pneumatics

A. 1. Gas Particles:

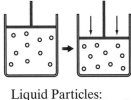

Liquid Particles:

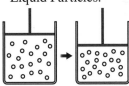

2. lots of
3. less
4. A gas has more compressibility than a liquid because the particles of gas are further apart from one another and there is somewhere for the particles to go. As the particles of liquid are closer to one another, they have less room to compress.
B. hydraulic system ; pneumatic system
C. a. A
   b. B
D. (Individual answers)

20 Using Fluids

A. 1. pressure
   2. pressure
   3. flow

4. flow
5. force
B. A and C
   B and D
C. (Suggested answer)
1. Medical hydraulic systems can save many lives, but the costs of tests and treatment are high, which means they are not available to everyone.
(Suggested answer)
2. Increased production
(Suggested answer)
3. They can cause habitat loss and water pollution.

Review

A. 1.

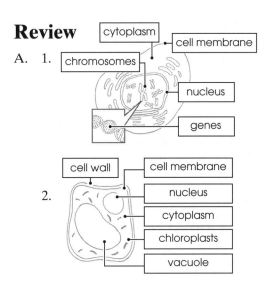

2.

3. nucleus ;
   chromosomes ;
   genes ;
   cell membrane
4. chloroplast ;
   plastid ;
   vacuole
B. Photosynthesis:
   carbon dioxide ; energy ; sugar ; oxygen
   Respiration:
   oxygen ; carbon dioxide ; water ; energy
C. 1. Diffusion: the movement of molecules from an area of high concentration to an area of low concentration
   Explanation: Molecules spread from an area of high concentration to an area of low concentration by the randomness of collisions. The process will not stop until the molecules are evenly distributed throughout a space.

2. Osmosis: the movement of water molecules from an area of high concentration to an area of low concentration through a semi-permeable membrane
Explanation: The concentration of water inside the cell is higher than outside. So, the water molecules pass across the cell membrane until the inside and outside of the cell have the same concentration of water. After the water leaves the cell, the cell will shrink.

D. 1. Wagon: mechanical system
Purpose: move things from one place to another
Input: push
Output: movement
2. Circulatory system: body system
Purpose: move oxygen to cells throughout the body
Input: energy
Output: pumps blood

E. 1. Work: 450 N x 10 m = 4500 J
2. Distance: 2100 J ÷ 600 N = 3.5 m
3. $75\% = \dfrac{24\,000}{\text{output}} \times 100\%$; output = 32 kJ

F. 1. Precipitation: condensed water vapour that falls to the Earth's surface
Runoff: the variety of ways by which water moves across the land
Evaporation: the transformation of water from liquid to gas
Condensation: the transformation of water vapour to liquid water droplets in the air, producing clouds
Groundwater: water located beneath the ground's surface
Transpiration: the evaporation of water from plants
2. Water on Earth moves in a continuous cycle, from the land to the sky and back again. This is called the water cycle.

G. 1.

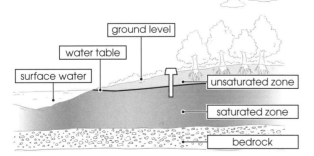

2. Heavy rainfall and water from melted snow and glaciers
3. Underground water can be found in the saturated zone.

H. 1. A: valley glacier
B: continental glacier
2. Changes in temperature, precipitation, and global climate cause the change in size of glaciers and ice caps.

I. 1. Density is the amount of matter in a given mass.

2a.

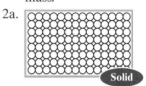

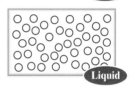

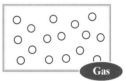

b. Solids
c. Gases
3. more

J. 1. A ; C ; D
2. B ; D ; E
3. A ; B ; D